Campus Wars

CAMPUS WARS

Multiculturalism and the Politics of Difference

edited by
John Arthur
Amy Shapiro

Westview Press
BOULDER • SAN FRANCISCO • OXFORD

Copyright © 1995 by Westview Press, Inc.

Published in 1995 in the United States of America by Westview Press, Inc., 5500 Central Avenue, Boulder, Colorado 80301-2877, and in the United Kingdom by Westview Press, 36 Lonsdale Road, Summertown, Oxford OX2 7EW

Library of Congress Cataloging-in-Publication Data
Campus wars : multiculturalism and the politics of difference / edited
    by John Arthur, Amy Shapiro.
      p.   cm.
    Includes bibliographical references.
    ISBN 0-8133-2480-7 — ISBN 0-8133-2481-5 (pbk.)
    1. Critical pedagogy—United States.   2. Multiculturalism—United
States.   3. Education, Higher—Political aspects—United States.
4. Social conflict—United States.   I. Arthur, John, 1946–   .
II. Shapiro, Amy, 1952–
LC196.5.U6C36   1995
370.19'0973—dc20
                                                                        94-29253
                                                                        CIP

Printed and bound in the United States of America

The paper used in this publication meets the requirements
of the American National Standard for Permanence of Paper
for Printed Library Materials Z39.48-1984.

10   9   8   7   6   5   4   3

Contents

Preface   vii

Introduction, *John Arthur and Amy Shapiro*   1

Part One
Multiculturalism and the College Curriculum

The Closing of the American Mind, *Allan Bloom*   9
What's All the Fuss About This Postmodernist Stuff?
   Barry W. Sarchett   19
Postmodernism and the Western Rationalist Tradition,
   John R. Searle   28
Is There a Text in This Class? *Stanley Fish*   49
Relativism, Deconstruction, and the Curriculum,
   Amy Gutmann   57

Part Two
Sex on Campus: Sexual Harassment and Date Rape

Sexuality, *Catharine A. MacKinnon*   71
Date Rape: A Feminist Analysis, *Lois Pineau*   87
An Interview About Sex and Date Rape, *Camille Paglia*   99

Part Three
Free Speech, Hate Speech, and Campus Speech Codes

Good Speech, Bad Speech—No, *Gerald Gunther*   109
Campus Speech Codes: *Doe v. University of Michigan*   114
Liberalism and Campus Hate Speech, *Andrew Altman*   122

Part Four
Race and Affirmative Action on Campus

Affirmative Action in Universities: *Regents of the University
   of California v. Bakke*   137
Affirmative Discrimination, *Lino A. Graglia*   144

A Cultural Pluralist Case for Affirmative Action,
   Duncan Kennedy   153
The Recoloring of Campus Life: Student Racism,
   Academic Pluralism, and the End of a Dream, *Shelby Steele*   176

Part Five
Identity, Assimilation, and Politics

Age, Race, Class, and Sex: Women Redefining Difference,
   Audre Lorde   191
Social Movements and the Politics of Difference,
   Iris Marion Young   199
The Disuniting of America: Reflections on a Multicultural Society,
   Arthur M. Schlesinger, Jr.   226
Separation or Assimilation? *Bernard R. Boxill*   235
The Politics of Recognition, *Charles Taylor*   249
Pragmatism, Relativism, and the Justification of Democracy,
   Hilary Putnam   264

About the Book and Editors   274
About the Contributors   275
List of Credits   277

Preface

This book grew out of our experiences teaching philosophy and history at a large state university. It addresses, we believe, many of the most controversial and troubling issues facing higher education.

Disputes about the educational curriculum and what should be included; sexual harassment and date rape; hate speech versus free speech; and affirmative action as well as the racial, ethnic, and gender issues underlying these disputes demand careful, thoughtful attention. To that end, we have sought to provide a balanced collection of essays that fairly represents all sides. We have no illusions that everyone will agree we have succeeded in this aim, much less applaud our specific selections. We do believe, however, that the authors are among the most important and thoughtful writers on these subjects. They represent a wide array of disciplines, including philosophy, history, literary theory, poetry, law, economics, and politics. We have also tried to blend familiar names with others who, though less well known, have something important to contribute to the discussion. And, finally, we have sought to make certain that one selection leads naturally to the next so that the discussion progresses in a logical fashion.

John Arthur
Amy Shapiro

Introduction

John Arthur

Amy Shapiro

Throughout its history, America's task has been the exhilarating one of forging community from multiplicity. From the beginning, the indigenous American population was augmented primarily by northern European settlers, black slaves, and later by immigrants from all the European nations. More recently, however, the descendants of these original settlers have been joined by immigrants whose roots extend from China and Vietnam to Africa, the Islamic World, and Latin America, so that it is sometimes even predicted that during the next century the descendants of European settlers will become a minority.

At the same time that the United States is becoming ethnically more diverse, those who have historically been marginalized in U.S. society are making broader claims for equality and power. With the opening of higher education to women, members of ethnic minorities, and those who could not have afforded it, issues of race, sex, and class have taken on a new urgency both as academic issues and in the day-to-day life of the university. Moreover, postmodernism and deconstruction, whose supporters can be found in both the social sciences and humanities, are questioning not only what is taught and by whom but the very nature of knowledge and the possibility of objectivity. Often these attacks on traditional ideals of knowledge and truth are undertaken explicitly in the name of furthering the political interests of traditionally marginalized groups.

The response to these changes has been varied and complicated, but four are of particular importance to campus life today. First, faculty and students on many campuses have demanded more women and minority professors, ethnic and gender studies departments, and a curriculum that includes voices not traditionally included in the "canon." These demands have often been met. Second, many universities have promulgated codes of conduct banning sexual harassment and date rape. Third, some institutions have abandoned the insistence on free speech that grew out of the student movements of the 1960s and enacted codes punishing racist, sexist, and harassing speech. Fourth, and finally, many schools have adopted affirmative action policies that give preference in hiring and admissions to women and persons of color.

The contributors to the first four parts of this volume provide a wide range of lively and provocative views on all of these topics. The authors included in the last part address these issues from a somewhat greater distance, asking more fundamental questions about the meaning and importance of group identity and the implications of the "politics of difference" for democratic institutions as well as for political theory.

Part One, "Multiculturalism and the College Curriculum," begins with a selection from Allan Bloom's book *The Closing of the American Mind*. Bloom is one of the most outspoken and influential defenders of the traditional canon, and his views have attracted wide criticism. One critic, Barry W. Sarchett, responds with a sympathetic discussion of the views of the new, "postmodernist" scholars in an essay titled "What's All the Fuss About This Postmodernist Stuff?" The next essay in this section, "Postmodernism and the Western Rationalist Tradition," written by John R. Searle, begins with a description and vigorous defense of the "Western Rationalist Tradition" along with its implicit commitments to objectivity, truth, and rationality. Searle then discusses postmodernism's rejection of traditional standards of truth and objectivity and its impact on the university, including the commitment to reform the curriculum, to redefine academic excellence, and to shift our understanding of the curriculum from a concern with "subjects to be investigated" toward "moral causes to be advanced." Among the issues raised by these authors is the nature of truth and the possibility of objectivity—a topic taken up in "Is There a Text in This Class?" by one of multiculturalism's best known defenders, literary and legal theorist Stanley Fish.

In an essay we titled "Relativism, Deconstruction, and the Curriculum," Amy Gutmann discusses the debate between traditional "essentialists" like Bloom and "deconstructionists" like Sarchett. She follows with an assessment of cultural relativism—a topic that is woven through the four preceding essays.

Part Two, "Sex on Campus: Sexual Harassment and Date Rape," begins with an essay titled "Sexuality" by one of feminism's leading theoreticians, Catharine A. MacKinnon. Placing sexual harassment in the context of a larger political and cultural system of oppression, MacKinnon discusses the nature of sex, gender, and rape and their relationship to the political system. Lois Pineau's article "Date Rape: A Feminist Analysis" discusses a range of issues associated with date tape, including myths about consent and sexuality that make conviction difficult. She defends what she terms a "communicative" mode of sexuality which, she argues, better describes the mutuality of sexual relationships and provides a better test for consent than the contractualist model she believes is currently used by the law. In the final selection, "An Interview About Sex and Date Rape," Camille Paglia argues that feminism's concern about date rape reflects a naive and unrealistic vision of male sexuality. Her understanding of sex marks a fascinating contrast with both MacKinnon and Pineau.

Part Three, "Free Speech, Hate Speech, and Campus Speech Codes," discusses the dispute over campus speech codes. Beginning with an account of his background in Nazi Germany, Gerald Gunther describes the importance of protecting even the most offensive and hurtful speech against censorship, especially on college campuses. The next selection, "Doe v. University of Michigan," is one of a number of cases in which a speech code was rejected on Constitutional grounds. In it, Judge Avern Cohen describes the principles behind free speech, the nature of the code in question, and the dual grounds—vagueness and overbreadth—on which he felt compelled to reject it.

The last selection, "Liberalism and Campus Hate Speech," by Andrew Altman, represents a careful attempt to defend limited restrictions on hate speech from the perspective of a liberal who is also deeply committed to freedom of speech. The fact that such a code is not viewpoint neutral, argues Altman, means that it cannot be justified because of harmful effects on its hearers. Nor, he claims, can hate speech be treated as a form of racial harassment, as others have suggested. Instead, says Altman, hate speech is best understood as an intentional act that is wrong because it treats an individual as a moral subordinate, that is, as a person whose interests are less important or worthy than those of others. He then argues that such a regulation, if narrowly drawn, is compatible with the three principles underlying liberalism's commitment to viewpoint neutrality.

The authors of the essays in the next part, "Race and Affirmative Action on Campus," offer differing perspectives on one of the most important, oft-discussed, and controversial issues facing higher education. The first selection is the leading constitutional case in this area, "Regents of the University of California v. Bakke." The next essay, "Affirmative Discrimination," by Lino A. Graglia, is a broad attack on the philosophical and political rationale behind affirmative action. In the next selection, "A Cultural Pluralist Case for Affirmative Action," Duncan Kennedy assesses what he terms "color-blind meritocratic fundamentalism." That familiar but mistaken position, according to Kennedy, emphasizes the contradiction between "merit" and "preferences" while claiming that institutions should strive to "produce" knowledge in accord with objective merit and therefore should ignore race, sex, class, and other "irrelevant" characteristics of authors and scholars. In response, Kennedy develops a political and cultural case for large-scale affirmative action based on the need to produce an intelligentsia that can both help subordinated cultural communities gain access to resources and improve the quality and social value of scholarship.

Beyond these ideas, he argues, is a "cultural pluralist" conception of American life that recognizes the importance of culture and ideology in judging scholarship.

The final essay in Part Four, "The Recoloring of Campus Life: Student Racism, Academic Pluralism, and the End of a Dream," by Shelby Steele, offers an assessment of where we have come in our understanding of race on campus as well as a description of affirmative action's impact on those whom it is meant to help. Based on his own experiences as a student and educator, Steele diagnoses racial tensions as arising from black fears of inferiority and white feelings of guilt. He goes on to question the recent emphasis on the politics of "difference" and the related campus moves toward affirmative action, race, and culturally based curricula, and the view that all minority students suffer victimization, arguing instead that universities should emphasize individual initiative, commonality, and integration.

Essays in the final part, "Identity, Assimilation, and Politics," are considerations of the theoretical issues beneath the surface of many of the previous discussions. These include the nature of individual identity and its connection with cultural membership, conflicts between assimilation and separatism, the political implications of the "politics of difference," and the prospects of liberal, democratic government in a divided, pluralistic society.

In the first essay, "Age, Race, Class, and Sex: Women Redefining Difference," poet Audre Lorde describes political and social reality as it appears from her perspective as a "forty-nine-year-old Black lesbian feminist socialist mother of two." Instead of denying the importance of "difference" and thus distorting its meaning, she claims, we must learn instead to acknowledge its importance in shaping our world. In the next essay, "Social Movements and the Politics of Difference," Iris Marion Young offers a wide-ranging and important discussion of the relevance of group difference to politics. Beginning with a critique of assimilation and the humanist ideal of impartiality, she goes on to describe the alternative, "relational" conception of difference and defend the "politics of difference" as the best means to achieve genuine emancipation. Young next defends various group-conscious policies to promote equality for women, Hispanics, and Indians. She concludes with a discussion of democratic government and the need to assure representation of oppressed groups.

In the next essay, taken from his book *The Disuniting of America: Reflections on a Multicultural Society*, noted historian Arthur M. Schlesinger, Jr., first raises questions about separatism, including bilingual education. He then addresses charges that Europe is "evil" and that the United States should reject its legacy. He argues that in fact the Western tradition itself provides the intellectual grounding and institutional protection on which modern multiculturalism rests. In "Separation or Assimilation?" Bernard R. Boxill considers the philosophical issues of assimilation and separatism against the backdrop of W.E.B. Dubois's defense of cultural pluralism. Boxill discusses the importance of black pride and black culture, the definition of race, and the role of cultural "authenticity," finally rejecting cultural pluralism in favor of individual autonomy.

The last two essays turn to the political question of governing a diverse society. In "The Politics of Recognition" Charles Taylor begins by tracing the historical and philosophical changes that, he argues, underlie the modern emphasis in multiculturalism and the "politics of recognition." Looking next to contemporary politics, he argues that the importance of equal respect has led to two different, sometimes conflicting political demands: universalism and the politics of difference. Taylor concludes with a brief discussion of the position that all cultures must be recognized as "equally valuable."

In the final selection, "Pragmatism, Relativism, and the Justification of Democracy," Hilary Putnam brings together a variety of themes that occupy the previous writers by discussing the political thought of American pragmatist John Dewey. Beginning with a description of democratic government as "the precondition for the full application of intelligence to the solution of social problems," Putnam then addresses the relativist's doubt whether moral and political claims—including those justifying democracy—can be rationally defended at all. He rejects what he terms the "noble savage" view of cultural relativists that immunizes oppression in non-Western cultures against criticism. Putnam argues that there are, in fact, better or worse solutions to human problems and, further, that democratic procedures are best suited to find them. He concludes with a brief description of Dewey's critical reflections—including Dewey's rejection of entrenched privilege and his insistence that the underprivileged be provided the opportunity to develop their capacities.

We said at the beginning that America's social and political task of building community out of diversity is an exhilarating one. We believe that the intellectual task of understanding the politics of diversity and its implications can be just as exciting. It is our hope that this generous and varied selection of readings will challenge students and their teachers to think more critically and creatively about the complex of issues we call "campus wars."

PART ONE

MULTICULTURALISM AND THE COLLEGE CURRICULUM

The Closing of the American Mind

There is one thing a professor can be absolutely certain of: almost every student entering the university believes, or says he believes, that truth is relative. If this belief is put to the test, one can count on the students' reaction: they will be uncomprehending. That anyone should regard the proposition as not self-evident astonishes them, as though he were calling into question 2 + 2 = 4. These are things you don't think about. The students' backgrounds are as various as America can provide. Some are religious, some atheists; some are to the Left, some to the Right; some intend to be scientists, some humanists or professionals or businessmen; some are poor, some rich. They are unified only in their relativism and in their allegiance to equality. And the two are related in a moral intention. The relativity of truth is not a theoretical insight but a moral postulate, the condition of a free society, or so they see it. They have all been equipped with this framework early on, and it is the modern replacement for the inalienable natural rights that used to be the traditional American grounds for a free society. That it is a moral issue for students is revealed by the character of their response when challenged—a combination of disbelief and indignation: "Are you an absolutist?," the only alternative they know, uttered in the same tone as "Are you a monarchist?" or "Do you really believe in witches?" This latter leads into the indignation, for someone who believes in witches might well be a witchhunter or a Salem judge. The danger they have been taught to fear from absolutism is not error but intolerance. Relativism is necessary to openness; and this is the virtue, the only virtue, which all primary education for more than fifty years has dedicated itself to inculcating. Openness—and the relativism that makes it the only plausible stance in the face of various claims to truth and various ways of life and kinds of human beings—is the great insight of our times. The true believer is the real danger. The study of history and of culture teaches that all the world was mad in the past; men always thought they were right, and that led to wars, persecutions, slavery, xenophobia, racism, and chauvinism. The point is not to correct the mistakes and really be right; rather it is not to think you are right at all.

9

The students, of course, cannot defend their opinion. It is something with which they have been indoctrinated. The best they can do is point out all the opinions and cultures there are and have been. What right, they ask, do I or anyone else have to say one is better than the others? If I pose the routine questions designed to confute them and make them think, such as, "If you had been a British administrator in India, would you have let the natives under your governance burn the widow at the funeral of a man who had died?," they either remain silent or reply that the British should never been there in the first place. It is not that they know very much about other nations, or about their own. The purpose of their education is not to make them scholars but to provide them with a moral virtue—openness. . . .

The old view was that, by recognizing and accepting man's natural rights, men found a fundamental basis of unity and sameness. Class, race, religion, national origin or culture all disappear or become dim when bathed in the light of natural rights, which give men common interests and make them truly brothers The immigrant had to put behind him the claims of the Old World in favor of a new and easily acquired education. This did not necessarily mean abandoning old daily habits or religions, but it did mean subordinating them to new principles. There was a tendency, if not a necessity, to homogenize nature itself.

The recent education of openness has rejected all that. It pays no attention to natural rights or the historical origins of our regime, which are now thought to have been essentially flawed and regressive. It is progressive and forward-looking. It does not demand fundamental agreement or the abandonment of old or new beliefs in favor of the natural ones. It is open to all kinds of men, all kinds of lifestyles, all ideologies. There is no enemy other than the man who is not open to everything. . . .

Liberalism without natural rights, the kind that we knew from John Stuart Mill and John Dewey, taught us that the only danger confronting us is being closed to the emergent, the new, the manifestations of progress. No attention had to be paid to the fundamental principles or the moral virtues that inclined men to live according to them. To use language now popular, civic culture was neglected. And this turn in liberalism is what prepared us for cultural relativism and the fact-value distinction, which seemed to carry that viewpoint further and give it greater intellectual weight. . . .

History and social science are used in a variety of ways to overcome prejudice. We should not be ethnocentric, a term drawn from anthropology, which tells us more about the meaning of openness. We should not think our way is better than others. The intention is not so much to teach the students about other times and places as to make them aware of the fact that their preferences are only that—accidents of their time and place. Their beliefs do not entitle them as individuals, or collectively as a nation, to think they are superior to anyone else. John Rawls is almost a parody of this tendency, writing hundreds of pages to persuade men, and proposing a scheme of government that would force them, not to despise anyone. In *A Theory of Justice,* he writes that the physicist or the poet should not look down on the man who spends his life counting blades of grass or performing any other frivolous or corrupt activity. Indeed, he should be esteemed, since esteem from others, as opposed to self-esteem, is a basic need of all men. So indiscriminateness is a moral imperative because its opposite is discrimination. This folly means that men are not permitted to seek for the natural human good and admire it when found, for such discovery is coeval with the discovery of the bad and contempt for it. Instinct and intellect must be suppressed by education. The natural soul is to be replaced with an artificial one.

At the root of this change in morals was the presence in the United States of men and women of a great variety of nations, religions, and races, and the fact that many were badly treated because they belonged to these groups. Franklin Roosevelt declared that we want "a society which leaves no one out." Although the natural rights inherent in our regime are perfectly adequate to the solution of this problem, provided these outsiders adhere to them (i.e., they become insiders by adhering to them), this did not satisfy the thinkers who influenced our educators, for the right to vote and the other political rights did not automatically produce social acceptance. The equal protection of the laws did not protect a man from contempt and hatred as a Jew, an Italian, or a Black.

The reaction to this problem was, in the first place, resistance to the notion that outsiders had to give up their "cultural" individuality and make themselves into that universal, abstract being who participates in natural rights or else be doomed to an existence on the fringe; in the second place, anger at the majority who imposed a "cultural" life on the nation to which the Constitution is indifferent. Openness was designed to provide a respectable place for these "groups" or "minorities"—to wrest respect from those who were not disposed to give it—and to weaken the sense of superiority of the dominant majority (more recently dubbed WASPs, a name the success of which shows something of the success of sociology in reinterpreting the national consciousness). That dominant majority gave the country a dominant culture with its traditions, its literature, its tastes, its special claim to know and supervise the language, and its Protestant religions. Much of the intellectual machinery of twentieth-century American political thought and social science was constructed for the purposes of making an assault on that majority. It treated the founding principles as impediments and tried to overcome the other strand of our political heritage, majoritarianism, in favor of a nation of minorities and groups each following its own beliefs and inclinations. In particular, the intellectual minority expected to enhance its status, presenting itself as the defender and spokesman of all the others.

This reversal of the founding intention with respect to minorities is most striking. For the Founders, minorities are in general bad things, mostly identical to factions, selfish groups who have no concern as such for the common good. Unlike older political thinkers, they entertained no hopes of suppressing factions and educating a united or homogeneous citizenry. Instead they constructed an elaborate machinery to contain factions in such a way that they would cancel one another and allow for the pursuit of the common good. The good is still the guiding consideration in their thought, although it is arrived at, less directly than in classical political thought, by tolerating faction. The Founders wished to achieve a national majority concerning the fundamental rights and then prevent that majority from using its power to overturn those fundamental rights. In twentieth-century social science, however, the common good disappears and along with it the negative view of minorities. The very idea of majority—now understood to be selfish interest—is done away with in order to protect the minorities. This breaks the delicate balance between majority and minority in Constitutional thought. In such a perspective, where there is no common good, minorities are no longer problematic, and the protection of them emerges as the central function of government. Where this leads is apparent. . . . Groups or individuals who really care, as opposed to those who have lukewarm feelings, deserve special attention or special rights for their "intensity" or "commitment," the new political validation, which replaces reason. The Founding Fathers wished to reduce and defang fanaticism, whereas [this] encourages it.

The appeal of the minority formula was enormous for all kinds of people, reactionary and progressive, all those who in the twenties and thirties still did not accept the political solution imposed the Constitution. The reactionaries did not like the suppression of class privilege and religious establishment. For a variety of reasons they simply did not accept equality. Southerners knew full well that the Constitution's heart was a moral commitment to equality and hence condemned segregation of blacks. The Constitution was not just a set of rules of government but implied a moral order that was to be enforced throughout the entire Union. Yet the influence, which has not been sufficiently noted, of Southern writers and historians on the American view of their history has been powerful. They were remarkably successful in characterizing their "peculiar institution" as part of a charming diversity and individuality of culture to which the Constitution was worse than indifferent. The ideal of openness, lack of ethnocentricity, is just what they needed for a modern defense of their way of life against all the intrusions of outsiders who claimed equal rights with the folks back home. The Southerners' romantic characterization of the alleged failings of the Constitution, and their hostility to "mass society" with its technology, its money-grubbing way of life, egoistic individuals and concomitant destruction of community, organic and rooted, appealed to malcontents of all political colorations. The New Left in the sixties expressed exactly the same ideology that had been developed to protect the South from the threat to its practices posed by the Constitutional rights and the Federal Government's power to enforce them. It is the old alliance of Right and Left against liberal democracy, parodied as "bourgeois society.". . .

Sexual adventurers like Margaret Mead and others who found America too narrow told us that not only must we know other cultures and learn to respect them, but we could also profit from them. We could follow their lead and loosen up, liberating ourselves from the opinion that our taboos are anything other than social constraints. We could go to the bazaar of cultures and find reinforcement for inclinations that are repressed by puritanical guilt feelings. All such teachers of openness had either no interest in or were actively hostile to the Declaration of Independence and the Constitution.

The civil rights movement provides a good example of this change in thought. In its early days almost all the significant leaders, in spite of tactical and temperamental differences, relied on the Declaration of Independence and the Constitution. They could charge whites not only with the most monstrous injustices but also with contradicting their own most sacred principles. The blacks were the true Americans in demanding the equality that belongs to them as human beings by natural and political right. The stance implied a firm conviction of the truth of the principles of natural right and of their fundamental efficacy within the Constitutional tradition, which, although tarnished, tends in the long run toward fulfilling those principles. They therefore worked through Congress, the Presidency, and, above all, the Judiciary. By contrast, the Black Power movement that supplanted the older civil rights movement—leaving aside both its excesses and its very understandable emphasis on self-respect and refusal to beg for acceptance—had at its core the view that the Constitutional tradition was always corrupt and was constructed as defense of slavery. Its demand was for black identity, not universal rights. Not rights but power counted. It insisted on respect for blacks as blacks, not as human beings simply.

Yet the Constitution does not promise respect for blacks, whites, yellows, Catholics, Protestants, or Jews. It guarantees the protection of the rights of individual human beings. This has not proved to be enough, however, to what is perhaps by now a majority of Americans.

The upshot of all this for the education of young Americans is that they know much less about American history and those who were held to be its heroes. This was one of the few things that they used to come to college with that had something to do with their lives. Nothing has taken its place except a smattering of facts learned about other nations or cultures and a few social science formulas. None of this means much, partly because little attention is paid to what is required in order truly to convey the spirit of other places and other times to young people, or for that matter to anyone, partly because the students see no relevance in any of it to the lives they are going to lead or to their prevailing passions. It is the rarest of occurrences to find a youngster who has been infused by this education with a longing to know all about China or the Romans or the Jews.

All to the contrary. There is an indifference to such things, for relativism has extinguished the real motive of education, the search for a good life. Young Americans have less and less knowledge of and interest in foreign places. In the past there were many students who actually knew something about and loved England, France, Germany, or Italy, for they dreamed of living there or thought their lives would be made more interesting by as-similating their languages and literatures. Such students have almost disap-peared, replaced at most by students who are interested in the political problems of Third World countries and in helping them to modernize, with due respect to their old cultures, of course. This is not learning from others but condescension and a disguised form of a new imperialism. It is the Peace Corps mentality, which is not a spur to learning but to a secularized version of doing good works.

Actually openness results in American conformism—out there in the rest of the world is a drab diversity that teaches only that values are relative, whereas here we can create all the life-styles we want. Our openness means we do not need others. Thus what is advertised as a great opening is a great closing. No longer is there a hope that there are great wise men in other places and times who can reveal the truth about life—except for the few remaining young people who look for a quick fix from a guru. Gone is the real historical sense of a Machiavelli who wrested a few hours from each busy day in which "to don regal and courtly garments, enter the courts of the ancients and speak with them."

None of this concerns those who promote the new curriculum. The point is to propagandize acceptance of different ways, and indifference to their real content is as good a means as any. It was not necessarily the best of times in America when Catholics and Protestants were suspicious of and hated one another; but at least they were taking their beliefs seriously, and the more or less satisfactory accommodations they worked out were not simply the result of apathy about the state of their souls. Practically all that young Americans have today is an insubstantial awareness that there are many cultures, accompanied by a saccharine moral drawn from that awareness: We should all get along. Why fight? . . .

One of the techniques of opening young people up is to require a college course in a non-Western culture. Although many of the persons teaching such courses are real scholars and lovers of the areas they study, in every case I have seen this requirement—when there are so many other things that can and should be learned but are not required, when philosophy and religion are no longer required—has a demagogic intention. The point is to force students to recognize that there are other ways of thinking and that Western ways are not better. It is again not the content that counts but the lesson to be drawn. Such requirements are part of the effort to establish a world community and train its member—the person devoid of prejudice. But if the students were really to learn something of the minds of any of these non-Western cultures—which they do not—they would find that each and every one of these cultures is ethnocentric. All of them think their way is the best way, and all other cultures are inferior. Herodotus tells us that the Persians thought that they were the best, that those nations bordering on them were next best, that those nations bordering on the nations bordering on them were third best, and so on, their worth declining as the concentric circles were farther from the Persian center. This is the very definition of ethnocentrism. Something like this is as ubiquitous as the prohibition against incest between mother and son.

Only in the Western nations, i.e., those influenced by Greek philosophy, is there some willingness to doubt the identification of the good with one's own way. One should conclude from the study of non-Western cultures that not only to prefer one's own way but to believe it best, superior to all others, is primary and even natural—exactly the opposite of what is intended by requiring students to study these cultures. What we are really doing is applying a Western prejudice—which we covertly take to indicate the superiority of our culture—and deforming the evidence of those other cultures to attest to its validity. The scientific study of other cultures is almost exclusively a Western phenomenon, and in its origin was obviously connected with the search for new and better ways, or at least for validation of the hope that our own culture really is the better way, a validation for which there is no felt need in other cultures. If we are to learn from those cultures, we must wonder whether such scientific study is a good idea. Consistency would seem to require professors of openness to respect the ethnocentrism or closedness they find everywhere else. However, in attacking ethnocentrism, what they actually do is to assert unawares the superiority of their scientific understanding and the inferiority of the other cultures which do not recognize it at the same time they reject all such claims to superiority. They both affirm and deny the goodness of their science. They face a problem akin to that faced by Pacal in the conflict between reason and revelation, without the intellectual intransigence that forced him to abandon science in favor of faith.

The reason for the non-Western closedness, or ethnocentrism, is clear. Men must love and be loyal to their families and their peoples in order to preserve them. Only if they think their own things are good can they rest content with them. A father must prefer his child to other children, a citizen his country to others. That is why there are myths—to justify these attachments. And a man needs a place and opinions by which to orient himself. This is strongly asserted by those who talk about the importance of roots. The problem of getting along with outsiders is secondary to, and sometimes in conflict with, having an inside, a people, a culture, a way of life. A very great narrowness is not incompatible with the health of an individual or a people, whereas with great openness it is hard to avoid decomposition. The firm binding of the good with one's own, the refusal to see a distinction between the two, a vision of the cosmos that has a special place for one's people, seem to be conditions of culture. This is what really follows from the study of non-Western cultures proposed for undergraduates. It points them back to passionate attachment to their own and away from the science which liberates them from it. Science now appears as a threat to culture and a dangerous uprooting charm. In short, they are lost in a no-man's land between the goodness of knowing and the goodness of culture, where they have been placed by their teachers who no longer have the resources to guide them. Help must be sought elsewhere.

Greek philosophers were the first men we know to address the problem of ethnocentrism. Distinctions between the good and one's own, between nature and convention, between the just and the legal are the signs of this movement of thought. They related the good to the fulfillment of the whole natural human potential and were aware that few, if any, of the nations of men had ways that allowed such fulfillment. They were open to the good. They had to use the good, which was not their own, to judge their own. This was a dangerous business because it tended to weaken wholehearted attachment to their own, hence to weaken their peoples as well as to expose themselves to the anger of family, friends, and countrymen. Loyalty versus quest for the good introduced an unresolvable tension into life. But the awareness of the good as such and the desire to possess it are priceless humanizing acquisitions.

This is the sound motive contained, along with many other less sound ones, in openness as we understand it. Men cannot remain content with what is given them by their culture if they are to be fully human. This is what Plato meant to show by the image of the cave in the *Republic* and by representing us as prisoners in it. A culture is a cave. He did not suggest going around to other cultures as a solution to the limitations of the cave. Nature should be the standard by which we judge our own lives and the lives of peoples. That is why philosophy, not history or anthropology, is the most important human science. Only dogmatic assurance that thought is culture-bound, that there is no nature, is what makes our educators so certain that the only way to escape the limitations of our time and place is to study other cultures. History and anthropology were understood by the Greeks to be useful only in discovering what the past and other peoples had to contribute to the discovery of nature. Historians and anthropologists were to put peoples and their conventions to the test, as Socrates did individuals, and go beyond them. These scientists were superior to their subjects because they saw a problem where others refused to see one, and they were engaged in the quest to solve it. They wanted to be able to evaluate themselves and others.

This point of view, particularly the need to know nature in order to have a standard, is uncomfortably buried beneath our human sciences, whether they like it or not, and accounts for the ambiguities and contradictions I have been pointing out. They want to make us culture-beings with the instruments that were invented to liberate us from culture. Openness used to be the virtue that permitted us to seek the good by using reason. It now means accepting everything and denying reason's power. The unrestrained and thoughtless pursuit of openness, without recognizing the inherent political, social, or cultural problem of openness as the goal of nature, has rendered openness meaningless. Cultural relativism destroys both one's own and the good. What is most characteristic of the West is science, particularly understood as the quest to know nature and the consequent denigration of convention—i.e., culture or the West understood as culture—in favor of what is accessible to all men as men through their common and distinctive faculty, reason. Science's latest attempts to grasp the human situation—cultural relativism, historicism, the fact-value distinction—are the suicide of science. Culture, hence closedness, reigns supreme. Openness to closedness is what we teach. . . .

conclusion

Cultural relativism succeeds in destroying the West's universal or intellectually imperialistic claims, leaving it to be just another culture. So there is equality in the republic of cultures. Unfortunately the West is defined by its need for justification of its ways or values, by its need for discovery of nature, by its need for philosophy and science. This is its cultural imperative. Deprived of that, it will collapse. The United States is one of the highest and most extreme achievements of the rational quest for the good life according to nature. What makes its political structure possible is the use of the rational principles of natural right to found a people, thus uniting the good with one's own. Or, to put it otherwise, the regime established here promised untrammeled freedom to reason—not to everything indiscriminately, but to reason, the essential freedom that justifies the other freedoms, and on the basis of which, and for the sake of which, much deviance is also tolerated. An openness that denies the special claim of reason bursts the mainspring keeping the mechanism of this regime in motion. And this regime, contrary to all claims to the contrary, was founded to overcome ethnocentrism, which is in no sense a discovery of social science.

It is important to emphasize that the lesson the students are drawing from their studies is simply untrue. History and the study of cultures do not teach or prove that values or cultures are relative. All to the contrary, that is a philosophical premise that we now bring to our study of them. This premise is unproven and dogmatically asserted for what are largely political reasons. History and culture are interpreted in the light of it, and then are said to prove the premise. Yet the fact that there have been different opinions about good and bad in different times and places in no way proves that none is true or superior to others. To say that it does so prove is as absurd as to say that the diversity of points of view expressed in a college bull session proves there is no truth. On the face of it, the difference of opinion would seem to raise the question as to which is true or right rather than to banish it. The natural reaction is to try to resolve the difference, to examine the claims and reasons for each opinion.

Only the unhistorical and inhuman belief that opinions are held for no reason would prevent the undertaking of such an exciting activity. Men and nations always think they have reasons, and it could be understood to be historians' and social scientists' most important responsibility to make explicit and test those reasons. It was always known that there were many and conflicting opinions about the good, and nations embodying each of them. Herodotus was at least as aware as we are of the rich diversity of cultures. But he took that observation to be an invitation to investigate all of them to see what was good and bad about each and find out what he could learn about good and bad from them. Modern relativists take that same observation as proof that such investigation is impossible and that we must be respectful of them all. Thus students, and the rest of us, are deprived of the primary excitement derived from the discovery of diversity, the impulse of Odysseus, who, according to Dante, traveled the world to see the virtues and vices of men. History and anthropology cannot provide the answers, but they can provide the material on which judgment can work.

I know that men are likely to bring what are only their prejudices to the judgment of alien peoples. Avoiding that is one of the main purposes of education. But trying to prevent it by removing the authority of men's reason is to render ineffective the instrument that can correct their prejudices. True openness is the accompaniment of the desire to know, hence of the awareness of ignorance. To deny the possibility of knowing good and bad is to suppress true openness. A proper historical attitude would lead one to doubt the truth of historicism (the view that all thought is essentially related to and cannot transcend its own time) and treat it as a peculiarity of contemporary history. . . .

BARRY W. SARCHETT

What's All the Fuss About This Postmodernist Stuff?

I have been asked to represent and explain "us": a new generation of academics which Lynne Cheney and her conservative allies refer to as "them." According to Cheney, William Bennett, and conservative think-tank journalists such as Dinesh D'Souza, "we" should be perceived as a monolithic, conspiratorial group of academic barbarians marching under various profane banners—deconstruction, poststructuralism, postmodernism, semiotics, marxism, feminism, multiculturalism, gay and lesbian studies—storming the barricades of Truth, Reason, Beauty, Western Civilization, and other capitalized self-evidently "transcendental" or "universal" Values. At least that's the way the mainstream national press has repeatedly posed the battles of the Culture Wars. Maybe it's the oldest tale of all, and it seems to be playing in Peoria as successfully as it played in Egypt and Rome. Us and Them.

If I told the so-called traditionalists of all the substantial differences among us, maybe they would feel better. But I don't think so. At any rate, if this is a war, I've been asked to take my shots. Yet my account of us can only necessarily be *my* account. One of the primary lessons of poststructuralism is to be *extremely* wary of speaking for others—something only those possessed of Truth or Universal Reason can do. So I don't pretend to be speaking for a we of any kind here. This is one professor's view.

One common charge is that the new theories and methods now so prevalent in the humanities and social sciences are somehow intellectually irresponsible, even faddish, deviations from such timeless norms as "The Tradition." In his book *Illiberal Education*, D'Souza states that "new forms of criticism" generate "an intellectual free fall" which "directly undermine[s] the notion that traditional academic criteria have any validity." D'Souza ignores the obvious fact that new scholarship and theories have been and continue to be subjected to endless academic review and debate. Changes in academic practice have come to be accepted by many precisely because, judged by "traditional academic criteria," they have seemed so persuasive and useful. Furthermore, as very few of the traditionalists acknowledge, much of the "new" thinking has its roots in a rigorous tradition of Western thought itself which can be traced from the Greek Sophists through David Hume's skepticism, the language theories of Nietzche and Wittgenstein, and American philosophical pragmatism. "The Tradition" itself has always been a tradition of debate and innovation. As Barbara Herrnstein Smith of Duke University has noted, those who fail to be enriched, informed, and transformed by new intellectual developments are those who will come to be seen as irresponsible.

Yet this observation does not preclude the cultural conservatives' sense that substantive changes are underway in the academy. However, like all cultural mutations, those in the academy are the products of complex inter-relations of demographic, political, as well as intellectual changes. Demographic changes in undergraduate and graduate schools are probably the most easy to identify. Since World War II women, people of color, children of immigrants, and other previously marginalized groups—including Jews, working-class children, and people who are openly gay—have entered the classrooms and the professions. They have brought with them sets of cultural experiences and values quite different from the relatively homogeneous group of genteel, middle-class males who had been the traditional recipients of post-graduate education. Thus, to take one rather notorious example, it's not hard to see why many of "us" tend to laugh off Allan Bloom's claim in *The Closing of the American Mind* that rock music threatens our souls.

New intellectual developments (what many people simply call "Theory") therefore didn't simply appear because a bunch of young scholars wanted to make up difficult new terms and methods in order to get tenure, which is often the preferred explanation of the Theory-Haters. As the British cultural critic Terry Eagleton puts it, theoretical activity "comes into being when the traditional rationales for a social or intellectual practice have broken down."

Theory is thus a rethinking of what was previously regarded as common sense or self-evident. I would argue that Theory is thinking reinvigorating itself, a cognitive discomfort with accepted forms of knowing and valuing. Theory is by nature perverse and intellectually abusive: in calling our thinking itself into question, it leaves little (if anything) which can be taken for granted. This accounts for much of the resistance to Theory (from some quarters of the left as well as the right). And the "new" theories, often lumped together as poststructuralism or postmodernism, are especially abusive.

I remember vividly my own initiation into the mysterious Land of the "Post's." In my second year of grad school I took a course in Contemporary

Aesthetics to see what all the fuss was about. The first text we read in the course, *S/Z* by the French critic Roland Barthes, struck me like the discovery of a new species might strike a biologist: not only did I have to struggle to understand what sort of critter this text was, but once I began to understand, it forced me to revise all my previous ways of thinking about the entire biosphere of books, reading, culture, and language. I discovered that a work of critical theory could challenge me as deeply as I had been challenged by Dostoyevsky or Faulkner.

In Barthes' hands, a seemingly straightforward short story by Balzac becomes a simmering surface of codes, multiplicities, implications, processes, and possibilities which can have no end or resolution. Barthes showed me how incredibly complicated the previously-taken-for-granted process of reading is, the exasperatingly multifaceted relations of readers to language. I found this prospect liberating rather than frustrating. I had been taught that only certain select texts were full of the "complexity" and "ambiguity" which mark the truly worthwhile literary work. But then I realized that an insightful and probing reader can make any text dance with possibility because reading itself puts into play so many diverse and complicated acts. Barthes, for example, has produced wonderfully suggestive "readings" of "texts," such as wrestling matches, striptease, and clothes.

At this point, all sorts of barriers and boundaries began breaking down in my thinking. Formerly self-evident distinctions between good and bad, high and low began to look more and more suspicious. "Texts" which I had always taken guilty pleasure in, such as Hollywood movies, detective novels, and (even!) TV shows and popular songs, and which I had been taught were not serious or mature, began to take on new life as rich, variegated cultural phenomena. Barthes had shown me that "reading" them involved the same sort of processes as reading the "great" works. So I began to suspect that what made something great might depend more on what texts particular sets of readers value than on any intrinsic literary attributes of the texts themselves. The more I have explored the nature of language and culture since that initial bout with *S/Z*, the more unstable and arbitrary traditional boundaries and standards have looked.

My subsequent attempts to digest a whole new world of formidable, nuanced, and rigorous critics and theorists has proven to be the most rewarding undertaking of my intellectual life. I learned that, roughly speaking, most new forms of analysis had arisen out of insights culled from 20th century linguistics, most notably the "structuralist" theory of language of Ferdinand de Saussure (1857–1913). Saussure's most influential conception involved the nature of the linguistic "sign." He argued that all signs are composed of a signifier (word) and a signified (concept to which the word refers). Furthermore, he noticed that the relationship between signifier and signified is arbitrary and culturally and historically determined. So different languages carve up the world of things and ideas in different ways which will be more or less incommensurable.

As Saussure says, "A linguistic system is a series of differences of sound combined with a series of differences of ideas." The signifier "tree" works as part of a sign because it is different from "free," "three," "tray," "brie," "trip," and so on. From a Saussurian viewpoint "tree" does not convey meaning because it has some innate connection to a "real" thing like "tree-ness" (some languages, for example, don't distinguish between "trees" and what we might call a "bush"), but because it exists in a system of different sounds and written marks.

This of course leads to the disconcerting possibility that language is a self-enclosed system which can have only a very murky relationship to a "real" world without words. Poststructuralists often point to the dictionary to demonstrate: for every signifier (word) we find several signifieds (referents), which in turn will be found as signifiers with their own bevy of signifieds, *ad infinitum*. This is what is known as the "chain of signification," in which a final and stable meaning (or signified) is forever deferred as signifiers relentlessly slide across and into other signifiers.

Lynne Cheney asserted . . . that it is an "enduring" or "transcendental" truth that "people love children." But what exactly does Cheney mean here? After all, a timeless truth must be very clear or how could it be true? So just what does "love" signify? Is there a universally shared intrinsic meaning here? But there are many possible meanings for this word, even if just the English language is considered. Which did she mean? We seem to be inundated lately with kinds of "love" for children of which "we" disapprove violently. So maybe we ought to agree that incestuous love or molestation isn't "love"? Surely that's not what Cheney meant by "love," was it? But this is a specific cultural agreement to limit the possible significations of the word—and the more we try to specify what Cheney means by her statement, the more we will have to come to a shared, highly qualified agreement that will become more and more specific and seems less and less universal. When does too much "love" cease to be love and become something like (to borrow a particularly unclear signifier) "co-dependency"? Or did Cheney mean that people and children are co-dependent? What amount of "love" is not enough and becomes something like "like"? What has happened to the possibilities of "people love children" by now? And does Cheney mean *all* people by "people"? W.C. Fields would disagree (let's keep his films out of the canon). Does Cheney mean that "people" (whoever that is, by now; *most* people? Just how many is that?) love *all* children? Or do we like some and love others? Does she mean babies as well as 17-year-olds (still legally children in our society)? People love minors but not necessarily 18-year-olds? Obviously, we could go on and on, and we haven't even left our culture (and dominant family structure) or our language yet. So our "enduring truth" now seems something like this: "some people love some children in particularly proper ways that are what I really mean by 'love' *if* we can agree on my definition." With universals like that, who needs particulars?

By acknowledging the unstable or undecidable nature of signification, poststructuralism calls into question any claims for a transparent mimetic language corresponding to the real world. This in turn calls into question any claims for a position outside or neutral or objective which is not already caught up in signifying systems itself (which holds for the position of poststructuralists as well, and that's another very interesting story).

In addition, galvanized by the work of French philosopher Jacques Derrida, poststructuralism has latched on to Saussure's concept of "difference"—*the* key word in recent theory—to show that meaning depends on binary systems of difference (man/woman, universal/particular, nature/culture, reason/belief, even identity/difference) in which one side of the binary is culturally "privileged" or "prior" and the other is merely nonessential or inferior. Derrida "deconstructs" these constructed hierarchies by showing that the privileged term in fact depends for its very meaning on the inferior term (in more exasperating terms, it is what it is not) and that any half of a binary can thus be redescribed as being a function of that which it claims to be prior to. This means that the very structures of meaning through which we "think" the world are arbitrarily stabilized and can be shown, through analyses of our language, to be fluid and self-contradictory.

When poststructralism is combined with the historical and political experience of the new generation of academics, it has turned out to be a very heady mixture. I would mention two crucial historical phenomena which rose to consciousness roughly in the sixties: the new social movements and the media. The civil rights movement and feminism, for example, have urged minorities and women to (re)discover their own voices and values rather than being defined through "scripts" or "discourses" written by the dominant white and patriarchal culture. Soon gays and lesbians discovered that they too had been "closeted" by dominant discourses which they sought to shed. These new social movements, in essence, have noticed that many voices have been occluded in both the academy and the larger culture, and they have insisted on being heard in terms of their own choosing.

In the humanities, this has resulted in new forms of reading which expose, for example, how particular patriarchal notions of gender roles have been coded as "universal" in many of our central cultural texts. It has meant the uncovering of previously ignored texts and the production of new forms of literature and history in which previously silenced voices try to find a language and vocabulary to articulate themselves.

Simultaneously, being raised in Marshall McLuhan's "global village" of the mass media, many of us learned that The Image is All. From the televised Kennedy assassination to the televised Vietnam War, it seemed to be widely recognized that "reality" is something manufactured or constructed, at least in so far as cultural *meanings* are concerned. It felt as if culture was essentially up for grabs. Yet the academy, especially in the humanities, seemed ill-equipped to understand the dynamics of the media, given its sacralization of "high culture" and Olympian disdain for the lived culture—advertisements, sitcoms, rap music, etc.—of the vast majority of people.

The new social movements provided a lived experience of "binary oppositions" such as masculine/feminine or civilized/primitive being questioned and deconstructed. The rise of the media neatly cohered with the theoretical insight that the signifier (image) has no stable or necessary relation to its signified (referent). Taken together, the result has been a thorough relativization of knowledge and value, a theoretical and experiential immersion in difference and the subtle but compelling connections between culture and power. The texts we read and how we read them, the images we see and what they mean, the knowledge we have and how (and to whom) it is transmitted—all these determine who is heard and who hears, who knows and who is merely known, who defines reality and who is defined by it.

The postmodern turn then requires that we pay as much attention to who is speaking and who is not authorized to speak as we do to what is being spoken. It requires a sense therefore that all knowledge and values depend on power differentials: some voices have cultural power to define good and bad, high and low, true and false, while others must live inside those definitions because they are relatively voiceless. When people talk about what is true or false, good or bad, the postmodern response is to pose more questions: better or worse for whom? In what context? For what purposes?

Notice I did *not* say that everything is as true or good as everything else; I am however implying that everything is *contingently* good or bad or true or false, and that judgments are *differently* validated. Thus I am quite willing to believe that for Allan Bloom and people more or less like him, given their personal economies, rock music would indeed harm their souls. Bloom's problem is that he takes his soul as some kind of universal soul, thus forever banishing me (and presumably the Soviet rock fans of recent events) from the realm of those who may live a "truly serious life" (his words). For Bloom then, education is a process of eradicating difference, since to have "real taste" and enjoy "real art" (his words again) means, as far as I can tell, to become like Allan Bloom. Excuse me if I opt out.

But what can a poststructuralist opt for? Since many people object that poststructuaralist approaches can only act negatively to demystify or de-

[handwritten margin note: core of response to Bloom. Yes, I am talking about relativistic values.]

construct, I take this question very seriously. I find that in my own discipline—English—new critical terms and methods have had an invigorating effect on scholarship and classroom practice. For one thing, they demand that students and teachers continually reflect on classroom practice itself: what values are being assumed in any particular reading or evaluation of a literary text? In the selection of the texts for the course? What questions are being asked and what kind of questions are therefore ignored or rendered illegitimate? What makes one reading or evaluation more acceptable than another—for whom and in what context?

As students discover that meaning is radically unstable, they feel more adventurous in their own readings. At the same time, as they learn the rules of discourse more or less accepted in the academic literary community, they realize how to persuade others in this particular context at this particular time without the helpless feeling that the rules have mysteriously appeared like a burning bush. They learn instead that the rules are fluid and in continual dispute among their own teachers. They discover that they are being introduced to a never-ending conversation in which meanings and values— and even the rules of conversing—are continually contested. To my mind, the cultural conservatives are upset precisely because voices previously excluded from the conversation have called into question many of the assumptions and values which propped up the authority and "universality" of previously dominant voices.

Students in a postmodern literary classroom should therefore even be encouraged to question the status of what counts as Literature or not, since that concept has varied widely over time. Forms previously relegated to the unworthy pile of the nonliterary or merely "popular" (guilty pleasures such as romances or detective novels) can be newly examined without condescension to either the texts or their readers. In such a classroom neither Shakespeare nor Dickinson is to be treated as sacred scripture containing a universal wisdom which can be properly decoded only by a self-selected *illuminati*. Instead, each has been interpreted and valued (or not valued) differently for different purposes by different people in different historical and cultural circumstances. In other words, "Shakespeare" and "Dickinson" are cultural constructions through which aesthetic, moral, and social values are contested. Literature thus assumes an important position in the web of social relations, and how it is defined and transmitted—what texts are read and valued and how they are read and valued—by students and teachers contributes in some measure to the ways we think of ourselves and our world (i.e., our signification practices) in terms of gender, ethnicity, age, class, and community. It matters both personally and politically how we conceive of Othello or Prospero or Queen Gertrude.

To treat literary works as timeless and universal statements seems to me the most boring, reductive method of teaching and reading imaginable. As the critic Myra Jehlen says, if we present students an Othello who embodies the general human condition, the complexities of human difference are submerged. Instead Jehlen argues for "explicating the particular."

Explicating the particular eventually requires, of course, a keen historical awareness of differences (which must include the differences of gender, race, and class) in Shakespearean England, the differences between then and now, and the different characterizations of Othello which have influenced our different senses of him today. A large undertaking, I'll admit, but one which complicates and expands Shakespeare's creation, inserts it back into the multifaceted and specific interactions of particular human beings at particular times. That is, we insert Shakespeare back into the messiness of political and cultural *life* not into the cloudy realms of "enduring truth."

A rather dramatic example of the political volatility and excitement of explicating the particular was brought home to me last spring in my Faulkner course. One of the texts we discussed at length was *Sanctuary*, one of Faulkner's most controversial and violent novels, which contains a notorious rape scene. When I explained why many critics have argued that Temple Drake, the female protagonist, is largely responsible for her rape, all of the women—and many of the men—in the class were vociferous in their condemnation of the novel. Some raised the very legitimate concern that Faulkner was in fact a misogynist and thus questioned his status as a major novelist. At the outset of the class, I had explained that the course's purpose was neither to enshrine Faulkner nor to accept his fiction as an expression of timeless wisdom, and the students had taken me at my word. Despite their growing admiration for Faulkner's narrative and stylistic virtuosity, many seemed ready to write him off as sanctioning violence against women.

I then asked several students to report on critical essays exploring *Sanctuary* and Temple from a feminist perspective. In these readings, the novel looks very different, and Temple does not emerge as a willing participant in her victimization. These essays sparked a great deal of impassioned and heated debate, in which the students not only examined Faulkner's novel, but fastened their sights on the particular ways our culture encodes "promiscuity," violence against women, and gender roles in general, and how these codes function in this particular text.

As for me, I kept trying to return the discussion to the problems of interpretation and signification, reminding the class that none of the various critics we read were stupid or inept readers. In fact, all of them had used textual evidence and critical thinking to support what were sometimes diametrically opposed readings. However, particular readers with different perceptual lenses had construed the novel differently, sometimes noticing details that others had missed, sometimes construing the same detail in different ways, given a different line of sight. Was Faulkner then a misogynist or (as some feminist critics have argued) a demystifier of patriarchal authority? Or, as a deconstructive reader might show, does the novel unravel each possibility? Or could it be that authors have little if any control over how their texts are construed because the signification process is so slippery, contingent, and particular?

Likewise, even if I wanted to (which I don't, and I don't even know of any of "us" who do, except those who insist on saluting Faulkner's "greatness"), I cannot finally control what each particular student will end up thinking of Faulkner or *Sanctuary.* I can't even predict how they will react to my repeated demonstrations of interpretive undecidability.

And so, in writing this article, I obviously hope that I have persuaded you of the "validity" of my position. But I can (probably) be assured of something else, given the process of signification. Each of you will read what I have said here and respond to it in more or less different ways: some may be upset and some may rush to Lynne Cheney's transcendental values for relief; some—I hope many—may cheer; some will be variously ambivalent; some may think me a misled radical; for some I'll appear not radical enough; some will want to know more; some will be bored. But none will construe what I have said in precisely the same way, nor will anyone fully construe it as I intended it be construed (whatever I did intend, which I myself cannot even fully know). Each of you will take from my article what you need to, and may in turn test your version against others' as they test theirs against yours—each of course (mis)construing the other in some way. This is what I find most exciting about life inside and outside the classroom: the endless proliferation of difference.

J O H N   R .   S E A R L E

Postmodernism and the Western Rationalist Tradition

Debates about the nature of higher education have been going on in American . . . universities for decades. There is nothing new about passionate controversies over the curriculum, over academic requirements, and even over the aims of higher education itself. But the current debates are in certain respects unusual. Unlike earlier academic reformers, many of the present challengers to the academic tradition have an explicitly leftist political agenda, and they seek explicit political goals. Furthermore, and more interestingly, they often present a challenge not just to the content of the curriculum but to the very conceptions of rationality, truth, objectivity, and reality that have been taken for granted in higher education, as they have been taken for granted in our civilization at large. I would not wish to exaggerate this point. The challengers of the tradition present a wide variety of different viewpoints and arguments. They are by no means united. But there has been a sea change in discussions of the aims of education in that the ideals which were previously shared by nearly everyone in the disputes—ideals of truth, rationality, and objectivity, for example—are rejected by many of the challengers, *even as ideals*. This is new.

In some of the disciplines in the humanities and social sciences, and even in some of the professional schools, there now are developing two more or less distinct faculty subcultures, one might almost say two different universities. The distinction between the two subcultures cuts across disciplinary boundaries, and it is not sharp. But it is there. One is that of the traditional university dedicated to the discovery, extension, and dissemination of knowledge as traditionally conceived. The second expresses a much more diverse set of attitudes and projects, but just to have a label, I will describe it as the subculture of "postmodernism." I do not mean to imply that this concept is well-defined or even coherent, but when describing any intellectual movement it is best to use terms the adherents themselves would accept, and this one appears to be accepted as a self-description by many of the people I will be discussing.

I referred above to "debates," but that is not quite accurate. There really is not much in the way of explicit debate going on between these two cultures over the central philosophical issues concerning the mission of the university and its epistemic and ontological underpinnings. There are lots of debates about specific issues such as multiculturalism and affirmative action, but not much in the way of a debate about the presuppositions of the traditional university and the alternatives. In journalistic accounts, the distinction between the traditional university and the discourse of postmodernism is usually described in political terms: the traditional university claims to cherish knowledge for its own sake and for its practical applications, and it attempts to be apolitical or at least politically neutral. The university of postmodernism thinks that all discourse is political anyway, and it seeks to use the university for beneficial rather than repressive political ends. This characterization is partly correct, but I think the political dimensions of this dispute can only be understood against a deeper dispute about fundamental philosophical issues. The postmodernists are attempting to challenge certain traditional assumptions about the nature of truth, objectivity, rationality, reality, and intellectual quality.

In what follows, I will try to identify some of the elements of the Western conceptions of rationality and realism that are now under challenge. My aim is not so much to resolve the disputes but to identify (at least some of) what exactly is in dispute. I will also briefly discuss some of the consequences different conceptions of rationality and realism have for higher education. These are not the only issues underlying the disputes in current debates about higher education, nor are these the only theoretical and philosophical issues in higher education, but they are worth discussing and as far as I know have not been addressed in quite these terms before.[1]

The Western Traditions: Some Preliminaries

There is a conception of reality, and of the relationships between reality on the one hand and thought and language on the other, that has a long history in the Western intellectual tradition. Indeed, this conception is so fundamental that to some extent it defines that tradition. It involves a very particular conception of truth, reason, reality, rationality, logic, knowledge, evidence, and proof. Without too much of an exaggeration one can describe this conception as "the Western Rationalistic Tradition." The Western Rationalistic Tradition takes different forms but it underlies the Western conception of science, for example. Most practicing scientists simply take it for granted. In the simplest conception of science, the aim of science is to get a set of true sentences, ideally in the form of precise theories, that are true because they correspond, at least approximately, to an independently existing reality. In some other areas, such as the law, the

Western Rationalistic Tradition has undergone some interesting permutations and it is certainly no longer in its pure form. For example, there are rules of procedure and evidence in the law which are adhered to even in cases where it is obvious to all concerned that they do not produce the truth. Indeed, they are adhered to even in cases when it is obvious that they prevent arriving at the truth. The Western Rationalistic Tradition is not a unified tradition in either its history or in its present application.

Two forms of disunity need special emphasis. First, at any given time the most cherished assumptions of the Western Rationalistic Tradition have been subject to challenge. There has seldom been unanimity or even consensus within it. Second, over time those assumptions have evolved, typically in response to challenges. For example, the role of sacred texts such as Scriptures in validating claims to knowledge, the role of mystical insight as a source of knowledge, and the role of the supernatural generally have declined spectacularly with the demystification of the world that began, roughly speaking, with the advent of the modern era in the seventeenth century. Any attempt to characterize the Western Rationalistic Tradition, therefore, inevitably suffers from some degree of oversimplification or even distortion. Furthermore, any attempt such as I am about to make to describe its present form is inevitably from the point of view of a particular thinker at a particular time and place—how it seems to him or her, then and there. And, by the way, the recognition of this limitation—that accuracy and objectivity are difficult to attain because of the fact that all representation is *from a point of view and under some aspects and not others—* is one of the central epistemic principles of the Western Rationalistic Tradition in its current incarnation.

I believe a decisive step in the creation of the Western Rationalistic Tradition was the Greek creation of the idea of a *theory*. It is important to state this point precisely. Many features of the Western Rationalistic Tradition—the presupposition of an independently existing reality, and the presupposition that language, at least on occasion, conforms to that reality—are essential to any successful culture. You cannot survive if you are unable to cope with the real world, and the ways that human beings characteristically cope with the real world essentially involve representing it to themselves in language. But the introduction of the idea of a theory allowed the Western tradition to produce something quite unique, namely systematic intellectual constructions that were designed to describe and to explain large areas of reality in a way that was logically and mathematically accessible. Euclid's *Elements* provides a model for the kind of logical relationships that have been paradigmatic in the Western tradition. Indeed, the Greeks had almost everything necessary for theory in the modern sense. One essential thing they lacked and which Europe did not get until the Renaissance was the idea of systematic experiments. The Greeks had logic, mathematics, rationality, systematicity, and the notion of a theoretical construct. But the idea of matching theoretical constructs against an independently existing reality through systematic experimentation really did not come in until much later. However, I am getting ahead of my story.

Another feature of Western Rationalistic Tradition is its self-critical quality. Elements within it have always been under challenge; it was never a unified tradition. The idea of *critique* was always to subject any belief to the most rigorous standards of rationality, evidence, and truth. Socrates is the hero of the intellectual branch of the Western Rationalistic Tradition . . . in large part because he accepted nothing without argument and was relentlessly critical of any attempts at solving philosophical problems. Recently, however, the self-critical element in the Western Rationalistic Tradition has had a peculiar consequence. If the point of the criticisms is to subject all beliefs, claims, prejudices, and assumptions to the most rigorous scrutiny through the magnifying glass of rationality, logic, evidence, etc., then why should the criticisms eventually not be directed at rationality or logic or evidence themselves? The heroic age of the Western Rationalistic Tradition came during and after the Renaissance when the faiths and dogmas of the Middle Ages were subjected to ever more savage criticisms, until finally we reached the European Enlightenment and the skepticism of Hume and Voltaire, for example. But now, why should we not also be skeptical of rationality, logic, evidence, truth, reality, etc., themselves? If the uncritical acceptance of a belief in God can be demolished, then why not also demolish the uncritical acceptance of the belief in the external world, the belief in truth, the belief in rationality, indeed, the belief in belief? At this point, the Western Rationalistic Tradition becomes not merely self-critical, but self-destructive. . . .

The Western Rationalistic Tradition: Some Basic Principles

Now I want to try to articulate some essential features of the Western Rationalistic Tradition in its contemporary incarnation. What is in dispute? What is under attack? What is presupposed by the intellectual tradition that stretches back to the Greeks? For example, the Western Rationalistic Tradition is sometimes accused of "logocentrism"; a few decades ago, the same style of objection was made to something called "linear thinking." What exactly does one accept when one is "logocentric," i.e., when one accepts the Greek ideal of "logos" or reason? What is one committed to when one engages in "linear thinking," i.e., when one tries to think straight? If we can understand the answers to these questions, we will know at least something of what is at stake in the current debates in higher education. . . .

For the sake of simplicity, I will state what I take to be some of the basic tenets of the Western Rationalistic Tradition as a set of propositions.

[1.] *Reality exists independently of human representations.* This view, called "realism," is the foundational principle of the Western Rationalistic Tradition. The idea is that though we have mental and linguistic representations of the world in the form of beliefs, experiences, statements, and theories, there is a world "out there" that is totally independent of these representations. This has the consequence, for example, that when we die, as we will, the world will in large part go on unaffected by our demise. It is consistent with realism to recognize that there are large areas of reality that are indeed social constructs. Such things as money, property, marriage, and governments are created and maintained by human cooperative behavior. Take away all of the human representations and you have taken away money, property, and marriage. But it is a foundational principle of the Western Rationalistic Tradition that there are also large sections of the world described by our representations that exist completely independently of those or any other possible representations. The elliptical orbit of the planets relative to the sun, the structure of the hydrogen atom, and the amount of snowfall in the Himalayas, for example, are totally independent of both the system and the actual instances of human representations of these phenomena.

This point needs to be stated carefully. The vocabulary or system of representation in which I can state these truths is a human creation, and the motivations that lead one to investigate such matters are contingent features of human psychology. Without a set of verbal categories I cannot make any statements about these matters or about anything else. Without a set of motivations, no one would bother. But the actual situations in the world that correspond to these statements are not human creations, nor are they dependent on human motivations. This conception of realism forms the basis of the natural sciences.

[2.] *At least one of the functions of language is to communicate meanings from speakers to hearers, and sometimes those meanings enable the communication to refer to objects and states of affairs in the world that exist independently of language.* The basic conception of language in the Western Rationalistic Tradition contains both the communicative and the referential character of language. The speaker can succeed in communicating thoughts, ideas, and meanings generally to a hearer; and language can be used by speakers to refer to objects and states of affairs that exist independently of the language and even of the speaker and the hearer. Understanding is possible because the speaker and the hearer can come to share the same thought, and that thought, on occasion at least, concerns a reality independent of both. . . .

How does it work? How is it possible that communication can take place? How is it possible that words and sentences relate? In the twentieth century, the philosophy of language became central to philosophy in general, both because of its own intrinsic interest and because it was central to other problems in philosophy such as the nature of knowledge and truth.

[3.] *Truth is a matter of the accuracy of representation.* In general, statements attempt to describe how things are in the world that exists independently of the statement, and the statement will be true or false depending on whether things in the world really are the way that the statement says they are.

So, for example, the statement that hydrogen atoms have one electron, or that the earth is 93 million miles from the sun, or that my dog is now in the kitchen are true or false depending on whether or not things in the hydrogen atom, solar system, and domestic canine line of business, respectively, are really the way these statements say that they are. Truth, so construed, admits of degrees. The statement about the sun, for example, is only *roughly true.*

In some versions, this idea is called the "correspondence theory of truth." It is often presented as a definition of "true" thus: *A statement is true if and only if the statement corresponds to the facts.*

In recent centuries, there has been a lot of debate among professional philosophers over the correspondence theory of truth. Much of this debate is about special problems concerning the notions of fact and correspondence. Does the notion of correspondence really *explain* anything? Are facts really independent of statements? Does every true statement really correspond to a fact? For example, are there moral facts? And if not, does that mean that there are no true statements in morals? . . .

The correspondence criterion makes it look as if there is a genuine relation between two independently identified entities—the statement and the fact. The difficulty, however, with this conception is that the two entities are not independently identifiable. You cannot answer the question, "which fact does the statement correspond to?," without stating a true statement. So, once I have identified the statement, "the dog is in the kitchen," and then I have identified the fact that the dog is in the kitchen, there is not anything else for me to do by way of comparing the statement to the fact to see if they really do correspond. The alleged correspondence relation has already been established by the very identification of the fact.

Is there any way to explain the correspondence theory which overcomes this difficulty? . . . I think that there is.

The word "fact" has evolved out of the Latin "facere" in such a way that it has come to mean that which corresponds to a true statement in virtue of which the statement is true. So the correspondence theory—a statement is true if and only if it corresponds to a fact—is a truism, a tautology, an analytic statement. But the grammar of the language then misleads us. We think that because "fact" is a noun, and nouns typically name things, and because "corresponds" typically names a relation between things, that therefore there must be a class of complicated objects, the facts, and a relation that true statements bear to these complicated objects, correspondence. But this picture does not work. It sounds plausible for the statement that the dog is in the kitchen but what about the true statement that the dog is not in the kitchen? Or the true statement that three-headed dogs have never existed? What complicated objects do they correspond to?

The mistake is to think that facts are a class of complicated objects, and that to find the truth we must first find the object and then compare it with a statement to see if they really do correspond. But that is not how language works in this area. The fact that the dog is not in the kitchen, or the fact that three-headed dogs have never existed are as much facts as any other, simply because the corresponding statements are true, and "fact" is *defined as* whatever it is that makes a statement true. . . .

The correspondence criterion tells us that the dog is in the kitchen is true if and only if it corresponds to a fact. But which fact? The only fact it could correspond to, if true, is the fact that the dog is in the kitchen. . . . The correspondence theory is trivially true and thus misleads us because we think correspondence must name some very general relation between language and reality, whereas in fact, I am suggesting, it is just a shorthand for all of the enormous variety of ways in which statements can accurately represent how things are. Statements are typically true in virtue of, or because of, features of the world that exist independently of the statement.

The upshot of this discussion, as far as the Western Rationalistic Tradition is concerned, is this: for the most part the world exists independently of language and one of the functions of language is to represent how things are in the world. One crucial point at which reality and language make contact is marked by the notion of truth. In general, statements are true to the extent that they accurately represent some feature of reality that exists independently of the statement.[2] . . .

[4.] *Knowledge is objective.* Because the content of what is known is always a true proposition, and because truth is in general a matter of accurate representation of an independently existing reality, knowledge does not depend on nor derive from the subjective attitudes and feelings of particular investigators. All representation is, as I said earlier, from a point of view and under certain aspects and not others. Furthermore, representations are made by particular investigators, subject to all the usual limitations of prejudice, ignorance, stupidity, venality, and dishonesty; they are made for all sorts of motives on the parts of the makers, some benign, some reprehensible, including desires to get rich, to oppress the oppressed, or even to get tenure. But if the theories put forward accurately describe an independently existing reality, none of this matters in the least. The point is that the objective truth or falsity of the claims made is totally independent of the motives, the morality, or even the gender, the race, or the ethnicity of the maker.

It is worth pausing to state the significance of this principle to some of the present debates. A standard argumentative strategy of those who reject the Western Rationalistic Tradition is to challenge some claim they find objectionable, by challenging the maker of the claim in question. Thus, the claim and its maker are said to be racist, sexist, phono-phallo-logocentric, and so forth. To those who hold the traditional conception of rationality, these challenges do not impress. They are, at best, beside the point. To those within the Western Rationalistic Tradition, these types of challenge have names. They are commonly called argumentum ad hominem and the genetic fallacy. Argumentum ad hominem is an argument against the person who presents a view rather than against the view itself, and the genetic fallacy is the fallacy of supposing that because a theory or claim has a reprehensible origin, the theory or claim itself is discredited. I hope it is obvious why anyone who accepts the idea of objective truth and therefore of objective knowledge thinks this is a fallacy and that an argumentum ad hominem is an invalid argument. If someone makes a claim to truth and can give that claim the right kind of support, and if that claim is indeed true, then that person genuinely knows something. The fact that the whole enterprise of claiming and validating may have been carried out by someone who is racist or sexist is just irrelevant to the truth of the claim. That is part of what is meant by saying that knowledge is objective. It is less obvious, but I hope still apparent, why anyone who denies the possibility of objective truth and knowledge might find *these* sorts of arguments appealing. If there is no such thing as objective truth, then the criteria for assessing claims have no essential connection with truth or falsity, and may as well be concerned with the maker of the argument, his or her motives, the consequences of making the claim, or other such issues.

[5.] *Logic and rationality are formal.* In the Western Rationalistic Tradition, there are traditionally supposed to be two kinds of reason: theoretical reason, which aims at what is reasonable to believe, and practical reason, which aims at what is reasonable to do. But it is, I believe, an essential part of the Western conception of rationality, reason, logic, evidence, and proof that they do not *by themselves* tell you what to believe or what to do. According to the Western conception, rationality provides one with a set of procedures, methods, standards, and canons that enables one to assess various claims in light of competing claims. Central to this view is the Western conception of logic. Logic does not by itself tell you what to believe. It only tells you what must be the case, given that your assumptions are true, and hence what you are committed to believing, given that you believe those assumptions. Logic and rationality provide standards of proof, validity, and reasonableness but the standards only operate on a previously given set of axioms, assumptions, goals, and objectives. Rationality as such makes no substantive claims.

Where practical reason is concerned, this point is sometimes made by saying that reasoning is always about means not about ends. This is not quite right, given the Western conception, because one can reason about whether or not one's ends are proper, appropriate or rational, but only in the light of other ends and other considerations such as consistency. The formal character of rationality has the important consequence that rationality as such cannot be "refuted" because it does not make any claim to refute.

On a natural interpretation, the previous five principles have the following consequence.

[6.] *Intellectual standards are not up for grabs. There are both objectively and intersubjectively valid criteria of intellectual achievement and excellence.* The previous five principles imply, in a fairly obvious way, a set of criteria for assessing intellectual products. Given a real world, a public language for talking about it, and the conceptions of truth, knowledge, and rationality that are implicit in the Western Rationalistic Tradition, there will be a complex, but not arbitrary, set of criteria for judging the relative merits of statements, theories, explanations, interpretations, and other sorts of accounts. Some of these criteria are "objective" in the sense that they are independent of the sensibilities of the people applying the criteria; others are "intersubjective" in the sense that they appeal to widely shared features of human sensibility. An example of objectivity in this sense is the criterion for assessing validity in propositional calculus. An example of intersubjectivity is the sort of criteria appealed to in debating rival historical interpretations of the American Civil War. There is no sharp dividing line between the two, and in those disciplines where interpretation is crucial, such as history and literary criticism, intersubjectivity is correspondingly central to the intellectual enterprise.

There are endless debates in the history of Western philosophy about these issues. In my own view, for example, even objectivity only functions relative to a shared "background" of cognitive capacities and hence is, in a sense, a form of intersubjectivity. However, for the present discussion what matters is that according to the Western Rationalistic Tradition there are rational standards for assessing intellectual quality. Except in a few areas, there is no algorithm that determines the standards and they are not algorithmic in their application. But all the same they are neither arbitrarily selected nor arbitrarily applied. Some disputes may be unsettleable—but that does not mean that anything goes.

For the traditional conception of the university this principle is crucial. For example, in the traditional university, the professor assigns Shakespeare and not randomly selected comic strips, and she does so in the belief that she could demonstrate that Shakespeare is better. No principle of the Western Rationalistic Tradition is more repulsive to the culture of postmodernism than this one, as we will soon see.

Some Consequences of Higher Education

One could continue this list of the essential claims of the Western Rationalistic Tradition for a long time. But even these six theses express a massive and powerful conception. Together they form a coherent picture of some of the relations between knowledge, truth, meaning, rationality, reality, and the criteria for assessing intellectual productions. They fit together. Knowledge is typically of a mind-independent reality. It is expressed in a public language, it contains true propositions—these propositions are true because they accurately represent that reality—and knowledge is arrived at by applying, and is subject to, constraints of rationality and logic. The merits and demerits of theories are largely a matter of meeting or failing to meet the criteria implicit in this conception.

All six of these principles are currently under attack in different forms, and I now want to explore some of the consequences, both of the principles and of the attacks. It is no exaggeration to say that our intellectual and educational tradition, especially in the research universities, is based on the Western Rationalistic Tradition. The scholarly ideal of the tradition is that of the *disinterested* inquirer engaged in the quest for *objective* knowledge that will have *universal* validity. Precisely this ideal is now under attack. . . .

In most academic disciplines it is fairly obvious how acceptance of the Western Rationalistic Tradition shapes both the content and the methods of higher education. As professors . . . we traditionally take ourselves as trying to advance and disseminate human knowledge and understanding, whether it be in physical chemistry, microeconomics, or medieval history. It is less obvious, but still intelligible, how standards of rationality, knowledge, and truth are supposed to apply to the study of fictional literature or the visual arts. Even in these areas the traditional assumptions by which they were studied and taught were of a piece with the rest of the Western Rationalistic Tradition. There were supposed to be intersubjective standards by which one could judge the quality of literary and artistic works, and the study of these works was supposed to give us knowledge not only of the history of literature and art but of the reality beyond to which they refer, if only indirectly. Thus, for example, it was commonly believed, at least until quite recently, that the study of the great classics of literature gave the reader insights into human nature and the human condition in general. It was, in short, something of a cliché that you could learn more about human beings from reading great novels than you could from most psychology courses. Nowadays, one does not hear much talk about "great classics of literature," and the idea of intersubjective standards of aesthetic quality is very much in dispute.

If the relation of the Western Rationalistic Tradition to the traditional ideals of the university is—more or less—obvious, the relation between attacks on the Western Rationalistic Tradition and proposals for educational reform is much less obvious. It is simply a fact that, in recent history, rejection of the Western Rationalistic Tradition has gone hand in hand with the proposals for politically motivated changes in the curriculum. So, what is the connection? I think the relationships are very complex, and I do not know of any simple answer to the question. But underlying all the complexity there is, I believe, this simple structure: those who want to use the universities, especially the humanities, for leftist political transformation correctly perceive that the Western Rationalistic Tradition is an obstacle in their path. In spite of their variety, most of the challengers to the traditional conception of education correctly perceive that if they are forced to conduct academic life according to a set of rules determined by constraints of truth, objectivity, clarity, rationality, logic, and the brute existence of the real world, their task is made more difficult, perhaps impossible. For example, if you think that the purpose of teaching the history of the past is to achieve social and political transformation of the present, then the traditional canons of historical scholarship—the canons of objectivity, evidence, close attention to the facts, and above all, truth—can sometimes seem an unnecessary and oppressive regime that stands in the way of achieving more important social objectives.

In my experience at least, the present multiculturalist reformers of higher education did not come to a revised conception of education from a refutation of the Western Rationalistic Tradition; rather they sought a refutation of the Western Rationalistic Tradition that would justify a revised conception of education that they already found appealing. For example, the remarkable interest in the work of Thomas Kuhn on the part of literary critics did not derive from a sudden passion in English departments to understand the transition from Newtonian Mechanics to Relativity Theory. Rather, Kuhn was seen as discrediting the idea that there is any such reality. If all of "reality" is just a text anyway, then the role of the textual specialist, the literary critic, is totally transformed. And if, as Nietzsche says, "There are not facts, but only interpretations," then what makes one interpretation better than another cannot be that one is true and the other false, but, for example, that one interpretation might help overcome existing hegemonic, patriarchal structures and empower previously underrepresented minorities.

I think in fact that the arguments against the Western Rationalistic Tradition used by a Nietzscheanized Left[3] are rather weak, but this does not matter as much as one might suppose because the refutation of the Western Rationalistic Tradition is not the primary goal. It is only necessary that the refutation have enough respectability to enable one to get on with the primary social and political goal. Historically, part of what happened is that in the late 1960s and 1970s a number of young people went into academic life because they thought that social and political transformation could be achieved through educational and cultural transformation, and that the political ideals of the 1960s could be achieved through education. In many disciplines, for example, analytic philosophy, they found the way blocked by a solid and self-confident professorial establishment committed to traditional intellectual values. But in some disciplines, primarily those humanities disciplines concerned with literary studies—English, French, and Comparative Literature especially—the existing academic norms were fragile, and the way was opened intellectually for a new academic agenda. . . .

Notice that the postmodernist-cultural Left differs from the traditional left-wing movements such as Marxism in that it makes no claims to being "scientific." Indeed it is, if anything, antiscientific, and Marxist-inspired philosophers who accept the Western Rationalistic Tradition, such as Jurgen Habermas, are much less influential in postmodernist subculture than, say, Derrida or Rorty.

There are now departments in some . . . universities that are ideologically dominated by antirealist and antirationalist conceptions, and these conceptions are beginning to affect both the content and the style of higher education. In cases where the objective is to use higher education as a device for political transformation, the usual justification given for this is that higher education has always been political anyway, and since the claim of the universities to impart to their students a set of objective truths about an independently existing reality is a sham hiding political motives, we should convert higher education into a device for achieving beneficial rather than harmful social and political goals.

So far I have argued that the biggest single consequence of the rejection of the Western Rationalistic Tradition is that it makes possible an abandonment of traditional standards of objectivity, truth, and rationality, and opens the way for an educational agenda, one of whose primary purposes is to achieve social and political transformation. I now want to explore the specific forms that this transformation is supposed to take. Most visibly in the humanities, it is now widely accepted that the race, gender, class, and ethnicity of the student defines his or her identity. On this view it is no longer one of the purposes of education, as it previously had been, to enable the student to develop an identity as a member of a larger universal human intellectual culture. Rather, the new purpose is to reinforce his or her pride in and self-identification with a particular subgroup. For this reason, *representativeness* in the structure of the curriculum, the assigned readings, and the composition of the faculty becomes crucial. If one abandons the commitment to truth and intellectual excellence that is the very core of the Western Rationalistic Tradition, then it seems arbitrary and elitist to think that some books are intellectually superior to others, that some theories are simply true and others false, and that some cultures have produced more important cultural products than others. On the contrary, it seems natural and inevitable to think that all cultures are created intellectually equal. In literary studies some of these features are indicated by a change in the vocabulary. One does not hear much about "the classics," "great works of literature," or even "works"; rather the talk nowadays is usually of "texts" with its leveling implication that one text is as much of a text as any other text.

Another form of transformation is this: we now commonly hear in the . . . universities that we must accept new and different conceptions of academic "excellence." We are urged to adopt different criteria of academic achievement. An argument sometimes given in favor of altering the traditional conception of academic excellence is that changes in the university brought about by changes in the larger society require new standards of excellence. A number of new faculty members were not recruited according to the traditional standards and did not enter the university with the idea of succeeding by those standards. Often they have been recruited for various social, political, or affirmative action needs. For these new interests and needs, new criteria of excellence have to be designed. However, the Western Rationalistic Tradition does not give you much room to maneuver where intellectual excellence is concerned. Intellectual excellence is already determined by a set of preexisting standards. In order to redefine excellence, you have to abandon certain features of the Western Rationalistic Tradition.

The connection between the attack on rationality and realism and curricular reform is not always obvious, but it is there to be found if you are willing to look closely enough. For example, many of the multiculturalist proposals for curricular reform involve a subtle redefinition of the idea of an academic subject from that of a *domain to be studied* to that of a *cause to be advanced*. Thus, for example, when Women's Studies departments were created some years ago, many people thought these new departments were engaged in the ("objective," "scientific") investigation of a domain, the history and present condition of women, in the same way that they thought that the new departments of Molecular Biology were investigating a domain, the molecular basis of biological phenomena. But in the case of Women's Studies, and several other such new disciplines, that is not always what happened. The new departments often thought of their purpose, at least in part, as advancing certain moral and political causes such as that of feminism.

And this shift from the territorial conception of an academic department to the moral conception in turn has further consequences down the line. Thus, traditionally the commitment to objectivity and truth was supposed to enable the scholar to teach a domain, whatever his or her moral attitudes about the domain. For example, you do not have to be a Platonist to do a good scholarly job of teaching Plato or a Marxist to do a good job of teaching Marx. But once the belief in objectivity and truth is abandoned and political transformation is accepted as a goal, then it seems that the appropriate person to teach Women's Studies would be a politically active feminist woman. On the traditional conception, there is no reason why Women's Studies should not be taught by a scholar who is male, even by a male who is unsympathetic with contemporary feminist doctrines; but in most Women's Studies departments in the United States that would now be out of the question. I hope it is obvious that analogous points could be made about Chicano Studies, Gay and Lesbian Studies, African American Studies, and other elements of the recent attempts at curricular reform.

Furthermore, the shift from domain-to-be-investigated to moral-cause-to-be-advanced is often not made explicit. When making the case to the general academic public for multiculturalist curriculum, the advocates often cite the uncharted academic territories that need to be investigated and taught, and the educational needs of a changing student population. Among themselves, however, they tend to emphasize the political transformations to be achieved, and these transformations include undermining certain traditional conceptions of the academic enterprise. Traditional "liberal" scholars are easily persuaded that new domains need to be investigated and new sorts of students need to be taught; they are often unaware that the main purpose is to advance a political cause.

I realize that the introduction of curricular reforms and even new academic departments to satisfy political demands is nothing new in the history of American universities. However, there is a difference between the traditional reforms and the new conception of education. Traditionally, the idea was that a new *science* of a particular area would help to solve some pressing political or social problem. For example, the development of political economy as a discipline was built in part around the conception of developing a scientific theory of economy and society that would help solve social problems. Part of the difference that I am pointing to is this: On the new conception, the very idea of "science" is itself regarded as repressive. The idea of developing a rigorous science to investigate, for example, gender and racial differences, is precisely the sort of thing that is under attack. In short, the idea is not to build a new policy on the basis of new scientific theory. Rather, the policy is given in advance and the idea is to develop a departmental and curricular base where that policy can be implemented in the university and extended to the society at large.

I do not wish these remarks to be misunderstood. There are many hardworking men and women engaged in solid traditional scholarship in these new disciplines, and they are committed to the highest standards of truth and objectivity as traditionally conceived. My point here is that they have a significant number of colleagues who do not share these values, and their rejection of these values is connected to their rejection of the Western Rationalistic Tradition.

The introduction of new academic departments is a visible sign of change. Less visible, but much more pervasive, is the change in the self-definition of the individual scholar. I mentioned earlier that there was an increase in the use of ad hominem arguments and genetic fallacies. If there is no such thing as objective truth and validity, than you might as well discuss the person making the argument and his motives for making it, as discuss its claims to validity and the alleged "truth" of its conclusions. But this is only the tip of the iceberg of a much larger shift in sensibility. The new sensibility is usually described (and excoriated) as "relativism," but I think a better term for it might be "politically motivated subjectivism." Previous scholars tried to overcome the limitations of their own prejudices and points of view. Now these are celebrated. For example, funding agencies such as the National Endowment for the Humanities (NEH) receive an increasing number of applications in which it is obvious that the scholar wants to write a book about his or her *politically motivated subjective reactions to, feelings about, and general "take on"* the Renaissance, the plight of women in the Middle Ages, minority novelists of the Pacific Northwest, transvestites in the eighteenth century.

Another scarcely noticed consequence of the rejection of the Western Rationalistic Tradition is the blurring of the distinction between high culture and popular culture in the teaching of the humanities. Traditionally, the humanities thought of themselves as conserving, transmitting, and interpreting the highest achievements of human civilization in general and Western civilization in particular. This view is now regarded as elitist, and there has now been a general abandonment of the idea that some works are qualitatively better than others. There is, rather, the assumption that all works are simply texts and can be treated as such.

On the traditional conception, the distinction between high culture and popular culture manifested itself in the fact that works of high culture were celebrated whereas works of popular culture were, if studied at all, treated as objects of sociological study or investigation. They were treated as symptomatic or expressive, but not themselves as achievements of the highest order. In the subtle shift that has been taking place, no works are celebrated as such. Rather, some works are regarded as important, significant, or valuable because of a political or social message that they convey.

Some Attacks on the Western Rationalistic Tradition

There are really too many kinds of attacks on the Western Rationalistic Tradition, and I am too unfamiliar with many of them, so I can only offer the briefest of surveys. There are deconstructionists, such as Derrida, inspired by Nietzsche and the later works of the German philosopher Martin Heidegger, who think that they can "deconstruct" the entire Western Rationalistic Tradition. There are some feminists who think that the tradition of rationality, realism, truth, and correspondence is essentially a kind of a masculinist device for oppression. There are some philosophers who think that we should stop thinking of science as corresponding to an independently existing reality. Rather, we should think that science in particular, and language in general, just gives us a set of devices for coping. On this view, language is for "coping," as opposed to "matching" or "corresponding." Thus according to Richard Rorty, the pragmatist "drops the notion of truth as correspondence with reality altogether, and says that modern science does not enable us to cope because it corresponds, it just plain enables us to cope."[4]

These attacks on the Western Rationalistic Tradition are peculiar in several respects. First, the movement in question is for the most part confined to various disciplines in the humanities, as well as some social sciences departments and certain law schools. The antirationalist component of the contemporary scene has—so far—had very little influence in philosophy, the natural sciences, economics, engineering, or mathematics. Though some of its heroes are philosophers, it has, in fact, little influence in American Philosophy departments. One might think that since the points at issue are in a very deep sense philosophical, the debates about the curriculum that are connected to the desire to overthrow the Western Rationalistic Tradition must be raging in philosophy departments. But at least in the major American research universities, this, as far as I can tell, is not so. Professional philosophers spend a lot of time fussing around the edges of the Western Rationalistic Tradition. They are obsessed by such questions as: "What is the correct analysis of truth?," "How do words refer to objects in the world?," and "Do the unobservable entities postulated by scientific theories actually exist?" Like the rest of us, they tend to take the core of the Western Rationalistic Tradition for granted even when they are arguing about truth, reference, or the philosophy of science. The philosophers who make an explicit point of rejecting the Western Rationalistic Tradition, such as Richard Rorty or Jacques Derrida, are much more influential in departments of literature than they are in philosophy departments.

A second, and perhaps more puzzling, feature is that it is very hard to find any clear, rigorous, and explicit arguments against the core elements of the Western Rationalistic Tradition. Actually, this is not so puzzling when one reflects that part of what is under attack is the whole idea of "clear, rigorous, and explicit arguments." Rorty has attacked the correspondence theory of truth, and Derrida has claimed that meanings are undecidable, but neither in their works, nor in the works of other favorites of the postmodernist subculture, will you find much by way of rigorous arguments that you can really sharpen your wits on. Somehow or other, there is the feeling that the Western Rationalistic Tradition has become superseded or obsolete, but actual attempts at refutations are rare. Sometimes we are said to be in a postmodern era, and have thus gone beyond the modern era that began in the seventeenth century; but this alleged change is often treated as if it were like a change in the weather, something that just happened without need of argument or proof. Sometimes the "arguments" are more in the nature of slogans and battlecries. But the general air of vaguely literary frivolity that pervades the Nietzscheanized Left is not regarded as a defect. Many of them think that is the way you are supposed to conduct intellectual life.

Two of the most commonly cited authors by those who reject the Western Rationalistic Tradition are Thomas Kuhn and Richard Rorty. I will digress briefly to say a little about them. Kuhn, in *The Structure of Scientific Revolutions,* is supposed to have shown that the claims of science to describe an independently existing reality are false, and that, in fact, scientists are more governed by crowd psychology than by rationality, and tend to flock from one "paradigm" to another in periodic scientific revolutions. There is no such thing as a real world to be described by science; rather each new paradigm creates its own world, so that, for example, as Kuhn says, "after a revolution scientists work in a different world."[5]

I think this interpretation is something of a caricature of Kuhn. But even if it were a correct interpretation, the argument would not show that there is no real world independent of our representations, nor would it show that science is not a series of systematic attempts, in varying degrees successful, to give a description of that reality. Even if we accept the most naive interpretation of Kuhn's account of scientific revolutions, it does not have any such spectacular ontological consequences. On the contrary, even the most pessimistic conception of the history of science is perfectly consistent with the view that there is an independently existing real world and the objective of science is to characterize it.

Rorty has many discussions of truth and correspondence and I could not attempt to do them justice here, but I will pick up on only one or two crucial aspects. He says repeatedly that "true" is just a term of commendation that we use to praise those beliefs that we think it is good to believe, and that truth is made and not discovered.[6] The difficulty with the first of these views is that in the ordinary sense of the word, there are lots of things that for one reason or another one thinks it is good to believe that are not true, and lots of things that are true but it would be better if they were not generally believed. I think, for example, that it is good that mothers believe the best of their children even though such beliefs often turn out false. Likewise, the persistence of religious beliefs is on balance a good thing, though most such beliefs are probably false. Rorty's claim suffers from the usual difficulty of such philosophical reductions: it is either circular or obviously false. On the one hand, the criterion of goodness can be defined as truth or correspondence to reality, in which case the analysis is circular. On the other hand, if one does not redefine "truth," there are lots of counterexamples, lots of propositions that it is good for one reason or another for people to believe but which are not true in the ordinary sense of the word; and there are propositions that for one reason or another it would be bad to believe but which are nonetheless true.

There is an ambiguity in Rorty's claim that truth is made and not discovered. Since truth is always in the form of true *statements* and true theories, then indeed true statements and true theories have to be made and formulated by human beings. But it does not follow from this fact that there is no independently existing reality to which their statements and theories correspond. So there is a sense in which truth is made—namely true statements are made. But there is also a sense, consistent with this, in which truth is discovered. What one discovers is that which makes the statements true (or false, as the case might be). In a word, true *statements* are made, but the truth of statements is not made, it is *discovered*.

Rorty's argument is typical of these discussions in that more is *insinuated* than is actually argued for. What is claimed, I guess, is that true statements, like all statements, are made by human beings. What is insinuated is much more serious: there are no facts in the real world that make our statements true, and perhaps the "real world" is just our creation.

The Status of the Western Rationalistic Tradition

I have not found any attacks on the Western Rationalistic Tradition—not in Rorty or Kuhn, much less in Derrida or Nietzsche—that seem to me at all convincing or even damaging to any of the basic principles I have enunciated. But the question naturally arises: is there anything to be said in *defense* of the Western Rationalistic Tradition? Is there any proof or argument that this is one possible right way to think and act? Certainly, alternative visions are possible, so why accept this one?

There is something puzzling about demanding an argument in favor of, or a proof of, the validity of a whole mode of sensibility and framework of presuppositions in which what we count as a proof and as an argument take place. The situation is a bit like the common occurrence of the 1960s in which one was asked to justify rationality: "What is your argument for rationality?" The notion of an argument already presupposes standards of validity and hence rationality. Something only counts as an argument given that it is subject to the canons of rationality. Another way to put this same point is: You cannot justify or argue for rationality, because there is no content to rationality as such, in a way that there is a content to particular claims made within a framework of rationality. You might show that certain canons of rationality are self-defeating or inconsistent, but there is no way to "prove" rationality.

It might seem that with realism the situation is different. Surely, one might say, the claim that reality exists independently of human representations is a factual claim and, as such, can be true or false. I want to suggest that in the actual operation of our linguistic, cultural, and scientific practices, all six principles function quite differently from ordinary empirical or scientific theses. Since realism is the foundation of the entire system, I will say a few words about it. I have presented the Western Rationalistic Tradition as if it consisted of a series of theoretical principles, as if it were simply one theory we might hold along with a number of others. Those of us brought up in our intellectual tradition find this mode of exposition almost inevitable, because our model of knowledge, as I remarked earlier, comes from the presentation of well-defined theses in systematic theoretical structures. But in order that we should be able to construct theories at all, we require a set of background presuppositions that are prior to any theorizing. For those of us brought up in our civilization, especially the scientific portions of our civilization, the principles that I have just presented as those of the Western Rationalistic Tradition do not function as *a theory*. Rather, they function as part of the taken-for-granted background of our practices. The conditions of intelligibility of our practices, linguistic and otherwise, cannot themselves be demonstrated as truths within those practices. To suppose they could was the endemic mistake of foundationalist metaphysics.

In "defense" of realism, the only thing that one can say is that it forms the presupposition of our linguistic and other sorts of practices. You cannot coherently deny realism and engage in ordinary linguistic practices, because realism is a condition of the normal intelligibility of those practices. You can see this if you consider any sort of ordinary communication. For example, suppose I call my car mechanic to find out if the carburetor is fixed; or I call the doctor to get the report of my recent medical examination. Now, suppose I have reached a deconstructionist car mechanic and he tries to explain to me that a carburetor is just a text anyway, and that there is nothing to talk about except the textuality of the text. Or suppose I have reached a postmodernist doctor who explains to me that disease is essentially a metaphorical construct. Whatever else one can say about such situations, one thing is clear: communication has broken down. The normal presuppositions behind our practical everyday communications, and a fortiori, behind our theoretical communications, require the presupposition of a preexisting reality for their normal intelligibility. Give me the assumption that these sorts of communication are even possible between human beings and you will see that you require the assumption of an independently existing reality. A public language presupposes a public world.

Realism does not function as a thesis, hypothesis, or supposition. It is, rather, the condition of the possibility of a certain set of practices, particularly linguistic practices. The challenge, then, to those who would like to reject realism is to try to explain the intelligibility of our practices in light of that rejection. Philosophers in the past who cared seriously about these matters, and who rejected realism, actually tried to do that. Berkeley, for example, tries to explain how it is possible that we can communicate with each other, given that on his view there are no independently existing material objects, but only ideas in minds. His answer is that God intervenes to guarantee the possibility of human communication. One interesting thing about the present theorists who claim to have shown that reality is a social construct, or that there is no independently existing reality, or that everything is really a text, is that they have denied one of the conditions of intelligibility of our ordinary linguistic practices without providing an alternative conception of that intelligibility.

Conclusion

There are many debates going on in the universities today and many proposals for educational change. I have not tried to explain or even describe most of what is going on. I have been concerned with only one issue: the philosophical presuppositions of the traditional conception of higher education and the educational consequences of accepting or denying those presuppositions. I have claimed that a deeper understanding of at least some of the headline issues can be gained by seeing them in their philosophical context.

However, there is one danger endemic to any such presentation. You are almost forced to present the issues as clearer and simpler than they really are. In order to describe the phenomena at all, you have to state them as more or less clear theses on each side: the subculture of the traditional university and the subculture of postmodernism. However, in real life people on both sides tend to be ambivalent and even confused. They are often not quite sure what they actually think. In light of this ambivalence, it is perhaps best to think of the present account not so much as a characterization of the thought processes of the participants in the current debates but as a description of what is at stake.

NOTES

1. I have discussed some related issues in two other articles. See John R. Searle, "The Storm Over The University," *New York Review of Books* XXVII (19) (6 December 1990): 34–42, and John R. Searle, "Is There a Crisis in American Higher Education?," *The Bulletin of the American Academy of Arts and Sciences* XLVI (4) (January 1993): 24–47.

2. I say "in general" because, for example, sometimes statements are self-referential; for example, "This sentence is in English."

3. I believe this expression was coined by Allan Bloom.

4. Richard Rorty, *Consequences of Pragmatism* (Minneapolis, Minn.: University of Minnesota Press, 1982).

5. Thomas S. Kuhn, *The Structure of Scientific Revolutions,* 2d ed. (Chicago, Ill.: University of Chicago Press, 1970), 135.

6. See especially Richard Rorty, *Objectivity, Relativism and Truth,* Philosophical Papers Vol. 1 (Cambridge and New York: Cambridge University Press, 1991.)

Is There a Text in This Class?

On the first day of the new semester a colleague at Johns Hopkins University was approached by a student who, as it turned out, had just taken a course from me. She put to him what I think you would agree is a perfectly straightforward question: "Is there a text in this class?" Responding with a confidence so perfect that he was unaware of it (although in telling the story, he refers to this moment as "walking into the trap"), my colleague said, "Yes; it's the *Norton Anthology of Literature*," whereupon the trap (set not by the student but by the infinite capacity of language for being appropriated) was sprung: "No, no," she said, "I mean in this class do we believe in poems and things, or is it just us?" Now it is possible (and for many tempting) to read this anecdote as an illustration of the dangers that follow upon listening to people like me who preach the instability of the text and the unavailability of determinate meanings; but in what follows I will try to read it as an illustration of how baseless the fear of these dangers finally is.

Of the charges levied against what Meyer Abrams has recently called the New Readers . . . the most persistent is that these apostles of indeterminacy and undecidability ignore, even as they rely upon, the "norms and possibilities" embedded in language, the "linguistic meanings" words undeniably have, and thereby invite us to abandon "our ordinary realm of experience in speaking, hearing, reading and understanding" for a world in which "no text can mean anything in particular" and where "we can never say just what anyone means by anything he writes."[1] The charge is that literal or normative meanings are overridden by the actions of willful interpreters. Suppose we examine this indictment in the context of the present example. What, exactly, is the normative or literal or linguistic meaning of "Is there a text in this class?"

Within the framework of contemporary critical debate . . . there would seem to be only two ways of answering this question: either there *is* a literal meaning of the utterance and we should be able to say what it is, or there are as many meanings as there are readers and no one of them is literal. But the answer suggested by my little story is that the utterance has *two* literal meanings: within the circumstances assumed by my colleague (I don't mean that he took the step of assuming them, but that he was already stepping within them) the utterance is obviously a question about whether or not there is a required textbook in this particular course; but within the circumstances to which he was alerted by his student's corrective response, the utterance is just as obviously a question about the instructor's position (within the range of positions available in contemporary literary theory) on the status of the text. Notice that we do not have here a case of indeterminacy or undecidability but of a determinacy and decidability that do not always have the same shape and that can, and in this instance do, change. My colleague was not hesitating between two (or more) possible meanings of the utterance; rather, he immediately apprehended what seemed to be an inescapable meaning, given his prestructured understanding of the situation, and then he immediately apprehended another inescapable meaning when that understanding was altered. Neither meaning was imposed (a favorite word in the anti-new-reader polemics) on a more normal one by a private, idiosyncratic interpretive act; both interpretations were a function of precisely the public and constituting norms (of language and understanding) invoked by Abrams. It is just that these norms are not embedded in the language (where they may be read out by anyone with sufficiently clear, that is, unbiased, eyes) but inhere in an institutional structure within which one hears utterances as already organized with reference to certain assumed purposes and goals. Because both my colleague and his student are situated in that institution, their interpretive activities are not free, but what constrains them are the understood practices and assumptions of the institution and not the rules and fixed meanings of a language system.

Another way to put this would be to say that neither reading of the question—which we might for convenience's sake label as "Is there a text in this class?"$_1$ and "Is there a text in this class?"$_2$—would be immediately available to any native speaker of the language. "Is there a text in this class?"$_1$ is interpretable or readable only by someone who already knows what is included under the general rubric "first day of class" (what concerns animate students, what bureaucratic matters must be attended to before instruction begins) and who therefore hears the utterance under the aegis of that knowledge, which is not applied after the fact but is responsible for the shape the fact immediately has. To someone whose consciousness is not already informed by that knowledge, "Is there a text in this class?"$_1$ would be just as unavailable as "Is there a text in this class?"$_2$ would be to someone who was not already aware of the disputed issues in contemporary literary theory. I am not saying that for some readers or hearers the question would be wholly unintelligible (indeed, in the course of this essay I will be arguing that unintelligibility, in the strict or pure sense, is an impossibility), but that there are readers and hearers for whom the intelligibility of the question would have neither of the shapes it had, in a temporal succession, for my colleague. It is possible, for example, to imagine someone who would hear or intend the question as an inquiry about the location of an object, that is, "I think I left my text in this class; have you seen it?" We would then have an "Is there a text in this class?"$_3$ and the possibility, feared by the defenders of the normative and determinate, of an endless succession of numbers, that is, of a world in which every utterance has an infinite plurality of meanings. But that is not what the example, however it might be extended, suggests at all. In any of the situations I have imagined (and in any that I might be able to imagine) the meaning of the utterance would be severely constrained, not after it was heard but in the ways in which it *could,* in the first place, be heard. An infinite plurality of meanings would be a fear only if sentences existed in a state in which they were not already embedded in, and had come into view as a function of, some situation or other. That state, if it could be located, would be the normative one, and it would be disturbing indeed if the norm were free-floating and indeterminate. But there is no such state; sentences emerge only in situations, and within those situations, the normative meaning of an utterance will always be obvious or at least accessible, although within another situation that same utterance, no longer the same, will have another normative meaning that will be no less obvious and accessible. (My colleague's experience is precisely an illustration.) This does not mean that there is no way to discriminate between the meanings an utterance will have in different situations, but that the discrimination will already have been made by virtue of our being in a situation (we are never not in one) and that in another situation the discrimination will also have already been made, but differently. In other words, while at any one point it is always possible to order and rank "Is there a text in this class?"$_1$ and "Is there a text in this class?"$_2$ (because they will always have already been ranked), it will never be possible to give them an immutable once-and-for-all ranking, a ranking that is independent of their appearance or nonappearance in situations (because it is only in situations that they do or do not appear).

Nevertheless, there is a distinction to be made between the two that allows us to say that, in a limited sense, one is more normal than the other: for while each is perfectly normal in the context in which their literalness is immediately obvious (the successive contexts occupied by my colleague), as things stand now, one of those contexts is surely more available, and therefore more likely to be the perspective within which the utterance is heard, than the other. Indeed, we seem to have here an instance of what I would call "institutional nesting": if "Is there a text in this class?"$_1$ is hearable only by those who know what is included under the rubric "first day of class," and if "Is there a text in this class?"$_2$ is hearable only by those whose categories of understanding include the concerns of contemporary literary theory, then it is obvious that in a random population presented with the utterance, more people would "hear" "Is there a text in this class?"$_1$ than "Is there a text in this class?"$_2$; and, moreover, that while "Is there a text in this class?"$_1$ could be immediately hearable by someone for whom "Is there a text in this class?"$_2$ would have to be laboriously explained, it is difficult to imagine someone capable of hearing "Is there a text in this class?"$_2$ who was not already capable of hearing "Is there a text in this class."$_1$ (One is hearable by anyone in the profession and by most students and by many workers in the book trade, and the other only by those in the profession who would not think it peculiar to find, as I did recently, a critic referring to a phrase "made popular by Lacan.") To admit as much is not to weaken my argument by reinstating the category of the normal, because the category as it appears in that argument is not transcendental but institutional; and while no institution is so universally in force and so perdurable that the meanings it enables will be normal for ever, some institutions or forms of life are so widely lived in that for a great many people the meanings they enable seem "naturally" available and it takes a special effort to see that they are the products of circumstances.

The point is an important one, because it accounts for the success with which an Abrams or an E. D. Hirsch can appeal to a shared understanding of ordinary language and argue from that understanding to the availability of a core of determinate meanings. When Hirsch offers "The air is crisp" as an example of a "verbal meaning" that is accessible to all speakers of the language, and distinguishes what is sharable and determinate about it from the associations that may, in certain circumstances, accompany it (for example, "I should have eaten less at supper," "Crisp air reminds me of my childhood in Vermont"),[2] he is counting on his readers to agree so completely with his sense of what that shared and normative verbal meaning is that he does not bother even to specify it; and although I have not taken a survey, I would venture to guess that his optimism, with respect to this particular example, is well founded. That is, most, if not all, of his readers immediately understand the utterance as a rough meteorological description predicting a certain quality of the local atmosphere. But the "happiness" of the example, far from making Hirsch's point (which is always, as he has recently reaffirmed, to maintain "the stable determinacy of meaning")[3] makes mine. The obviousness of the utterance's meaning is not a function of the values its words have in a linguistic system that is independent of context; rather, it is because the words are heard as already embedded in a context that they have a meaning that Hirsch can then cite as obvious. One can see this by embedding the words in another context and observing how quickly another "obvious" meaning emerges. Suppose, for example, we came upon "The air is crisp" (which you are even now hearing as Hirsch assumes you hear it) in the middle of a discussion of music ("When the piece is played correctly the air is crisp"); it would immediately be heard as a comment on the performance by an instrument or instruments of a musical air. Moreover, it would *only* be heard that way, and to hear it in Hirsch's way would require an effort on the order of a strain. It could be objected that in Hirsch's text "The air is crisp"₁ has no contextual setting at all; it is merely presented, and therefore any agreement as to its meaning must be because of the utterance's acontextual properties. But there *is* a contextual setting and the sign of its presence is precisely the absence of any reference to it. That is, it is impossible even to think of a sentence independently of a context, and when we are asked to consider a sentence for which no context has been specified, we will automatically hear it in the context in which it has been most often encountered. Thus Hirsch invokes a context by not invoking it; by not surrounding the utterance with circumstances, he directs us to imagine it in the circumstances in which it most likely to have been produced; and to so imagine it is already to have given it a shape that seems at the moment to be the only one possible.

What conclusions can be drawn from these two examples? First of all, neither my colleague nor the reader of Hirsch's sentence is constrained by the meanings words have in a normative linguistic system; and yet neither is free to confer on an utterance any meaning he likes. Indeed, "confer" is exactly the wrong word because it implies a two stage procedure in which a reader or hearer first scrutinizes an utterance and *then* gives it a meaning. The argument of the preceding pages can be reduced to the assertion that there is no such first stage, that one hears an utterance within, and not as preliminary to determining, a knowledge of its purposes and concerns, and that to so hear it is already to have assigned it a shape and given it a meaning. In other words, the problem of how meaning is determined is only a problem if there is a point at which its determination has not yet been made, and I am saying that there is no such point. . . .

Let me recall you to . . . the contention of Abrams and others that authority depends upon the existence of a determinate core of meanings because in the absence of such a core there is no normative or public way of construing what anyone says or writes, with the result that interpretation becomes a matter of individual and private construings none of which is subject to challenge or correction. In literary criticism this means that no interpretation can be said to be better or worse than any other, and in the classroom this means that we have no answer to the student who says my interpretation is as valid as yours. It is only if there is a shared basis of agreement at once guiding interpretation and providing a mechanism for deciding between interpretations that a total and debilitating relativism can be avoided.

But the point of my analysis has been to show that while "Is there a text in this class?" does not have a determinate meaning, a meaning that survives the sea change of situations, in any situation we might imagine the meaning of the utterance is either perfectly clear or capable, in the course of time, of being clarified. What is it that makes this possible, if it is not the "possibilities and norms" already encoded in language? How does communication ever occur if not by reference to a public and stable norm? The answer, implicit in everything I have already said, is that communication occurs within situations and that to be in a situation is already to be in possession of (or to be possessed by) a structure of assumptions, of practices understood to be relevant in relation to purposes and goals that are already in place; and it is within the assumption of these purposes and goals that any utterance is *immediately* heard. I stress immediately because it seems to me that the problem of communication, as someone like Abrams poses it, is a problem only because he assumes a distance between one's receiving of an utterance and the determination of its meaning—a kind of dead space when one has only the words and then faces the task of construing them. If there were such a space, a moment before interpretation began, then it would be necessary to have recourse to some mechanical and algorithmic procedure by means of which meanings could be calculated and in relation to which one could recognize mistakes. What I have been arguing is that meanings come already calculated, not because of norms embedded in the language but because language is always perceived, from the very first, within a structure of norms. That structure, however, is not abstract and independent but social; and therefore it is not a single structure with a privileged relationship to the process of communication as it occurs in any situation but a structure that changes when one situation, with its assumed background of practices, purposes, and goals, has given way to another. In other words, the shared basis of agreement sought by Abrams and others is never not already found, although it is not always the same one.

Many will find in this last sentence, and in the argument to which it is a conclusion, nothing more than a sophisticated version of the relativism they fear. It will do no good, they say, to speak of norms and standards that are context specific, because this is merely to authorize an infinite plurality of norms and standards, and we are still left without any way of adjudicating between them and between the competing systems of value of which they are functions. In short, to have many standards is to have no standards at all.

On one level this counterargument is unassailable, but on another level it is finally beside the point. It is unassailable as a general and theoretical conclusion: the positing of context- or institution-specific norms surely rules out the possibility of a norm whose validity would be recognized by everyone, no matter what his situation. But it is beside the point for any particular individual, for since everyone is situated somewhere, there is no one for whom the absence of an asituational norm would be of any practical consequence, in the sense that his performance or his confidence in his ability to perform would be impaired. So that while it is generally true that to have many standards is to have none at all, it is not true for anyone in particular (for there is no one in a position to speak "generally"), and therefore it is a truth of which one can say "it doesn't matter."

In other words, while relativism is a position one can entertain, it is not a position one can occupy. No on can *be* a relativist, because no one can achieve the distance from his own beliefs and assumptions which would result in their being no more authoritative *for him* than the beliefs and assumptions held by others, or, for that matter, the beliefs and assumptions he himself used to hold. The fear that in a world of indifferently authorized norms and values the individual is without a basis for action is groundless because no one is indifferent to the norms and values that enable his consciousness. It is in the name of personally held (in fact they are doing the holding) norms and values that the individual acts and argues, and he does so with the full confidence that attends belief. When his beliefs change, the norms and values to which he once gave unthinking assent will have been demoted to the status of opinions and become the objects of an analytical and critical attention; but that attention will itself be enabled by a new set of norms and values that are, for the time being, as unexamined and undoubted as those they displace. The point is that there is never a moment when one believes nothing, when consciousness is innocent of any and all categories of thought, and whatever categories of thought are operative at a given moment will serve as an undoubted ground.

Here, I suspect, a defender of determinate meaning would cry "solipsist" and argue that a confidence that had its source in the individual's categories of thought would have no public value. That is, unconnected to any shared and stable system of meanings, it would not enable one to transact the verbal business of everyday life; a shared intelligibility would be impossible in a world where everyone was trapped in the circle of his own assumptions and opinions. The reply to this is that an individual's assumptions and opinions are not "his own" in any sense that would give body to the fear of solipsism. That is, *he* is not their origin (in fact it might be more accurate to say that they are his); rather, it is their prior availability which delimits in advance the paths that his consciousness can possibly take. When my colleague is in the act of construing his student's question ("Is there a text in this class?"), none of the interpretive strategies at his disposal are uniquely his, in the sense that he thought them up; they follow from his preunderstanding of the interests and goals that could possibly animate the speech of someone functioning within the institution of academic America, interests and goals that are the particular property of no one in particular but which link everyone for whom their assumption is so habitual as to unthinking. They certainly link my colleague and his student, who are able to communicate and even to reason about one another's intentions, not, however, because their interpretive efforts are constrained by the shape of an independent language but because their shared understanding of what could possibly be at stake in a classroom situation results in language appearing to them in the same shape (or successions of shapes). That shared understanding is the basis of the confidence with which they speak and reason, but its categories are their own only in the sense that as actors within an institution they automatically fall heir to the institution's way of making sense, its systems of intelligibility. That is why it is so hard for someone whose very being is defined by his position within an institution (and if not this one, then some other) to explain to someone outside it a practice or a meaning that seems to him to require no explanation, because he regards it as natural. Such a person, when pressed, is likely to say, "but that's just the way it's done" or "but isn't it obvious" and so testify that the practice or meaning in question is community property, as, in a sense, he is too.

We see then that (1) communication does occur, despite the absence of an independent and context-free system of meanings, that (2) those who participate in this communication do so confidently rather than provisionally (they are not relativists), and that (3) while their confidence has its source in a set of beliefs, those beliefs are not individual-specific or idiosyncratic but communal and conventional (they are not solipsists).

Of course, solipsism and relativism are what Abrams and Hirsch fear and what lead them to argue for the necessity of determinant meaning. But if, rather than acting on their own, interpreters act as extensions of an institutional community, solipsism and relativism are removed as fears because they are not possible modes of being. That is to say, the condition required for someone to be a solipsist or relativist, the condition of being independent of institutional assumptions and free to originate one's own purposes and goals, could never be realized, and therefore there is no point in trying to guard against it. Abrams, Hirsch, and company spend a great deal of time in a search for the ways to limit and constrain interpretation, but if the example of my colleague and his student can be generalized (and obviously I think it can be), what they are searching for is never not already found. It short, my message to them is finally not challenging, but consoling—not to worry.

NOTES

1. M. H. Abrams, "The Deconstructive Angel," *Critical Inquiry,* 3, no. 3 (Spring 1977), 431, 434.

2. *Validity in Interpretation* (New Haven: Yale University Press, 1967), pp. 218–219.

3. *The Aims of Interpretation* (Chicago: University of Chicago Press, 1976), p. 1.

Relativism, Deconstruction, and the Curriculum

I. Essentialists and Deconstructionists

Consider the opening lines of an op-ed piece that ran in the *Wall Street Journal* in the midst of the controversy that raged over Stanford University's core curriculum: "The intellectual heritage of the West goes on trial at Stanford University today. Most predict it will lose." The controversy referred to by the author of the piece, Isaac Barchas, a Stanford classics major, revolved around the content of Stanford's only year-long requirement in "Western Culture." Students were required to choose one of eight courses, all of which shared a core reading list of fifteen works by classical thinkers such as Plato, Homer, Dante, and Darwin.

If Barchas's characterization is correct, the intellectual heritage of the West lost at Stanford three years ago, with remarkably little opposition from the faculty. The faculty voted, 39 to 4, to replace the requirement in Western Culture with one called "Culture, Ideas, and Values" that adds works of some non-European cultures and works by women, African-Americans, Hispanics, Asians, and Native Americans to a contracted core of the classics. The Old and New Testament, Plato, Saint Augustine, Machiavelli, Rousseau, and Marx remain in the new core.

In the ensuing public debate over whether to change the content of such core courses, one side—call them "essentialists"—argued that to dilute the core with new works for the sake of including previously unheard voices would be to forsake the values of Western civilization for the standardlessness of relativism, the tyranny of the social sciences, lightweight trendiness, and a host of related intellectual and political evils. Another, diametrically opposed side—call them " deconstructionists"—argued that to preserve the core by excluding contributions to civilization by women, African-Americans, Hispanics, Asians, and Native Americans as if the classical canon were sacred, unchanging, and unchangeable would be to denigrate the identities of members of these previously excluded groups and to close off Western civilization from the influences of unorthodox and challenging ideas for the sake of perpetuating sexism, racism, Eurocentrism, closed-mindedness, the tyranny of Truth (with a capital "T"), and a host of related intellectual and political evils.

Much more is at issue, and of value, here than meets the ear in the public debate between essentialists and deconstructionists. If the intellectual heritage of the West went on trial at Stanford and other campuses that have considered changing their core curricula, then the intellectual heritage of the West lost before the trials began. Neither the intellectual heritage of the West nor the liberal democratic ideal of higher education can be preserved by a decision to require or not to require of every university student several courses in fifteen, thirty, or even a hundred great books. Nor can our heritage be eradicated by a decision to decrease the number of canonical books to make room for newer, less established, less widely esteemed or even less lasting works that speak more explicitly to the experiences or better express the sense of social alienation of women and minorities. The reason is not that Western civilization will not stand or fall on such small decisions. A long train of seemingly small abuses can create a large revolution, as we Americans, of all people, should know.

There is another reason, which has been lost in the public debate. Liberal education, an education adequate to serve the life of a free and equal citizen in any modern democracy, requires far more than the reading of great books, although great books are an indispensable aid. We also need to read and think about books, and therefore to teach them, in a spirit of free and open inquiry, the spirit of both democratic citizenship and individual freedom. The cultivation of that spirit is aided by immersion in profound and influential books, like Plato's *Republic,* which expose us to eloquently original, systematically well-reasoned, intimidating, and unfamiliar visions of the good life and good society. But liberal education fails if intimidation leads to blind acceptance of those visions or if unfamiliarity leads us to blind rejection.

These two signs of failure are too often reflected in the public debate over multiculturalism on college and university campuses. In resisting the substitution of new works for old ones, essentialists suggest that the insights and truths of the old will be lost by even partial substitution, which is typically what is at stake in controversies like the one at Stanford. But preservation of tried-and-true verities is not among the best reasons for including the classics in any list of required reading at the university level. Why not say that great books like Plato's *Republic* or Aristotle's *Politics* are among the most challenging to anyone who wants to think carefully, systematically, and critically about politics? It is intellectual idolatry, and not philosophical openness and acuity, that supports the claim, frequently articulated but rarely defended, that the greatest philosophical works—judged by such standards as originality and eloquence, systematic reasoning, depth of moral, psychological, or political understanding, and influence on our inherited social understandings—contain the greatest wisdom now available to us on all significant subjects.

Is Aristotle's understanding of slavery more enlightening than Frederick Douglass's? Is Aquinas's argument about civil disobedience more defensible than Martin Luther King's or John Rawls's? If not, then why not assign students *The Autobiography of Frederick Douglass,* "Letter from Birmingham City Jail," and *A Theory of Justice* alongside the *Politics* and *Summa Theologiae?* Although Rousseau's understanding of women challenges contemporary feminism, it is far less credible or compelling on intellectual grounds than Virginia Woolf's, Simone de Beauvoir's, or Toni Morrison's insights on women. Similarly, Hannah Arendt offers a perspective on political evil that goes beyond that of any canonical political philosopher. Were essentialists explicitly to open their public argument to the possibility that the classics do not contain comprehensive or timeless truths on all significant subjects, they could moderate their critique and recognize the reasonableness of some proposed reforms that create more multicultural curricula.

A significant internal obstacle that stands in the way of moderation is the belief held in reserve by some essentialists that the classics, especially the works of Plato and Aristotle, are the key to timeless moral and political truths, the truths of human nature. In the spirit of Robert Maynard Hutchins, essentialists often invoke Plato, Aristotle, and "nature" as critical standards. The argument, explicitly made by Hutchins but only intimated by Allan Bloom and other contemporary critics, goes roughly as follows: The highest form of human nature is the same in America as in Athens, as should be the content of higher eduction, if it is to be true to the highest in human nature, the intellectual virtues cultivated to their greatest perfection. Here is Hutchins' succinct formulation: "Education implies teaching. Teaching implies knowledge. Knowledge is truth. The truth is everywhere the same. Hence eduction should be everywhere the same. I do not overlook the possibilities of differences in organization, in administration, in local habits and customs. These are details."[1] Essentialists honor and invoke the great books as the critical standard for judging both "lesser" works and societies that inevitably fail to live up to Platonic or Aristotelian standards.

One need not in any way denigrate the great books or defend a standardless relativism to worry about the way in which the essentialist critique of multiculturalism partakes of intellectual idol worship. Compare the essentialist defense of the canon to Ralph Waldo Emerson's approach to books, as argued in "The American Scholar." Emerson's perspective serves as an important challenge to essentialism, and yet no contemporary critic takes up this challenge: "The theory of books is noble. . . . But none is quite perfect. As no air-pump can by any means make a perfect vacuum, so neither can any artist entirely exclude the conventional, the local, the perishable from his book, or write a book of pure thought, that shall be as efficient, in all respects, to a remote posterity, as to contemporaries, or rather to the second age."[2] Emerson is not saying that because even the best books are to some significant extent conventional and rooted in a particular social context, we should read them primarily for what they reflect about their own times rather than what they can say to us and our times. We can still learn a lot about the human condition from Plato's *Republic,* or about our obligation to the state from the *Crito.* But we cannot learn everything profound about obligation, let alone everything worth knowing about the human condition, from reading Plato, Aristotle, or the entire corpus of canonical works.

"Each age," Emerson concludes, "must write its own books."[3] Why? Because well-educated, open-minded people and liberal democratic citizens must think for themselves. In liberal democracies, a primary aim of liberal arts universities is not to create bookworms, but to cultivate people who are willing and able to be self-governing in both their political and personal lives. "Books are the best of things, well used," Emerson argues, "abused, among the worst. What is the right use? . . . They are for nothing but to inspire."[4]

It would also be a form of intellectual idolatry to take Emerson's words as gospel. Books do more than inspire. They also unite us in a community, or communities, of learning. They teach us about our intellectual heritage, our culture, as well as about foreign cultures. American universities may aspire to be more international, but to the extent that our liberal arts curriculum along with our student body is still primarily American, it is crucial . . . that universities recognize who "we" are when they defend a core curriculum that speaks to "our" circumstances, culture, and intellectual heritage. Not because students can identify only with works written by authors of the same race, ethnicity, or gender, but because there are books by and about women, African-Americans, Asian-Americans, and Native Americans that speak to neglected pars of our heritage and human condition, and speak more wisely than do some of the canonical works. Although social injustices concern us all, neglect of noncanonical literature is more acutely perceived by people who identify themselves with the neglected, and the exclusion of such works is not unreasonably thought to reflect lack of respect for members of these groups, or disregard for part of their cultural identities. Criticism of the canon per se should not therefore be equated with tribalism or particularism. Emerson was guilty of neither when he argued that each age must write, and presumably also read, its own books.

Radically opposed to essentialism, deconstructionists erect a different obstacle to liberal democratic education when they deny the desirability of shared intellectual standards, which scholars and students of diverse cultural backgrounds might use to evaluate our common education. Although deconstructionists do not deny the possibility of shared standards, they view common standards as masks for the will to political power of dominant, hegemonic groups. This reductionist argument about intellectual standards is often made on behalf of groups that are underrepresented in the university and disadvantaged in society, but it is hard to see how it can come to the aid of anyone. The argument is self-undermining, both logically and practically. By its internal logic, deconstructionism has nothing more to say for the view that intellectual standards are masks for the will to political power than that it too reflects the will to power of deconstructionists. But why then bother with intellectual life at all, which is not the fastest, surest, or even most satisfying path to political power, if it is political power that one is really after?

Deconstructionism is also impractical. If intellectual standards are political in the sense of reflecting the antagonistic interests and will to power of particular groups, then disadvantaged groups have no choice but to accept the hegemonic standards that society imposes on the academy and the academy in turn imposes on them. The less powerful cannot possibly hope to have their standards win out, especially if their academic spokespersons publicize the view that intellectual standards are nothing more than assertions or reflections of the will to power.

The deconstructionist outlook on the academy not only deconstructs itself, it does so in a dangerous way. Deconsructionists do not *act* as if they believed that common standards are impossible. They act, and often speak, as if they believed that the university curriculum *should* include works by and about disadvantaged groups. And some version of this position, as we have seen, is defensible on universalistic grounds. But the reduction of all intellectual disagreements to conflicts of group interests is not. It does not stand up to evidence or reasoned argument. Anyone who doubts this conclusion might try to demonstrate in a nontautological way that the *strongest* arguments for and against legalizing abortion, not the arguments offered by politicians but the most careful and compelling philosophical arguments, simply reflect the will to power, class and gender interests of their proponents.

Reductionism of intellect and argument to political interest threatens to politicize the university more profoundly and destructively than ever before. I say "threatens" because deconstructionism has not actually "taken over" the academy, as some critics claim. But the anti-intellectual, politicizing threat it poses is nonetheless real. A great deal of intellectual life, especially in the humanities and the "soft" social sciences, depends upon dialogue among reasonable people who disagree on the answers to some fundamental questions about the value of various literary, political,

economic, religious, educational, scientific, and aesthetic understandings
and achievements. Colleges and universities are the only major social institutions dedicated to fostering knowledge, understanding, intellectual dialogue, and the pursuit of reasoned argument in the many directions that it
may lead. The threat of deconstructionism to intellectual life in the academy is twofold: (1) it denies *a priori* that there are any reasonable answers
to fundamental questions, and (2) it reduces every answer to an exercise of
political power.

Taken seriously, on its own terms, the deconstructionist defense of a
more multicultural curriculum itself appears as an assertion of political
power in the name of the exploited and oppressed, rather than as an intellectually defensible reform. And deconstructionism represents critics and
criticisms of multiculturalism, however reasonable, as politically retro-
grade and unworthy of intellectual respect. Whereas essentialists react to
reasonable uncertainty and disagreement by invoking rather than defending timeless truths, deconstructionists react by explaining away our different viewpoints, presuming they are equally indefensible on intellectual
grounds. Intellectual life is deconstructed into a political battlefield of
class, gender, and racial interests, an analogy that does not do justice to
democratic politics at its best, which is not merely a contest of competing
interest groups. But the image conveyed of academic life, the real arena of
deconstructionist activity, is more dangerous still because it can create its
own reality, converting universities into political battlefields rather than
mutually respectful communities of substantial, sometimes even fundamental, intellectual disagreement.

Deconstructionists and essentialists disagree about the value and content
of a multicultural curriculum. The disagreement is exacerbated by the zero-
sum nature of the choice between canonical and newer works, when a few
required core courses become the focus in academic and public discussions
of what constitutes a good education. But disagreement about what books
should be required and how they should be read is not in itself terribly
troubling. No university curriculum can possibly include all the books or
represent all the cultures worthy of recognition in a liberal democratic education. Nor can any free society, let alone any university of independent
scholars and teachers, expect to agree on hard choices between competing
goods. The cause for concern about the ongoing controversies over multiculturalism and the curriculum is rather that the most vocal parties to these
disputes appear unwilling to defend their views before people with whom
they disagree, and to entertain seriously the possibility of change in the face
of well-reasoned criticism. Instead, in an equal and opposite reaction, essentialists and deconstructionists express mutual disdain rather than respect for their differences. And so they create two mutually exclusive and
disrespecting intellectual cultures in academic life, evincing an attitude of
unwillingness to learn anything from the other or recognize any value in

the other. In political life writ large, there is a parallel problem of disrespect and lack of constructive communication among the spokespersons for ethnic, religious, and racial groups, a problem that all too often leads to violence.

The survival of many mutually exclusive and disrespecting cultures is not the moral promise of multiculturalism, in politics or in education. Nor is it a realistic vision: neither universities nor polities can effectively pursue their valued ends without mutual respect among the various cultures they contain. But not every aspect of cultural diversity is worthy of respect. Some differences—racism and anti-Semitism are obvious examples—ought not to be *respected* even if expressions of racist and anti-Semitic views must be *tolerated*.

The controversy on college campuses over racist, ethnic, sexist, homophobic, and other forms of offensive speech directed against members of disadvantaged groups exemplifies the need for a shared moral vocabulary that is richer than our rights to free speech. Suppose one grants that members of a university community should have the right to express racist, anti-Semitic, sexist, and homophobic views provided they do not threaten anyone. What is left to say about the racist, anti-Semitic, sexist, and homophobic remarks that have become increasingly common on college campuses? Nothing, if our shared moral vocabulary is limited to the right of free speech, unless one challenges racist and anti-Semitic statements on free speech grounds. But then the public issue will quickly shift from the pernicious content of the speech to the speaker's right of free speech.

Everything is left to say, however, if we can distinguish between tolerating and respecting differences. Toleration extends to the widest range of views, so long as they stop short of threats and other direct and discernible harms to individuals. Respect is far more discriminating. Although we need not agree with a position to respect it, we must understand it as reflecting a moral point of view. Someone with a pro-choice position on abortion, for example, should be able to understand how a morally serious person without ulterior motives might be opposed to legalizing abortion. There are serious moral arguments to be made against legalization. And vice versa. A multicultural society is bound to include a wide range of such respectable moral disagreements, which offers us the opportunity to defend our views before morally serious people with whom we disagree and thereby learn from our differences. . . .

II. Multiculturalism and Relativism

My [next] aim . . . is to understand the constitutive challenge posed by multiculturalism to social justice. . . . The challenge is that different cultures contain apparently different ethical standards that yield conflicting judgments concerning social justice. To take a striking example, some cultures defend polygamy, while others deem polygamy unjust and subject to governmental prohibition. In light of an apparent conflict in judgment about the justice of an institution as important as the family, a conflict associated with cultural differences, should we not reconsider what justice requires?

The Response of Cultural Relativism

Suppose you believe that your society is justified in recognizing only monogamous marriages. You then discover that polygamous marriages are recognized by some cultures, not your own. Your own cultural background predisposes you to believe that it is right for a government to forbid anyone to marry more than one person at a time. Long after the formation of your basic moral predispositions, you learn that members of some other cultures consider polygamy just and its prohibition unjust, as just as you consider state enforcement of monogamy and as unjust as you would consider its prohibition. Do you have any reason to reconsider your belief in the justice of state-enforced monogamy? Should I reconsider my beliefs about the justice of gender integration in light of learning about purdah, the Muslim practice of gender segregation, which includes the mandatory veiling of women?

Suppose that standards of justice are relative to particular cultural understandings such that the cultural meaning of each social good is what defines its just distribution. Cultural relativism, so understood, challenges the view that some seemingly conflicting practices sanctioned by different cultures, such as enforced monogamy and polygamy or gender integration and purdah, actually pose moral conflicts and on reflection call for criticism of one or both of the conflicting practices. If justice is relative to particular cultural understandings, then polygamy can be unjust for members of my culture and just for members of another culture whose social understandings of marital responsibility and kinship are radically different. Our views on social justice as they apply to our culture are justified (or not) relative to its social understandings. Views on social justice that apply to members of other cultures must be judged by *their* social understandings, not ours. We should ask not whether social practices like polygamy and purdah are justified by the moral considerations that *we* find most compelling, but rather whether they are sanctioned by the relevant social understandings of the cultures within which they are practiced. There is no reason to assume that our moral principles, which we typically learn in relation to problems and practices of our own culture, are the same principles that should apply to other cultures, whose understandings of social goods such as kinship and gender relations differ dramatically from our own.

Cultural relativism claims that the question we should be asking is not what *should* people choose between (state-enforced) monogamy and (state-permitted) polygamy, sexual integration and purdah, religious toleration and shunning, but rather what *do* people who share a culture—and therefore share substantive understandings of social goods as far ranging as kinship and love, education, jobs, health care, and divine grace—choose? Social justice, according to cultural relativism, is the distribution of goods according to their cultural meaning.

What must modern cultures be like for the distributive principle of cultural relativism to work? Each culture must contain a set of social understandings that govern the distribution of goods for that culture. For each good, such as kinship, gender relations, health care, or eduction, there must be an internal social understanding that governs the distribution of that good.[5] Meanings change over time, but at any given time in any given culture, we must be able to locate one relevant meaning for each good. If there are multiple meanings for any given good, then a culture will not sanction a given meaning, and cultural relativism will require reformulation to deal with multiple and competing meanings, a problem to which I will return.

First we should ask what modern cultures are actually like in this regard. A fair test for cultural relativism are modern cultures that are likely to meet this standard of internal agreement. Among the many detailed historical accounts of such cultures, even the apparently most homogeneous contained conflicting understandings of important social goods. Consider the case of Mormonism, which the critic Harold Bloom considers the model of an internally homogeneous, communitarian culture, "a *total* system of belief and behavior, dedicated to particular hopes, dreams, and interpretations."[6]

What do detailed historical investigations of Mormon beliefs reveal about this prototypically nonpluralistic culture? Since the 1840s, when Joseph Smith advocated the duty of polygamy as "the most holy and important doctrine ever revealed to man on earth," Mormons have disagreed about its legitimacy.[7] Historical accounts reveal that long before polygamy was outlawed in the United States, even during the period of greatest devotion to "polygamous duty" (1856–1857), Mormons were internally divided over the legitimacy of the practice.[8] We also have evidence in the testimony of both Mormon men and women, about as good evidence as one ever gets, that nineteenth-century Mormons differed in their beliefs about the desirability of polygamy. Here is a not uncommon set of nineteenth-century Mormon attitudes toward polygamy, expressed by two sister-wives, Becky and Sadie Jacobson. Becky Jacobson says that she has been "happy and blessed as a polygamist wife," whereas Sadie says: "If anyone in this world thinks plural marriage is not a trial, they are wrong. The Lord said he would have a tried people."[9] There are also some rare accounts, even more revealing, like that of a Mormon elder's efforts to marry a second wife. The elder's first wife had told him that if he ever brought a second wife in the front door, she would go out the back one. When another elder from southern Utah pressed upon him a potential second wife, the elder still hesitated to confront his first wife. "Finally," this account goes, "he told her he had had a revelation to marry a certain girl and that in the face of such divine instructions, she must give her consent." The next morning his first wife announced that she too had had a revelation, to "shoot any woman who became his plural wife." He remained monogamous.[10]

In 1890, twelve years following the Supreme Court decision *Reynolds v. United States*[11] that upheld state prohibition of polygamy, the Mormon church officially reversed course and prohibited polygamy, again on doctrinal grounds. Yet approximately 30,000 Mormons today, so-called Mormon fundamentalists, still believe in polygamy and practice it despite plenty of pressure to the contrary. Nor does the practice of polygamy simply split along class lines. Some Mormon women with professional careers today claim that polygamy is "the ideal way for a woman to have a career and children. As I see it, if this life style didn't already exist, it would have to be invented to accommodate career women." Elizabeth Joseph, a lawyer and one of Alex Joseph's nine wives, believes that "polygamy is good feminism." Alex Joseph's reasons are more religious: "Every writer in the Old Testament, except for Daniel, was a polygamist. The way I see it, if you're going to get a degree in electrical engineering, then you have to learn a little something about engineering. And if you're going to understand the Bible, you have to adopt the life style of those who wrote it."[12] None of these views represents *the* Mormon understanding of kinship because there is no single such social understanding endemic to Mormonism, either today or for any significant period of Mormon history, despite the fact that Mormonism has long been seen by outsiders as a nonpluralistic, monolithic culture.

Cultures are often distinguished by a set of dominant social understandings. During most periods, a particular understanding of marriage dominates Mormon culture and contributes to its identity. Faced with the problem of indeterminacy created by multiple understandings of a good within a single culture, cultural relativism might specify that the dominant understanding should rule: polygamy, or the choice between polygamy and monogamy, when sanctioned by the Mormon church and widely accepted among Mormons, state-enforced monogamy after 1890; mandatory veiling when Islamic authorities command the practice and most Moslems comply, voluntary veiling or no veiling when the authoritative or hegemonic consensus breaks down. Even when the dominant understanding is widely shared, it may still, causally speaking, be the standard of the most powerful ("dominant") groups in society, who by virtue of dominating socialization and education also shape social understandings. Hegemony, one might say, characterizes a culture in which the understandings of a dominant group or groups not only prevail but also are widely considered to be just because those understandings appear to be *the* social understandings of that culture.

While presupposing a single shared cultural understanding is false, relying upon the dominant understanding is dangerous. The danger follows not from our always knowing that a dominant understanding is the standard of a dominant group or groups, but rather from our rarely knowing that it is *not* and often having reason to think that it is (even if we cannot prove it). Every culture we know contains significant and systematic disparities of power by race, class, gender, or ethnicity that influence whose or what understandings dominate. The danger of domination exists in any such culture even if we cannot be sure that these disparities account for the dominant understandings. If cultural relativism relies upon the standard of dominant understandings, it threatens to identify justice with the social understandings of dominant groups, and in so doing, implicitly denies that justice can serve as a critical standard to assess dominant understandings.

There is a closely related and still more basic problem that concerns the moral standing of social criticism within a cultural relativist framework. The dominant understandings of justice typically consist of critical standards; they claim adequately to protect the well-being of everyone governed by them. The moral claims of powerful groups are not that their social understandings are ipso facto justified because they are dominant, regardless of the content of those understandings. Consider the social understanding, once dominant in many cultures, that a woman's place is necessarily in the family and not in the public sphere because she is by nature unfit for public life but well suited for, and satisfied by, raising children and caring for her husband. The cultural relativist claim that this social understanding could be justified by virtue of being the dominant understanding (even if the claim about woman's unfitness for public life is demonstrably false) creates a tension with the very content of the understanding itself, that a woman's place is in the home *because* of her natural social function, not because men (or for that matter most men and women) sincerely believe that a woman's place is in the home. The cultural relativist can avoid any logical contradiction here by stipulating that distributions are justified by a social consensus about the justificatory grounds for social understandings even if that consensus is demonstrably false. By protecting itself from an internal contradiction, however, cultural relativism, succumbs to solipsism. Why claim that there is no referent beyond social consensus when the justificatory reasons actually offered by that social consensus refer beyond themselves? Reasons may be rationalizations, in this case of male self-interest, or demonstrably fallacious, for example, on empirical grounds. Exposing reasons as rationalizations or as fallacious calls into question the principles of distributive justice that they claim to support.

Social understandings that serve as the basis of distributive principles—including understandings about the just distribution of labor, love, kinship, money, citizenship, and education—often have a content that calls into question the claim that the dominant social understanding should govern by virtue of its dominance. The same problem applies to social understandings that are not merely dominant but truly shared among all members of a culture. The problem may be harder to discern in the absence of dissent, and certainly more difficult to overcome. A complete social consensus on slavery, assuming one ever existed, would not in itself justify slavery. The social understandings that have been used to justify slavery contain claims about the nature of human beings and the benefits of slavery that stand or fall independently of a social consensus. If cultural relativists agree that there can be standards for judging justice that are independent of social consensus, then they give up the distinctive premise of cultural relativism. . . .

NOTES

1. Robert Maynard Hutchins, *The Higher Learning in America* (New Haven: Yale University Press, 1936), p. 66.

2. Ralph Waldo Emerson, "The American Scholar," in *Selected Essays,* ed. Larzer Ziff (New York: Viking Penguin, 1982), p. 87.

3. Ibid.

4. Ibid., p. 88.

5. The internal social understanding may be to permit people to choose among various options, such as whether to enter into polygamous or monogamous marriages. If agreement exists that people should be free to choose between polygamy and monogamy, then this counts as a single social understanding. If, on the other hand, some people believe the state should enforce monogamy and others that it should permit polygamy (as well as monogamy), then social understandings are divided. To make sense, cultural relativism requires singularity of social understandings, not social practices.

6. Harold Bloom, *The American Religion: The Emergence of the Post-Christian Nation* (New York: Simon and Schuster, 1992), p. 91.

7. Richard S. Van Wagoner, *Mormon Polygamy: A History* (Salt Lake City: Signature Books, 1986), p. iii.

8. Ibid., chaps. 6–7. During this period, fewer than forty percent of Mormon families were polygamous. Although some monogamous Mormons probably . . . accepted polygamy as a legitimate marital choice, others did not.

9. Ibid., pp. 93–94.

10. Ibid., p. 97. The original account is found in Kimball Young, *Isn't One Wife Enough? The Story of Mormon Polygamy* (New York: Henry Holt, 1954), p. 123.

11. 98 U.S. 145 (1878).

12. *New York Times,* Tuesday, April 9, 1991, p. A22.

PART TWO

SEX ON CAMPUS: SEXUAL HARASSMENT AND DATE RAPE

CATHARINE A. MacKINNON

Sexuality

What is it about women's experience that produces a distinctive perspective on social reality? How is an angle of vision and an interpretive hermeneutics of social life created in the group, women? What happens to women to give them a particular interest in social arrangements, something to have a consciousness of? How are the qualities we know as male and female socially created and enforced on an everyday level? Sexual objectification of women—first in the world, then in the head, first in visual appropriation, then in forced sex, finally in sexual murder—provides answers.

Male dominance is sexual. Meaning: men in particular, if not men alone, sexualize hierarchy; gender is one. As much a sexual theory of gender as a gendered theory of sex, this is the theory of sexuality that has grown out of consciousness raising. Recent feminist work, both interpretive and empirical, on rape, battery, sexual harassment, sexual abuse of children, prostitution and pornography, support it. These practices, taken together, express and actualize the distinctive power of men over women in society; their effective permissibility confirms and extends it. If one believes women's accounts of sexual use and abuse by men; if the pervasiveness of male sexual violence against women substantiated in these studies is not denied, minimized, or excepted as deviant or episodic; if the fact that only 7.8 percent of women in the United States are not sexually assaulted or harassed in their lifetimes is considered not ignorable or inconsequential;[1] if the women to whom it happens are not considered expendable; if violation of women is understood as sexualized on some level—then sexuality itself can no longer be regarded as unimplicated. Nor can the meaning of practices of sexual violence be categorized away as violence not sex. The male sexual role, this information and analysis taken together suggest, centers on aggressive intrusion on those with less power. Such acts of dominance are experienced a sexually arousing, as sex itself. They therefore are. The new knowledge on the sexual violation of women by men thus frames an inquiry into the place of sexuality in gender and of gender in sexuality.

A feminist theory of sexuality based on these data locates sexuality within a theory of gender inequality, meaning the social hierarchy of men over women. To make a theory feminist, it is not enough that it be authored by a biological female, nor that it describe female sexuality as

71

different from (if equal to) make sexuality, or as if sexuality in women in-eluctably exists in some realm beyond, beneath, above, behind—in any event, fundamentally untouched and unmoved by—an unequal social order. A theory of sexuality becomes feminist methodologically, meaning feminist in the post-marxist sense, to the extent it treats sexuality as a so-cial construct of male power: defined by men, forced on women, and con-stitutive of the meaning of gender. Such an approach centers feminism on the perspective of the subordination of women to men as it identifies sex—that is, the sexuality of dominance and submission—as crucial, as a funda-mental, as on some level definitive, in that process. Feminist theory be-comes a project of analyzing that situation in order to face it for what it is, in order to change it.

Focusing on gender inequality without a sexual account of its dynamics, as most work has, one could criticize the sexism of existing theories of sex-uality and emerge knowing that men author scripts to their own advantage, women and men act them out; that men set conditions, women and men have their behavior conditioned; that men develop developmental catego-ries through which men develop, and women develop or not; that men are socially allowed selves hence identities with personalities into which sexu-ality is or is not well integrated, women being that which is or is not inte-grated, that through the alterity of which a self experiences itself as having an identity; that men have object relations, women are the objects of those relations; and so on. Following such critique, one could attempt to invert or correct the premises or applications of these theories to make them gen-der neutral, even if the reality to which they refer looks more like the theo-ries—once their gender specificity is revealed—than it looks gender neu-tral. Or, one could attempt to enshrine a distinctive "women's reality" as if it really were permitted to exist as something more than one dimension of women's response to a condition of powerlessness. Such exercises would be revealing and instructive, even deconstructive, but to limit feminism to correcting sex bias by acting in theory as if male power did not exist in fact, including by valorizing in writing what women have had little choice but to be limited to becoming in life, is to limit feminist theory the way sexism limits women's lives: to a response to terms men set.

A distinctive feminist theory conceptualizes social reality, including sex-ual reality, on its own terms. The question is, what are they? If women have been substantially deprived not only of their own experience but of terms of their own in which to view it, then a feminist theory of sexuality which seeks to understand women's situation in order to change it must first identify and criticize the construct "sexuality" as a construct that has circumscribed and defined experience as well as theory. This requires cap-turing it in the world, in its situated social meanings, as it is being con-structed in life on a daily basis. It must be studied in its experienced empirical existence, not just in the texts of history (as Foucault does), in the social psyche (as Lacan does), or in language (as Derrida does). Sexual meaning is not made only, or even primarily, by words and in texts. It is made in social relations of power in the world, through which process gender is also produced. In feminist terms, the fact that male power has power means that the interests of male sexuality construct what sexuality as such means, including the standard way it is allowed and recognized to be felt and expressed and experienced, in a way that determines women's biographies, including sexual ones. Existing theories, until they grasp this, will not only misattribute what they call female sexuality to women as such, as if it were not imposed on women daily; they will also participate in enforcing the hegemony of the social construct "desire," hence its product, "sexuality," hence its construct "woman," on the world.

The gender issue, in this analysis, becomes the issue of what is taken to be "sexuality"; what sex means and what is meant by sex, when, how, with whom, and with what consequences to whom. Such questions are almost never systematically confronted, even in discourses that purport feminist awareness. What sex is—how it comes to be attached and attributed to what it is, embodied and practiced as it is, contextualized in the ways it is, signifying and referring to what it does—is taken as a baseline, a given, except in explanations of what happened when it is thought to have gone wrong. It is as if "erotic," for example, can be taken as having an understood referent, although it is never defined, except to imply that it is universal yet individual, ultimately variable and plastic, essentially indefinable but overwhelmingly positive. "Desire," the vicissitudes of which are endlessly extolled and philosophized in culture high and low, is not seen as fundamentally problematic or as calling for explanation on the concrete, interpersonal operative level, unless (again) it is supposed to be there and is not. To list and analyze what seem to be the essential elements for male sexual arousal, what has to be there for the penis to work, seems faintly blasphemous, like a pornographer doing market research. Sex is supposed both too individual and too universally transcendent for that. To suggest that the sexual might be continuous with something other than sex itself—something like politics—is seldom done, is treated as detumescent, even by feminists. It is as if sexuality comes from the stork.

Sexuality, in feminist light, is not a discrete sphere of interaction or feeling or sensation or behavior in which preexisting social divisions may or may not be played out. It is a pervasive dimension of social life, one that permeates the whole, a dimension along which gender occurs and through which gender is socially constituted; it is a dimension along which other social divisions, like race and class, partly play themselves out. Dominance eroticized defines the imperatives of its masculinity, submission eroticized defines its femininity. So many distinctive features of women's status as second class—the restriction and constraint and contortion, the servility and the display, the self-mutilation and requisite presentation of self as a beautiful thing, the enforced passivity, the humiliation—are made into the content of sex for women. Being a thing for sexual use is fundamental to it. This approach identifies not just a sexuality that is shaped under conditions of gender inequality but reveals this sexuality itself to be the dynamic of the inequality of the sexes. It is to argue that the excitement at reduction of a person to a thing, to less than a human being, as socially defined, is its fundamental motive force. It is to argue that sexual difference is a function of sexual dominance. It is to argue a sexual theory of the distribution of social power by gender, in which this sexuality that is sexuality is substantially what makes the gender division be what it is, which is male dominant, wherever it is, which is nearly everywhere.

Across cultures, in this perspective, sexuality is whatever a given culture or subculture defines it as. The next question concerns its relation to gender as a division of power. Male dominance appears to exist cross-culturally, if in locally particular forms. Across cultures, is whatever defines women as "different" the same as whatever defines women as "inferior" the same as whatever defines women's "sexuality"? Is that which defines gender inequality as merely the sex difference also the content of the erotic, cross-culturally? In this view, the feminist theory of sexuality is its theory of politics, its distinctive contribution to social and political explanation. To explain gender inequality in terms of "sexual politics" is to advance not only a political theory of the sexual that defines gender but also a sexual theory of the political to which gender is fundamental.

In this approach, male power takes the social form of what men as a gender want sexually, which centers on power itself, as socially defined. In capitalist countries, it includes wealth. Masculinity is having it; feminity is not having it. Masculinity precedes male as femininity precedes female, and male sexual desire defines both. Specifically, "woman" is defined by what male desire requires for arousal and satisfaction and is socially tautologous with "female sexuality" and "the female sex." In the permissible ways a woman can be treated, the ways that are socially considered not violations but appropriate to her nature, one finds the particulars of male sexual interests and requirements. In the concomitant sexual paradigm, the ruling norms of sexual attraction and expression are fused with gender identity formation and affirmation, such that sexuality equals heterosexuality equals the sexuality of (male) dominance and (female) submission.

Post-Lacan, actually post-Foucault, it has become customary to affirm that sexuality is socially constructed. Seldom specified is what, socially, it is constructed of, far less who does the constructing or how, when, or where. When capitalism is the favored social construct, sexuality is shaped and controlled and exploited and repressed by capitalism; not, capitalism creates sexuality as we know it. When sexuality is a construct of discourses of power, gender is never one of them; force is central to its deployment but through repressing it, not through constituting it; speech is not concretely investigated for its participation in this construction process. Power is everywhere therefore nowhere, diffuse rather than pervasively hegemonic. "Constructed" seems to mean influenced by, directed, channeled, as a highway constructs traffic patterns. Not: Why cars? Who's driving? Where's everybody going? What makes mobility matter? Who can own a car? Are all these accidents not very accidental? Although there are partial exceptions (but disclaimers notwithstanding) the typical model of sexuality which is tacitly accepted remains deeply Freudian and essentialist: sexuality is an innate sui generis primary natural prepolitical unconditioned drive divided along the biological gender line, centering on heterosexual intercourse, that is, penile intromission, full actualization of which is repressed by civilization. Even if the sublimation aspect of this theory is rejected, or the reasons for the repression are seen to vary (for the survival of civilization or to maintain fascist control or to keep capitalism moving), sexual expression is implicitly seen as the expression of something that is to a significant extent pre-social and is socially denied its full force. Sexuality remains largely pre-cultural and universally invariant, social only in that it needs society to take socially specific forms. The impetus itself is a hunger, an appetite founded on a need; what it is specifically hungry for and how it is satisfied is then open to endless cultural and individual variance, like cuisine, like cooking.

Allowed/not allowed is this sexuality's basic ideological axis. The fact that sexuality is ideologically bounded is known. That these are its axes, central to the way its "drive" is driven, and that this is fundamental to gender and gender is fundamental to it, is not. Its basic normative assumption is that whatever is considered sexuality should be allowed to be "expressed." Whatever is called sex is attributed to a normatively positive valence, an affirmative valuation. This *ex cathedra* assumption, affirmation of which appears indispensable to one's credibility on any subject that gets near the sexual, means that sex as such (whatever it is) is good—natural, healthy, positive, appropriate, pleasurable, wholesome, fine, one's own, and to be approved and expressed. This, sometimes characterized as "sex-positive," is, rather obviously, a value judgment.

Kinsey and his followers, for example, clearly thought (and think) the more sex the better. Accordingly, they trivialize even most of those cases of rape and child sexual abuse they discern as such, decry women's sexual refusal as sexual inhibition, and repeatedly interpret women's sexual disinclination as "restrictions" on men's natural sexual activity, which left alone would emulate (some) animals. Followers of the neo-Freudian derepression imperative have similarly identified the frontier of sexual freedom with the transgression of social restraints on access, with making the sexually disallowed allowed, especially male sexual access to anything. The struggle to have everything sexual allowed in a society we are told would collapse if it were, creates a sense of resistance to, and an aura of danger around, violating the powerless. If we knew the boundaries were phony, existed only to eroticize the targeted transgressable, would penetrating them feel less sexy? Taboo and crime may serve to eroticize what would otherwise feel about as much like dominance as taking candy from a baby. Assimilating actual powerlessness to male prohibition, to male power, provides the appearance of resistance, which makes overcoming possible, while never undermining the reality of power, or its dignity, by giving the powerless actual power. The point is, allowed/not allowed becomes the ideological axis along which sexuality is experienced when and because sex—gender and sexuality—is about power.

One version of the derepression hypothesis that purports feminism is: civilization having been male dominated, female sexuality has been repressed, not allowed. Sexuality as such still centers on what would otherwise be considered the reproductive act, on intercourse: penetration of the erect penis into the vagina (or appropriate substitute orifices), followed by thrusting to male ejaculation. If reproduction actually had anything to do with what was sex was for, it would not happen every night (or even twice a week) for forty or fifty years, nor would prostitutes exist. "We had sex three times" typically means the man entered the woman three times and orgasmed three times. Female sexuality in this model refers to the presence of this theory's "sexuality," or the desire to be so treated, in biological females; "female" is somewhere between an adjective and a noun, half possessive and half biological ascription. Sexual freedom means women are allowed to behave as freely as men to express this sexuality, to have it allowed, that is (hopefully) shamelessly and without social constraints to initiate genital drive satisfaction through heterosexual intercourse. Hence, the liberated woman. Hence, the sexual revolution.

The pervasiveness of such assumptions about sexuality throughout otherwise diverse methodological traditions is suggested by the following comment by a scholar of violence against women:

> If women were to escape the culturally stereotyped role of disinterest in and
> resistance to sex and to take on an assertive role in expressing their own
> sexuality, rather than leaving it to the assertiveness of men, it would
> contribute to the reduction of rape . . . First, and most obviously, voluntary
> sex would be available to more men, thus reducing the "need" for rape.
> Second, and probably more important, it would help to reduce the confounding of sex and aggression.[2]

In this view, somebody must be assertive for sex to happen. Voluntary sex—sexual equality—means equal sexual aggression. If women freely expressed "their own sexuality," more heterosexual intercourse would be initiated. Women's "resistance" to sex is an imposed cultural stereotype, not a form of political struggle. Rape is occasioned by women's resistance, not by men's force; or, male force, hence rape, is created by women's resistance to sex. Men would rape less if they got more voluntarily compliant sex from women. Corollary: the force in rape is not sexual to men.

Underlying this quotation lurks the view, as common as it is tacit, that if women would just accept the contact men now have to rape to get—if women would stop resisting or (in one of the pornographers' favorite scenarios) become sexual aggressors—rape would wither away. On one level, this is a definitionally obvious truth. When a woman accepts what would be rape if she did not accept it, what happens is sex. If women were to accept forced sex as sex, "voluntary sex would be available to more men." If such a view is not implicit in this text, it is a mystery how women equally aggressing against men sexually would eliminate, rather than double, the confounding of sex and aggression. Without such an assumption, only the confounding of sexual aggression with gender would be eliminated. If women no longer resisted male sexual aggression, the confounding of sex with aggression would, indeed, be so epistemologically complete that it would be eliminated. No woman would ever be sexually violated, because sexual violation would be sex. The situation might resemble the one evoked by a society categorized as "rape-free" in part because the men assert there is no rape there: "our women never resist." Such pacification also occurs in "rape-prone" societies like the United States, where some force may be perceived as force, but only above certain threshold standards.

While intending the opposite, some feminists have encouraged and participated in this type of analysis by conceiving rape as violence, not sex. While this approach gave needed emphasis to rape's previously effaced elements of power and dominance, it obscured its elements of sex. Aside from failing to answer the rather obvious question, if it is violence not sex, why didn't he just hit her? this approach made it impossible to see that violence is sex when it is practiced as sex. This is obvious once what sexuality is, is understood as a matter of what it means and how it is interpreted. To say rape is violence not sex preserves the "sex is good" norm by simply distinguishing forced sex as "not sex," whether it means sex to the perpetrator or even, later, to the victim, who has difficulty experiencing sex without reexperiencing the rape. Whatever is sex cannot be violent; whatever is violent cannot be sex. This analytic wish-fulfillment makes it possible for rape to be opposed by those who would save sexuality from the rapists while leaving the sexual fundamentals of male dominance intact.

While much previous work on rape has analyzed it as a problem of inequality between the sexes but not as a problem of unequal sexuality on the basis of gender, other contemporary explorations of sexuality that purport to be feminist lack comprehension either of gender as a form of social power or of the realities of sexual violence. For instance, the editors of *Powers of Desire* take sex "as a central form of expression, one that defines identity and is seen as a primary source of energy and pleasure."[3] This may be how it "is seen," but it is also how the editors, operatively, see it. As if women choose sexuality as definitive of identity. As if it is as much a form of women's "expression" as it is men's. As if violation and abuse are not equally central to sexuality as women live it.

The *Diary* of the Barnard conference on sexuality pervasively equates sexuality with "pleasure." "Perhaps the overall question we need to ask is: how do women . . . negotiate sexual pleasure?"[4] As if women under male supremacy have power to. As if "negotiation" is a form of freedom. As if pleasure and how to get it, rather than dominance and how to end it, is the "overall" issue sexuality presents feminism. As if women do just need a good fuck. In these texts, taboos are treated as real restrictions—as things that really are not allowed—instead of as guises under which hierarchy is eroticized. The domain of the sexual is divided into "restriction, repression, and danger" on the one hand and "exploration, pleasure, and agency" on the other. This division parallels the ideological forms through which dominance and submission are eroticized, variously socially coded as heterosexuality's male/female, lesbian culture's butch/femme, and sadomasochism's top/bottom. Speaking in role terms, the one who pleasures in the illusion of freedom and security within the reality of danger is the "girl"; the one who pleasures in the reality of freedom and security within the illusion of danger is the "boy." That is, the *Diary* uncritically adopts as an analytic tool the central dynamic of the phenomenon it purports to be analyzing. Presumably, one is to have a sexual experience of the text.

The terms of these discourses preclude or evade crucial feminist questions. What do sexuality and gender inequality have to do with each other? How do dominance and submission become sexualized, or, why is hierarchy sexy? How does it get attached to male and female? Why does sexuality center on intercourse, the reproductive act by physical design? Is masculinity the enjoyment of violation, femininity the enjoyment of being violated? Is that the social meaning of intercourse? Do "men love death"? Why? What is the etiology of heterosexuality in women? Is its pleasure women's stake in subordination?

Taken together and taken seriously, feminist inquiries into the realities of rape, battery, sexual harassment, incest, child sexual abuse, prostitution, and pornography answer these questions by suggesting a theory of the sexual mechanism. Its script, learning, conditioning, developmental logos, imprinting of the microdot, its deus ex machina, whatever sexual process term defines sexual arousal itself, is force, power's expression. Force is sex, not just sexualized; force is the desire dynamic, not just a response to the desired object when desire's expression is frustrated. Pressure, gender socialization, withholding benefits, extending indulgences, the how-to books, the sex therapy are the soft end; the fuck, the fist, the street, the chains, the poverty are the hard end. Hostility and contempt, or arousal of master to slave, together with awe and vulnerability, or arousal of slave to master— these are the emotions of this sexuality's excitement. "Sadomasochism is to sex what war is to civil life: the magnificent experience," wrote Susan Sontag.[5] "[I]t is hostility—the desire, overt or hidden, to harm another person—that generates and enhances sexual excitement," wrote Robert Stoller.[6] Harriet Jacobs, a slave, speaking of her systematic rape by her master, wrote, "It seems less demeaning to give one's self, than to submit to compulsion."[7] It is clear from the data that the force in sex and the sex in force is a matter of simple empirical description—unless one accepts that force in sex is not force anymore, it is just sex; or, if whenever a woman is forced it is what she really wants, or it or she does not matter; or, unless prior aversion or sentimentality substitutes what one wants sex to be, or will condone or countenance as sex, what is actually happening.

To be clear: what is sexual is what gives a man an erection. Whatever it takes to make a penis shudder and stiffen with the experience of its potency is what sexuality means culturally. Whatever else does this, fear does, hostility does, hatred does, the helplessness of a child or a student or an infantilized or restrained or vulnerable woman does, revulsion does, death does. Hierarchy, a constant creation of person/thing, top/bottom, dominance/ subordination relations, does. What is understood as violation, conventionally penetration and intercourse, defines the paradigmatic sexual encounter. The scenario of sexual abuse is: you do what I say. These textualities and these relations, situated within as well as creating a context of power in which they can be lived out, become sexuality. All this suggests that what is called sexuality is the dynamic of control by which male dominance—in forms that range from intimate to institutional, from a look to a rape—eroticizes and thus defines man and woman, gender identity and sexual pleasure. It is also that which maintains and defines male supremacy as a political system. Male sexual desire is thereby simultaneously created and serviced, never satisfied once and for all, while male force is romanticized, even sacralized, potentiated and naturalized, by being submerged into sex itself.

In contemporary philosophical terms, nothing is "indeterminate" in the post-structuralist sense here; it is all too determinate. Nor does its reality provide just one perspective on a relativistic interpersonal world that could mean anything or its opposite. The reality of pervasive sexual abuse and its erotization does not shift relative to perspective, although whether or not one will see it or accord it significance may. Interpretation varies relative to place in sexual abuse, certainly; but the fact that women are sexually abused as women, located in a social matrix of sexualized subordination, does not go away because it is often ignored or authoritatively disbelieved or interpreted out of existence. Indeed, some ideological supports for its persistence rely precisely upon techniques of social indeterminacy: no language but the obscene to describe the unspeakable; denial by the powerful casting doubt on the facticity of the injuries; actually driving its victims insane. . . .

Male sexuality is apparently activated by violence against women and expresses itself in violence against women to a significant extent. If violence is seen as occupying the most fully achieved end of a dehumanization continuum on which objectification occupies the least express end, one question that is raised is whether some form of hierarchy—the dynamic of the continuum—is currently essential for male sexuality to experience itself. If so, and if gender is understood to be a hierarchy, perhaps the sexes are unequal so that men can be sexually aroused. To put it another way, perhaps gender must be maintained as a social hierarchy so that men will be able to get erections; or, part of the male interest in keeping women down lies in the fact that it gets men up. Maybe feminists are considered castrating because equality is not sexy.

Recent inquiries into rape support such suspicions. Men often rape women, it turns out, because they want to and enjoy it. The act, including the dominance, is sexually arousing, sexually affirming, and supportive of the perpetrator's masculinity. Many unreported rapists report an increase in self-esteem as a result of the rape. Indications are that reported rapists perceive that getting caught accounts for most of the unpleasant effects of raping. About one-third of all men say they would rape a woman if they knew they would not get caught. That the low conviction rate may give them confidence is supported by the prevalence rate. Some convicted rapists see rape as an "exciting" form of interpersonal sex, a recreational activity or "adventure," or as a means of revenge or punishment on all women or some subgroup of women or an individual woman. Even some of those who did the act out of bad feelings make it clear that raping made them feel better. "Men rape because it is rewarding to do so." If rapists experience rape as sex, does that mean there can be nothing wrong with it?

Once an act is labeled rape there is an epistemological problem with seeing it as sex. Indeed, this is a major social function served by labeling acts rape. Rape becomes something a rapist does, as if he were a separate species. But no personality disorder distinguishes most rapists from normal men. Psychopaths do rape, but only about 5 percent of all known rapists are diagnosed psychopathic. In spite of the numbers of victims, the normalcy of rapists, and even given the fact that most women are raped by men they know (making it most unlikely that a few lunatics know around half of the women in the United States), rape remains considered psychopathological and therefore not about sexuality.

Add this to rape's pervasiveness and permissibility, together with the belief that it is both rare and impermissible. Combine this with the similarity between the patterns, rhythms, roles, and emotions, not to mention acts, which make up rape (and battery) on the one hand and intercourse on the other. All this makes it difficult to sustain the customary distinctions between pathology and normalcy, parophilia and nomophilia, violence and sex, in this area. Some researchers have previously noticed the centrality of force to the excitement value of pornography but have tended to put it down to perversion. Robert Stoller, for example, observes that pornography today depends upon hostility, voyeurism, and sadomasochism and calls perversion "the erotic form of hatred."[8] If the perverse in this context is seen not as the other side of a bright normal/abnormal line but as an undiluted expression of a norm that permeates many ordinary interactions, hatred of women—that is, misogyny—becomes a dynamic of sexual excitement itself.

Compare victims' reports of rape with women's reports of sex. They look a lot alike. Compare victims' reports of rape with what pornography says is sex. They look a lot alike. In this light, the major distinction between intercourse (normal) and rape (abnormal) is that the normal happens so often that one cannot get anyone to see anything wrong with it. Which also means that anything sexual that happens often and one cannot get anyone to consider wrong is intercourse, not rape, no matter what was done. The distinctions that purport to divide this territory look more like the ideological supports for normalizing the usual male use and abuse of women as "sexuality" through authoritatively pretending that whatever is exposed of it is deviant. This may have something to do with the conviction rate in rape cases (making all those unconvicted men into normal men, and all those acts into sex). It may have something to do with the fact that most convicted rapists, and many observers, find rape convictions incomprehensible. And with the fact that marital rape is considered by many to be a contradiction in terms ("But if you can't rape your wife, who can you rape?"). And with the fact that so many rape victims have trouble with sex afterward.

What effect does the pervasive reality of sexual abuse of women by men have on what are deemed the more ordinary forms of sexual interaction? How do these material experiences create interest and point of view? Consider women. Recall that more than one-third of all girls experience sex, perhaps are sexually initiated, under conditions that even this society recognizes are forced or at least unequal. Perhaps they learn this process of sexualized dominance as sex. Top-down relations feel sexual. Is sexuality throughout life then ever not on some level a reenactment of, a response to, that backdrop? Rape, adding more women to the list, can produce similar resonance. Sexually abused women—most women—seem to become either sexually disinclined or compulsively promiscuous or both in series, trying to avoid the painful events, or repeating them over and over almost addictively, or both, in an attempt to reacquire a sense of control or to make them come out right. Women also widely experience sexuality as a means to male approval; male approval translates into nearly all social goods. Violation can be sustained, even sought out, to this end. Sex can, then, be a means of trying to feel alive by redoing what has made one feel dead, of expressing a denigrated self-image seeking its own reflection in self-action in order to feel fulfilled, or of keeping up one's stock with the powerful. . . .

Women often begin alienating themselves from their body's self-preserving reactions under conditions under which they cannot stop the pain from being inflicted, and then find the deadening process difficult to reverse. Some then seek out escalating pain to feel sexual or to feel alive or to feel anything at all. One particularly devastating and confusing consequence of sexual abuse for women's sexuality—and a crisis for consciousness—occurs when one's body experiences abuse as pleasurable. Feeling loved and aroused and comforted during incest, or orgasm during rape, are examples. Because body is widely regarded as access to unmediated truth in this culture, women feel betrayed by their bodies and seek mental justifications (Freudian derepression theory provides an excellent one) for why their body's reactions are their own true reactions, and their values and consciousness (which interprets the event as a violation) are socially imposed. That is, they come to believe they really wanted the rape or the incest and interpret violation as their own sexuality.

Interpreting women's responses to pornography, in which there is often a difference between so-called objective indices of arousal, such as vaginal secretions, and self-reported arousal, raises similar issues. Repression is the typical explanation. It seems at least as likely that women disidentify with their bodies' conditioned responses. Not to be overly behavioral, but does anyone think Pavlov's dogs were really hungry every time they salivated at the sound of the bell? If it is possible that hunger is inferred from salivation, perhaps humans experience sexual arousal from pornographic cues and, since sexuality is social, that is sexual arousal. Identifying that as a conditioned response to a set of social cues, conditioned to what it is for political reasons, is not the same as considering the response proof of sexual truth simply because it physically happens. Further, research shows that sexual fetishism can be experimentally induced readily in "normal" subjects. If this can be done with sexual responses that the society does not condone out front, why is it so unthinkable that the same process might occur with those sexual responses it does?

If the existing social model and reality of sexuality center on male force, and if that sex is socially learned and ideologically considered positive and is rewarded, what is surprising is that not all women eroticize dominance, not all love pornography, and many resent rape. As Valerie Heller has said of her use in incest and pornography, both as a child and as an adult, "I believed I existed only after I was turned on, like a light switch by another person. When I needed to be nurtured I thought I wanted to be used . . . Marks and bruises and being used was the way I measured my self worth. You must remember that I was taught that because men were fucking my body and using it for their needs it meant I was loved."[9] Given the pervasiveness us such experiences, the truly interesting question becomes why and how sexuality in women is ever other than masochistic.

All women live in sexual objectification the way fish live in water. Given the statistical realities, all women live all the time under the shadow of the threat of sexual abuse. The question is, what can life as a woman mean, what can sex mean, to targeted survivors in a rape culture? Given the statistical realities, much of women's sexual lives will occur under posttraumatic stress. Being surrounded by pornography—which is not only socially ubiquitous but often directly used as part of sex—makes this a relatively constant condition. Women cope with objectification through trying to meet the male standard, and measure their self-worth by the degree to which they succeed. Women seem to cope with sexual abuse principally by denial or fear. On the denial side, immense energy goes into defending sexuality as just fine and getting better all the time, and into trying to make sexuality feel all right, the way it is supposed to feel. Women who are compromised, cajoled, pressured, tricked, blackmailed, or outright forced into sex (or pornography) often respond to the unspeakable humiliation, coupled with the sense of having lost some irreplaceable integrity, by claiming that sexuality as their own. Faced with no alternatives, the strategy to acquire self-respect and pride is: I chose it.

Consider the conditions under which this is done. This is a culture in which women are socially expected—and themselves necessarily expect and want—to be able to distinguish the socially, epistemologically, indistinguishable. Rape and intercourse are not authoritatively separated by any difference between the physical acts or amount of force involved but only legally, by a standard that centers on the man's interpretation of the encounter. Thus, although raped women, that is, most women, are supposed to be able to feel every day and every night that they have some meaningful determining part in having their sex life—their life, period—not be a series of rapes, the most they provide is the raw data for the man to see as he sees it. And he has been seeing pornography. Similarly, "consent" is supposed to be the crucial line between rape and intercourse, but the legal standard for it is so passive, so acquiescent, that a woman can be dead and have consented under it. The mind fuck of all of this makes liberalism's complicitous collapse into "I chose it" feel like a strategy for sanity. It certainly makes a woman at one with the world.)

On the fear side, if a woman has ever been beaten in a relationship, even if "only once," what does that do to her everyday interactions, or her sexual interactions, with that man? With other men? Does her body ever really forget that behind his restraint he can do that any time she pushes an issue, or for no reason at all? Does her vigilance ever really relax? If she tried to do something about it, as many women do, and if nothing was done, as it usually is not, does she ever forget that that is what can be done to her at any time and nothing will done about it? Does she smile at men less—or more? If she writes at all, does she imitate men less—or more? If a woman has ever been raped, ever, does a penis ever enter her without some body memory, if not a flashback then the effort of keeping it back; or does she hurry up or keep trying, feeling something gaining on her, trying to make it come out right? If a woman has ever been raped, does she ever fully regain the feeling of physical integrity, of self-respect, of having what she wants count somewhere, of being able to make herself clear to those who have not gone through what she has gone through, of living in a fair society, of equality?

Given the effects of learning sexuality through force or pressure or imposition; given the constant roulette of sexual violence; given the daily sexualization of every aspect of a woman's presence—for a woman to be sexualized means constant humiliation or threat of it, being invisible as human being and center stage as sex object, low pay, and being a target for assault or being assaulted. Given that this is the situation of all women, that one never knows for sure that one is not next on the list of victims until the moment one dies (and then, who knows?), it does not seem exaggerated to say that women are sexual, meaning that women exist, in a context of terror. Yet most professionals in the area of sexuality persist in studying the inexplicabilities of what is termed female sexuality acontextually, outside the context of gender inequality and its sexual violence—navel gazing, only slightly further down.

The general theory of sexuality emerging from this feminist critique does not consider sexuality to be an inborn force inherent in individuals, nor cultural in the Freudian sense, in which sexuality exists in a cultural context but in universally invariant stages and psychic representations. It appears instead to be culturally specific, even if so far largely invariant because male supremacy is largely universal, if always in specific forms. Although some of its abuses (like prostitution) are accentuated by poverty, it does not vary by class, although class is one hierarchy it sexualizes. Sexuality becomes, in this view, social and relational, constructing and constructed of power. Infants, though sensory, cannot be said to possess sexuality in this sense because they have not had the experiences (and do not speak the language) that give it social meaning. Since sexuality is its social meaning, infant erections, for example, are clearly sexual in the sense that this society centers its sexuality on them, but to relate to a child as though his erections mean what adult erections have been conditioned to mean is a form of child abuse. Such erections have the meaning they acquire in social life only to observing adults. . . .

There may be a feminist unconscious, but it is not the Freudian one. Perhaps equality lives there. Its laws, rather than a priori, objective, or universal, might as well be a response to the historical regularities of sexual subordination, which under bourgeois ideological conditions require that the truth of male dominance be concealed in order to preserve the belief that women are sexually self-acting: that women want it. The feminist psychic universe certainly recognizes that people do not always know what they want, have hidden desires and inaccessible needs, lack awareness of motivation, have contorted and opaque interactions, and have an interest in obscuring what is really going on. But this does not essentially conceal that what women really want is more sex. It is true, as Freudians have persuasively observed, that many things are sexual that do not present themselves as such. But in ways Freud never dreamed.

At risk of further complicating the issues, perhaps it would help to think of women's sexuality as women's like Black culture is Blacks': it is, and it is not. The parallel cannot be precise in part because, owing to segregation, Black culture developed under more autonomous conditions than women, intimately integrated with men by force, have had. Still, both can be experienced as a source of strength, joy, expression, and as an affirmative badge of pride. Both remain nonetheless stigmatic in the sense of a brand, a restriction, a definition as less. This is not because of any intrinsic content or value, but because the social reality is that their shape, qualities, texture, imperative, and very existence are a response to powerlessness. They exist as they do because of lack of choice. They are created out of social conditions of oppression and exclusion. They may be part of a strategy for survival or even of change. But, as is, they are not the whole world, and it is the whole world that one is entitled to. This is why interpreting female sexuality as an expression of women's agency and autonomy, as if sexism did not exist, is always denigrating and bizarre and reductive, as it would be to interpret Black culture as if racism did not exist. As if Black culture just arose freely and spontaneously on the plantations and in the ghettos of North America, adding diversity to American pluralism.

So long as sexual inequality remains unequal and sexual, attempts to value sexuality as women's, possessive as if women possess it, will remain part of limiting women to it, to what women are now defined as being. Outside of truly rare and contrapuntal glimpses (which most people think they live almost their entire sex life within), to seek an equal sexuality without political transformation is to seek equality under conditions of inequality. Rejecting this, and rejecting the glorification of settling for the best that inequality has to offer or has stimulated the resourceful to invent, are what Ti-Grace Atkinson meant to reject when she said: "I do not know any feminist worthy of that name who, if forced to choose between free-dom and sex, would choose sex. She'd choose freedom every time."[10]

NOTES

1. This figure was calculated at my request by Diana E. H. Russell on the ran-dom-sample date base of 930 San Francisco households discussed in *The Secret Trauma,* pp. 20–37, and *Rape in Marriage,* pp. 27–41. The figure includes all the forms of rape or other sexual abuse or harassment surveyed, noncontact as well as contact, from gang rape by strangers and marital rape to obscene phone calls, unwanted sexual advances on the street, unwelcome requests to pose for pornog-raphy, and subjection to peeping toms and sexual exhibitionists (flashers).

2. A third reason is also given: "to the extent that sexism in societal and family structure is responsible for the phenomena of 'compulsive masculinity' and struc-tured antagonism between the sexes, the elimination of sexual inequality would reduce the number of 'power trip' and 'degradation ceremony' motivated rapes"; M. Straus, "Sexual Inequality, Cultural Norms, and Wife-Beating," *Victimology: An International Journal* 1 (1976): 54–76. Note that these structural factors seem to be considered nonsexual, in the sense that "power trip" and "degradation cere-mony" motivated rapes are treated as not erotic to the perpetrators *because* of the elements of dominance and degradation, nor is "structured antagonism" seen as an erotic element of rape or sex (or family).

3. A. Snitow, C. Stansell, and S. Thompson, Introduction to *Powers of Desire: The Politics of Sexuality* (New York: Monthly Review Press, 1983), p. 9.

4. C. Vance, "Concept Paper: Toward a Politics of Sexuality," in *Diary of a Conference on Sexuality,* ed. H. Alderfer, B. Jaker, and M. Nelson (Record of the planning committee of the conference "The Scholar and the Feminist IX: Toward a Politics of Sexuality," April 24, 1982), p. 27: to address "women's sexual pleasure, choice, and autonomy, acknowledging that sexuality is simultaneously a domain of restriction, repression and danger as well as a domain of exploration, pleasure and agency." Parts of the *Diary,* with the conference papers, were later published in C. Vance, ed., *Pleasure and Danger: Exploring Female Sexuality* (London: Routledge & Kegan Paul, 1984).

5. Susan Sontag, "Fascinating Fascism," in *Under the Sign of Saturn* (New York: Farrar, Straus and Giroux, 1980), p. 103.

6. Robert Stoller, *Sexual Excitement: Dynamics of Erotic Life* (New York: Pan-theon Books, 1979), p. 6.

7. Harriet Jacobs quoted in Rennie Simpson, "The Afro-American Female: The Historical Context of the Construction of Sexual Identity," in Snitow, Stansell, Thompson, eds., *Powers of Desire,* p. 231.

8. Robert Stoller, *Perversion: The Erotic Form of Hatred* (New York: Pantheon, 1975), p. 87.

9. Speech at March for Women's Dignity, New York City, May 1984.

10. Ti-Grace Atkinson, "Why I'm Against S/M Liberation," in *Against Sado-masochism,* ed. E. Linden (Palo Alto: Frog in the Well, 1982), p. 91.

Date Rape:
A Feminist Analysis

Date rape is nonaggravated sexual assault, nonconsensual sex that does not involve physical injury, or the explicit threat of physical injury. But because it does not involve physical injury, and because physical injury is often the only criterion that is accepted as evidence that the *actus reas* is nonconsensual, what is really sexual assault is often mistaken for seduction. . . .

However, if a man is to be convicted, it does not suffice to establish that the *actus reas* was nonconsensual. In order to be guilty of sexual assault a man must have the requisite *mens rea,* i.e., he must either have believed that his victim did not consent or that she was probably not consenting. . . .

The following statements by self-confessed date rapists reveal how our lack of a solution for dealing with date rape protects rapists by failing to provide their victims with legal recourse:

> All of my rapes have been involved in a dating situation where I've been out with a woman I know. . . . I wouldn't take no for an answer. I think it had something to do with my acceptance of rejection. I had low self-esteem and not much self-confidence and when I was rejected for something which I considered to be rightly mine, I became angry and I went ahead anyway. And this was the same in any situation, whether it was rape or it was something else.[1]
>
> When I did date, when I was younger, I would pick up a girl and if she didn't come across I would threaten her or slap her face then tell her she was going to fuck—that was it. But that's because I didn't want to waste time with any come-ons. It took too much time. I wasn't interested because I didn't like them as people anyway, and I just went with them just to get laid. Just to say that I laid them.[2]

There is, at this time, nothing to protect women from this kind of unscrupulous victimization. A woman on a casual date with a virtual stranger has almost no chance of bringing a complaint of sexual assault before the courts. One reason for this is the prevailing criterion for consent. According to this criterion, consent is implied unless some emphatic episodic sign of resistance occurred, and its occurrence can be established. But if no episodic act occurred, or if it did occur, and the defendant claims that it didn't, or if the defendant threatened the plaintiff but won't admit it in court, it is almost impossible to find any evidence that would support the plaintiff's word against the defendant. . . .

The Problem of the Criterion

The reasoning that underlies the present criterion of consent is entangled in a number of mutually supportive mythologies which see sexual assault as masterful seduction, and silent submission as sexual enjoyment. Because the prevailing ideology has so much informed our conceptualization of sexual interaction, it is extraordinarily difficult for us to distinguish between assault and seduction, submission and enjoyment, or so we imagine. At the same time, this failure to distinguish has given rise to a network of rationalizations that support the conflation of assault with seduction, submission with enjoyment. I therefore want to begin my argument by providing an example which shows both why it is so difficult to make this distinction, and that it exists. Later, I will identify and attempt to unravel the lines of reasoning that reinforce this difficulty.

> The woman I have in mind agrees to see someone because she feels an initial attraction to him and believes that he feels the same way about her. She goes out with him in the hope that there will be mutual enjoyment and in the course of the day or evening an increase of mutual interest. Unfortunately, these hopes of *mutual* and *reciprocal* interest are not realized. We do not know how much interest she has in him by the end of their time together, but whatever her feelings she comes under pressure to have sex with him, and she does not want to have the kind of sex he wants. She may desire to hold hands and kiss, to engage in more intense caresses or in some form of foreplay, or she may not want to be touched. She may have reasons unrelated to desire for not wanting to engaged in the kind of sex he is demanding. She may have religious reservations, concerns about pregnancy or disease, a disinclination to be just another conquest. She may be engaged in a seduction program of her own which sees abstaining from sexual activity as a means of building an important emotional bond. She feels she is desirable to him, and she knows, and he knows that he will have sex with her if he can. And while she feels she doesn't owe him anything, and that it is her prerogative to refuse him, this feeling is partly a defensive reaction

against a deeply held belief that if he is in need, she should provide. If she buys into the myth of insistent male sexuality she may feel he is suffering from sexual frustration and that she is largely to blame.

We do not know how much he desires her, but we do know that his desire for erotic satisfaction can hardly be separated from his desire for conquest. He feels no dating obligation, but has a strong commitment to scoring. He uses the myth of "so hard to control" male desire as a rhetorical tactic, telling her how frustrated she will leave him. He becomes overbearing. She resists, voicing her disinclination. He alternates between telling her how desirable she is and taking a hostile stance, charging her with misleading him, accusing her of wanting him, and being coy, in short of being deceitful, all the time engaging in rather aggressive body contact. It is late at night, she is tired and a bit queasy from too many drinks, and he is reaffirming her suspicion that perhaps she has misled him. She is having trouble disengaging his body from hers, and wishes he would just go away. She does not adopt a strident angry stance, partly because she thinks he is acting normally and does not deserve it, partly because she feels she is partly to blame, and partly because there is always the danger that her anger will make him angry, possibly violent. It seems that the only thing to do, given his aggression, and her queasy fatigue, is to go along with him and get it over with, but this decision is so entangled with the events in process it is hard to know if it is not simply a recognition of what is actually happening. She finds the whole encounter a thoroughly disagreeable experience, but he does not take notice, and wouldn't have changed course if he had. He congratulates himself on his sexual prowess and is confirmed in his opinion that aggressive tactics pay off. Later she feels that she has been raped, but paradoxically tells herself that she let herself be raped.

The paradoxical feelings of the woman in our example indicate her awareness that what she feels about the incident stands in contradiction to the prevailing cultural assessment of it. She knows that she did not want to have sex with her date. She is not so sure, however, about how much her own desires count, and she is uncertain that she has made her desires clear. Her uncertainty is reinforced by the cultural reading of this incident as an ordinary seduction.

As for us, we assume that the woman did not want to have sex, but just like her, we are unsure whether her mere reluctance, in the presence of high-pressure tactics, constitutes nonconsent. We suspect that submission to an overbearing and insensitive lout is no way to go about attaining sexual enjoyment, and we further suspect that he felt no compunction about providing it, so that on the face of it, from the outside looking in, it looks like a pretty unreasonable proposition for her.

Let us look at this reasoning more closely. Assume that she was not attracted to the kind of sex offered by the sort of person offering it. Then it would be *prima facie* unreasonable for her to agree to have sex, unreasonable, that is, unless she were offered some pay-off for her stoic endurance, money perhaps, or tickets to the opera. The reason is that in sexual matters, agreement is closely connected to attraction. Thus, where the presumption is that she was not attracted, we should at the same time presume that she did not consent. Hence, the burden of proof should be on her alleged assailant to show that she had good reasons for consenting to an unattractive proposition.

This is not, however, the way such situations are interpreted. In the unlikely event that the example I have described should come before the courts, there is little doubt that the law would interpret the woman's eventual acquiescence or "going along with" the sexual encounter as consent. But along with this interpretation would go the implicit understanding that she had consented because when all was said and done, when the "token" resistances to the "masterful advances" had been made, she had wanted to after all. Once the courts have constructed this interpretation, they are then forced to conjure up some horror story of feminine revenge in order to explain why she should bring charges against her "seducer." . . .

The position of the courts is supported by the widespread belief that male aggression and female reluctance are normal parts of seduction. Given their acceptance of this model, the logic of their response must be respected. For if sexual aggression is a part of ordinary seduction, then it cannot be inconsistent with the legitimate consent of the person allegedly seduced by this means. And if it is normal for a woman to be reluctant, then this reluctance must be consistent with her consent as well. The position of the courts is not inconsistent just so long as they allow that some sort of protest on the part of a woman counts as refusal. As we have seen, however, it frequently happens that no sort of a protest would count as a refusal. Moreover, if no sort of protest, or at least if precious few count, then the failure to register these protests will amount to "asking for it," it will amount, in other words, to agreeing.

The court's belief in "natural" male aggression and "natural" female reluctance has increasingly come under attack by feminist critics who see quite correctly that the entire legal position would collapse if, for example, it were shown empirically that men were not aggressive, and that women, at least when they wanted sex, were. This strategy is of little help, however, so long as aggressive men can still be found, and relics of reluctant women continue to surface. Fortunately, there is another strategy. The position collapses through the weakness of its internal logic. The next section traces the several lines of this logic.

Rape Myths

... In what follows, I propose to excavate the logical support for popular attitudes that are tolerant of date rape. These myths are not just popular, however, but often emerge in the arguments of judges who acquit date rapists, and policemen who refuse to lay charges.

The claim that the victim provoked a sexual incident, that "she asked for it," is by far the most common defence given by men who are accused of sexual assault. ...

Attempts to explain that women have a right to behave in sexually provocative ways without suffering dire consequences still meet with surprisingly tough resistance. Even people who find nothing wrong or sinful with sex itself, in any of its forms, tend to suppose that women must not behave sexually unless they are prepared to carry through on some fuller course of sexual interaction. The logic of this response seems to be that at some point a woman's behaviour commits her to following through on the full course of a sexual encounter as it is defined by her assailant. At some point she has made an agreement, or formed a contract, and once that is done, her contractor is entitled to demand that she satisfy the terms of that contract. Thus, this view about sexual responsibility and desert is supported by other assumptions about contracts and agreement. But we do not normally suppose that casual nonverbal behaviour generates agreements. Nor do we normally grant private persons the right to enforce contracts. What rationale would support our conclusion in this case?

The rationale, I believe, comes in the form of a belief in the especially insistent nature of male sexuality, an insistence which lies at the root of natural male aggression, and which is extremely difficult, perhaps impossible, to contain. At a certain point in the arousal process, it is thought, a man's rational will gives way to the prerogatives of nature. His sexual need can and does reach a point where it is uncontrollable, and his natural masculine aggression kicks in to assure that this need is met. Women, however, are naturally more contained, and so it is their responsibility not to provoke the irrational in the male. If they do go so far as that, they have both failed in their responsibilities, and subjected themselves to the inevitable. One does not go into the lion's cage and expect not to be eaten. Natural feminine reluctance, it is thought, is no protection against a sexually aroused male.

This belief about the normal aggressiveness of male sexuality is complemented by common knowledge about female gender development. Once, women were taught to deny their sexuality and to aspire to ideals of chastity. Things have not changed so much. Women still tend to eschew conquest mentalities in favour of a combination of sex and affection. Insofar as this is thought to be merely a cultural requirement, however, there is an expectation that women will by coy about their sexual desire. The assumption that women both want to indulge sexually, and are inclined to sacrifice this desire for higher ends, gives rise to the myth that they want to be raped. After all, doesn't rape give them the sexual enjoyment they *really* want, at the same time that it relieves them of the responsibility for admitting to and acting upon what they want? And how then can we blame men, who have been socialized to be aggressively seductive precisely for the purpose of overriding female reserve? If we find fault at all, we are inclined to cast our suspicions on the motives of the woman. For it is on her that the contradictory roles of sexual desirer and sexual denier have been placed. Our awareness of the contradiction expected of her makes us suspect her honesty. In the past, she was expected to deny her complicity because of the shame and guilt she felt at having submitted. This expectation persists in many quarters today, and is carried over into a general suspicion about her character, and the fear that she might make a false accusation out of revenge, or some other low motive. . . .

Dispelling the Myths

. . . The belief that a woman generates some sort of contractual obligation whenever her behaviour is interpreted as seductive is the most indefensible part of the mythology of rape. In law, contracts are not legitimate just because a promise had been made. In particular, the use of pressure tactics to extract agreement is frowned upon. . . .

Even if we assume that a woman has initially agreed to an encounter, her agreement does not automatically make all subsequent sexual activity to which she submits legitimate. If during coitus a woman should experience pain, be suddenly overcome with guilt or fear of pregnancy, or simply lose her initial desire, those are good reasons for her to change her mind. Having changed her mind, neither her partner nor the state has any right to force her to continue. But then if she is forced to continue she is assaulted. Thus, establishing that consent occurred at a particular point during a sexual encounter should not conclusively establish the legitimacy of the encounter. What is needed is a reading of whether she agreed throughout the encounter.

If the "she asked for it" contractual view of sexual interchange has any validity, it is because there is a point at which there is no stopping a sexual encounter, a point at which that encounter becomes the inexorable outcome of the unfolding of natural events. If a sexual encounter is like a slide on which I cannot stop halfway down, it will be relevant whether I enter the slide of my own free will, or am pushed.

But there is no evidence that the entire sexual act is like a slide. While there may be a few seconds in the "plateau" period just prior to orgasm in which people are "swept" away by sexual feelings to the point where we could justifiably understand their lack of heed for the comfort of their partner, the greater part of a sexual encounter comes well within the bounds of morally responsible control or our own actions. Indeed, the available evidence shows that most of the activity involved in sex has to do with building the requisite level of desire, a task that involves the proper use of foreplay, the possibility of which implies control over the form that foreplay will take. Modern sexual therapy assumes that such control is universally accessible, and so far there has been no reason to question that assumption. Sexologists are unanimous, moreover, in holding that mutual sexual enjoyment requires an atmosphere of comfort and communication, a minimum of pressure, and an ongoing check-up on one's partner's state. They maintain that different people have different predilections, and that what is pleasurable for one person is very often anathema to another. These findings show that the way to achieve sexual pleasure, at any time at all, let alone with a casual acquaintance, decidedly does not involve overriding the other person's express reservations and providing them with just any kind of sexual stimulus. . . . In this case science seems to concur with women's perception that aggressive incommunicative sex is not what they want. But if science and the voice of women concur, if aggressive seduction does not lead to good sex, if women to not like it or want it, then it is not rational to think that they would agree to it. Where such sex takes place, it is therefore rational to presume that the sex was not consensual. . . .

In conclusion, there are no grounds for the "she asked for it" defence. Sexually provocative behaviour does not generate sexual contracts. Even where there are sexual agreements, they cannot be legitimately enforced either by the State, or by private right, or by natural prerogative. Secondly, all the evidence suggests that neither women nor men find sexual enjoyment in rape or in any form of non-communicative sexuality. Thirdly, male sexual desire is containable, and can be subjected to moral and rational control. Fourthly, since there is no reason why women should not be sexually provocative, they do not "deserve" any sex they do not want. This last is a welcome discovery. The taboo on sexual provocativeness in women is a taboo both on sensuality and on teasing. But sensuality is a source of delight, and teasing is playful and inspires wit. What a relief to learn that it is not sexual provocativeness, but its enemies, that constitutes a danger to the world.

Communicative Sexuality:
Reinterpreting the Kantian Imperative

The present criterion of consent sets up sexual encounters as contractual events in which sexual aggression is presumed to be consented to unless there is some vigorous act of refusal. As long as we view sexual interaction on a contractual model, the only possibility for finding fault is to point to the presence of such an act. But it is clear that whether or not we can determine such a presence, there is something strongly disagreeable about the sexual aggression described above.

In thinking about sex we must keep in mind its sensual ends, and the facts show that aggressive high-pressure sex contradicts those ends. Consensual sex in dating situations is presumed to aim at mutual enjoyment. It may not always do this, and when it does, it might not always succeed. There is no logical incompatibility between wanting to continue a sexual encounter, and failing to derive sexual pleasure from it.

But it seems to me that there is a presumption in favour of the connection between sex and sexual enjoyment, and that if a man wants to be sure that he is not forcing himself on a woman, he has an obligation either to ensure that the encounter really is mutually enjoyable, or to know the reasons why she would want to continue the encounter in spite of her lack of enjoyment. A closer investigation of the nature of this obligation will enable us to construct a more plausible norm of sexual conduct. . . .

The obligation to promote the sexual ends of one's partner implies the obligation to know what those ends are, and also the obligation to know how those ends are attained. Thus, the problem comes down to a problem of epistemic responsibility, the responsibility to know. The solution, in my view, lies in the practice of a communicative sexuality, one which combines the appropriate knowledge of the other with respect for the dialectics of desire.

So let us, for a moment, conceive of sexual interaction on a communicative rather than a contractual model. Let us look at it the way I think it should be looked at, as if it were a proper conversation rather than an offer from the Mafia. . . .

The communicative interaction involved in conversation is concerned with a good deal more than didactic content and argument. Good conversationalists are intuitive, sympathetic, and charitable. Intuition and charity aid the conversationalist in her effort to interpret the words of the other correctly and sympathy enables her to enter into the other's point of view. Her sensitivity alerts her to the tone of the exchange. Has her point been taken good-humouredly or resentfully? Aggressively delivered responses are taken as a sign that *ad hominems* are at work, and that the respondent's self-worth has been called into question. Good conversationalists will know to suspend further discussion until this sense of self-worth has been reestablished. Angry responses, resentful responses, bored responses, even over-enthusiastic responses require that the emotional ground be cleared before the discussion be continued. Often it is better to change the topic, or to come back to it on another day under different circumstances. Good conversationalists do not overwhelm their respondents with a barrage of their own opinions. While they may be persuasive, the forcefulness of their persuasion does not lie in their being overbearing, but rather in their capacity to see the other's point of view, to understand what it depends on, and so to address the essential point, but with tact and clarity.

Just as communicative conversationalists are concerned with more than didactic content, persons engaged in communicative sexuality will be concerned with more than achieving coitus. They will be sensitive to the responses of their partners. They will, like good conversationalists, be intuitive, sympathetic, and charitable. Intuition will help them to interpret their partner's responses; sympathy will enable them to share what their partner is feeling; charity will enable them to care. Communicative sexual partners will not overwhelm each other with the barrage of their own desires. They will treat negative, bored, or angry responses as a sign that the erotic ground needs to be either cleared or abandoned. Their concern with fostering the desire of the other must involve an ongoing state of alertness in interpreting her responses.

Just as a conversationalist's prime concern is for the mutuality of the discussion, a person engaged in communicative sexuality will be most concerned with the mutuality of desire. As such, both will put into practice a regard for their respondent that is guaranteed no place in the contractual language of rights, duties, and consent. The dialectics of both activities reflect dialectics of desire insofar as each person's interest in continuing is contingent upon the other person wishing to do so too, and each person's interest is as much fueled by the other's interest as it is by her own. . . .

Cultural Presumptions

. . . Traditionally, the decision to date indicates that two people have an initial attraction to each other, that they are disposed to like each other, and look forward to enjoying each other's company. Dating derives its implicit meaning from this tradition. It retains this meaning unless other aims are explicitly stated, and even then it may not be possible to alienate this meaning. It is a rare woman who will not spurn a man who states explicitly, right at the onset, that he wants to go out with her solely on the condition that he have sexual intercourse with her at the end of the evening, and that he has no interest in her company apart from gaining that end, and no concern for mutual satisfaction.

Explicit protest to the contrary aside, the conventions of dating confer on it its social meaning, and this social meaning implies a relationship which is more like friendship than the cutthroat competition of opposing teams. As such, it requires that we do more than stand on our rights with regard to each other. As long as we are operating under the auspices of a dating relationship, it requires that we behave in the mode of friendship and trust. But if a date is more like friendship than a business contract, then clearly respect for the dialectics of desire is incompatible with the sort of sexual pressure that is inclined to end in date rape. And clearly, also, a conquest mentality which exploits a situation of trust and respect for purely selfish ends is morally pernicious. Failure to respect the dialectics of desire when operating under the auspices of friendship and trust is to act in flagrant disregard of the moral requirement to avoid manipulative, coercive, and exploitive behaviour. Respect for the dialectics of desire is *prima facie* inconsistent with the satisfaction of one person at the expense of the other. The proper end of friendship relations is mutual satisfaction. But the requirement of mutuality means that we must take a communicative approach to discovering the ends of the other, and this entails that we respect the dialectics of desire.

But now that we know what communicative sexuality is, and that it is morally required, and that it is the only feasible means to mutual sexual enjoyment, why not take this model as the norm of what is reasonable in sexual interaction? The evidence of sexologists strongly indicates that women whose partners are aggressively uncommunicative have little chance of experiencing sexual pleasure. But it is not reasonable for women to consent to what they have little chance of enjoying. Hence it is not reasonable for women to consent to aggressive noncommunicative sex. Nor can we reasonably suppose that women have consented to sexual encounters which we know and they know they do not find enjoyable. With the communicative model as the norm, the aggressive contractual model should strike us as a model of deviant sexuality, and sexual encounters patterned on that model should strike us as encounters to which *prima facie* no one would reasonably agree. But if acquiescence to an encounter counts as consent only if the acquiescence is reasonable, something to which a reasonable person, in full possession of knowledge relevant to the encounter, would agree, then acquiescence to aggressive noncommunicative sex is not reasonable. Hence, acquiescence under such conditions should not count as consent.

Thus, where communicative sexuality does not occur, we lack the main ground for believing that the sex involved was consensual. Moreover, where a man does not engage in communicative sexuality, he acts either out of reckless disregard, or out of willful ignorance. For he cannot know, except through the practice of communicative sexuality, whether his partner has any sexual reason for continuing the encounter. And where she does not, he runs the risk of imposing on her what she is not willing to have. All that is needed then, in order to provide women with legal protection from "date rape," is to make both reckless indifference and willful ignorance a sufficient condition of *mens rea* and to make communicative sexuality the accepted norm of sex to which a reasonable woman would agree. Thus, the appeal to communicative sexuality as a norm for sexual encounters accomplishes two things. It brings the aggressive sex involved in "date rape" well within the realm of sexual assault, and it locates the guilt of date rapists in the failure to approach sexual relations on a communicative basis.

The Epistemological Implications

Finding a proper criterion for consent is one problem, discovering what really happened, after the event, when the only eyewitnesses give conflicting accounts is another. But while there is no foolproof way of getting the unadulterated truth, it can make a significant difference to the outcome of a prosecution what sort of facts we are seeking. On the old model of aggressive seduction we sought evidence of resistance. But on the new model of communicative sexuality what we want is evidence of an ongoing positive and encouraging response on the part of the plaintiff. This new goal will require quite different tactics on the part of the cross-examiners, and quite different expectations on the part of juries and judges. Where communicative sexuality is taken as the norm, and aggressive sexual tactics as a presumption against consent, the outcome for the example that I described above would be quite different. It would be regarded as sexual assault rather than seduction. . . .

Conclusion

In sum, using communicative sexuality as a model of normal sex has several advantages over the "aggressive-acquiescence" model of seduction. The new model ties the presumption that consensual sex takes place in the expectation of mutual desire much more closely to the facts about how that desire actually functions. Where communicative sex does not occur, this establishes a presumption that there was no consent. The importance of this presumption is that we are able, in criminal proceedings, to shift the burden of proof from the plaintiff, who on the contractual model must show that she resisted or was threatened, to the defendant, who must then give some reason why she should consent after all. The communicative model of sexuality also enables us to give a different conceptual content to the concept of consent. It sees consent as something more like an ongoing cooperation than the one-shot agreement which we are inclined to see it as on the contractual model. Moreover, it does not matter, on the communicative model, whether a woman was sexually provocative, what her reputation is, what went on before the sex began. All that matters is the quality of communication with regard to the sex itself.

But most importantly, the communicative model of normal sexuality gives us a handle on a solution to the problem of date rape. If noncommunicative sexuality establishes a presumption of non-consent, then where there are no overriding reasons for thinking that consent occurred, we have a criterion for a category of sexual assault that does not require evidence of physical violence or threat. If we are serious about date rape, then the next step is to take this criterion as objective grounds for establishing that a date rape has occurred. The proper legislation is the shortest route to establishing this criterion.

NOTES

1. *Why Men Rape,* Sylvia Levine and Joseph Loenig, eds. (Toronto: Macmillan, 1980), p. 83.
2. *Ibid.,* p. 77.

An Interview About Sex and Date Rape

From a two-part interview with Celia Farber, *SPIN*, September and October 1991.

Part One

Paglia: . . . My views on sex are coming from the fact that I am a football fan and I am a rock fan. Rock and football are revealing something true and permanent and eternal about male energy and sexuality. They are revealing the fact that women, in fact, *like* the idea of flaunting, strutting, wild masculine energy. . . . This date-rape propaganda has been primarily coming out of the elite schools, where the guys are all these cooperative, literate, introspective, sit-on-their-ass guys, whereas you're not getting it that much down in the football schools where people accept the fact of the beauty and strength of masculinity. You see jocks on the campus all the time—they understand what manhood is down there. It's only up here where there is this idea that they can get men on a leash. It's these guys in the Ivy League schools who get used to obeying women. They're sedentary guys. It's ironic that you're getting the biggest bitching about men from the schools where the men are just eunuchs and bookworms.

SPIN: That point about primordial male sexuality is also at odds with much contemporary pop psychology. I'm referring to the twelve-step, women-who-love-too-much school of thought, which insists that a woman's attraction to an "untamed" man, as it were, is necessarily a sign of sickness—a sign of a warped emotional life that invariably traces back to childhood, and the attention span of the father. It never considers such an attraction to be a naturally occurring phenomenon—a force of nature. I think the approach to remedying the problem is simplistic, even dangerously so at times.

Paglia: I agree. I'm a Freudian. I like Freud very much, even though I adapt him and add things to him. But his system of analysis is extremely accurate. It's a conflict-based system that allows for paradox. It's also very self-critical and self-analytical. I've watched therapy getting more and more mushy in the past fifteen years in America. . . . It's become what I call coercive compassion. It's disgusting, it's condescending, it's insulting, it's coddling, it keeps everyone in an infantile condition rather than in the adult condition that was postulated as the ultimate goal of Freudian analysis. You were meant to be totally self-aware as a Freudian. Now, it's everyone who will help you, the group will help you. It's awful. It's a return to the Fifties conformist model of things. It's this victim-centered view of the world, which is very pernicious. We cannot have a world where everyone is a victim. "I'm this way because my father made me this way. I'm this way because my husband made me this way." Yes, we are indeed formed by traumas that happened to us. But then you must take charge, you must take over, you are responsible. Personal responsibility is at the heart of my system. But today's system is this whining thing, "Why won't you help me, Mommy and Daddy?" It's like this whole thing with date rape.

SPIN: One point that hasn't been made in the whole rape debate is women's role over men, sexually. In the case of a rape, a man has to use brute force to obtain something that a woman has—her very sex. So naturally she's weaker physically, and will always be oppressed by him physically. But in that moment when he decides that the only way he can get what he wants from her emotionally, or sexually, or whatever, is to rape her, he is confessing to a weakness that is all-encompassing. She is abused, but he is utterly tragic and pathetic. One is temporary and the other is permanent. I was raped once and it helped me to think of it like that. Not at all to apologize for him, but to focus on my power instead of my helplessness. It was a horrible experience, but it certainly didn't destroy my whole life or my psyche, as much as contemporary wisdom insisted it must have.

Paglia: Right, we *have* what they want. I think woman is the dominant sex. Men have to do all sorts of stuff to prove that they are worthy of a woman's attention. It's very interesting what you said about the rape, because one of the German magazine reporters who came to talk to me— she's been living in New York for ten years—she came to talk to me about two weeks ago and she told me a very interesting story, very similar to yours. She lives in Brooklyn, and she let this guy in whom she shouldn't have, and she got raped. She said that, because she's a feminist, of course she had to go for counseling. She said it was awful, that the minute she arrived there, the rape counselors were saying, "You will never recover from this, what's happened to you is so terrible." She said, what the hell, it was a terrible experience, but she was going to pick herself up, and it wasn't that big a deal. The whole system now is designed to make you feel that you are maimed and mutilated forever if something like that happens.

She said it made her feel worse. It's absolutely American—it is not European—and the whole system is filled with these clichés about sex. I think there is a fundamental prudery about sex in all this. Rape is one of the risk factors in getting involved with men. It's a risk factor. It's like driving a car. My attitude is, it's like gambling. If you go to Atlantic City—these girls are going to Atlantic City, and when they lose, it's like "Oh, Mommy and Daddy, I lost." My answer is stay home and do your nails, if that's the kind of person you are. My Sixties attitude is, yes, go for it, take the risk, take the challenge—if you get raped, if you get beat up in a dark alley in a street, it's okay. That was part of the risk of freedom, that's part of what we've demanded as women. Go with it. Pick yourself up, dust yourself off, and go on. We cannot regulate male sexuality. The uncontrollable aspect of male sexuality is part of what makes sex interesting. And yes, it can lead to rape in some situations. What feminists are asking for is for men to be castrated, to make eunuchs out of them. The powerful, uncontrollable force of male sexuality has been censored out of white middle-class homes. But it's still there in black culture, and in Spanish culture.

Part Two

SPIN: In the first part of our interview, the section about rape upset every single woman who read it—in the offices at *SPIN* and even at the typesetters. They all seemed to feel that you were defending the rapist.

Paglia: No, that's not it at all. The point is, these white, upper-middle-class feminists believe that a pain-free world is achievable. I'm saying that a pain-free world will be achievable only under totalitarianism. There is no such thing as risk-free anything. In fact, all valuable human things come to us from risk and loss. Therefore we value beauty and youth because they are transient. Part of the sizzle of sex is the danger, the risk of loss of identity in love. That's part of the drama of love. My generation demanded no more overprotection of women. We wanted women to be able to freely choose sex, to freely have all the adventures that men could have. So women began to hike on mountain paths and do all sorts of dangerous things. That's the risk of freedom. If women break their legs on mountain bikes, that's the risk factor. I'm not defending the rapist—I'm defending the freedom to risk rape. I don't want sexual experience to be protected by society. A part of it is that since women are physically weaker than men, in our sexual freedom, women are going to get raped. We should be angry about it, but it's a woman's personal responsibility now, in this age of sexual liberation, to make herself physically fit, so that she can fight off as best she can man's advances. She needs to be alert in her own mind to any potential danger. It's up to the woman to give clear signals of what her wishes are. If she does not want to be out to control of the situation, she should not get drunk, she should not be in a private space with a man whom she does not know. Rape does not destroy you forever. It's like getting beaten up. Men get beat up all the time.

SPIN: But don't you think that people see a man getting beat up and a woman getting raped as completely different? Do you think rape should be considered as serious a crime as murder?

Paglia: That's absurd. I dislike anything that treats women as if they are special, frail little creatures. We don't need special protection. Rape is an assault. If it is a totally devastating psychological experience for a woman, then she doesn't have a proper attitude toward sex. It's this whole stupid feminist thing about how we are basically nurturing, benevolent people, and sex is a wonderful thing between two equals. With that kind of attitude, then of course rape is going to be a total violation of your entire life, because you have had a stupid, naïve, Mary Poppins view of life to begin with. Sex is a turbulent power that we are not in control of; it's a dark force. The sexes are at war with each other. That's part of the excitement and interest of sex. It's the dark realm of the night. When you enter the realm of the night, horrible things can happen there. You can be attacked on a dark street. Does that mean we should never go into dark streets? Part of my excitement as a college student in the Sixties was coming out of the very protective Fifties. I was wandering those dark streets understanding that not only could I be raped, I could be killed. It's like the gay men going down to the docks and having sex in alleyways and trucks; it's the danger. Feminists have no idea that some women like to flirt with danger because there is a sizzle in it. You know what gets me sick and tired? The battered-woman motif. It's so misinterpreted, the way we have to constantly look at it in terms of male oppression and tyranny, and female victimization. When, in fact, everyone knows throughout the world that many of these working-class relationships where women get beat up have hot sex. They ask why she won't leave him? Maybe she won't leave him because the sex is very hot. I say we should start looking at the battered-wife motif in terms of sex. If gay men go down to bars and like to get tied up, beaten up, and have their asses whipped, how come we can't allow that a lot of wives like the kind of sex they are getting in these battered-wife relationships? We can't consider that women might have kinky tastes, can we? No, because women are naturally benevolent and nurturing, aren't they? Everything is so damn Mary Poppins and sanitized.

SPIN: What do you think is the main quality that women have within them that they aren't using?

Paglia: What women have to realize is their dominance as a sex. That women's sexual powers are enormous. All cultures have seen it. Men know it. Women know it. The only people who don't know it are feminists. Desensualized, desexualized, neurotic women. I wouldn't have said this twenty years ago because I was a militant feminist myself. But as the years have gone on, I begin to see more and more that the perverse, neurotic psychodrama projected by these women is coming from their own problems with sex.

Interview with Sonya Friedman, *Sonya Live,* CNN Television, December 13, 1991.

Friedman: Do you see this as liberated feminism, Camille?

Paglia: I see a liberated feminism that takes full responsibility for the woman's part in the sexual encounter or the potentially sexual encounter. Yes, I do. You see, in the old days, you did have a system where fathers and brothers protected women, essentially. Men knew that if they devirginized a woman, they could end up dead within twenty-four hours. These controls have been removed.

Friedman: I'm so lost here, Camille. What I hear is not something that is either modern or egalitarian. What I hear is a woman going back into *veils,* in effect.

Paglia: No, no! I'm encouraging women: *accept* the adventure of sex, *accept* the danger!

Friedman: Do you see a difference between sex and rape?

Paglia: I think this is one of the biggest pieces of propaganda coming out of feminism, the idea that rape is a crime of violence but not of sex. *All* rape is erotic. *All* rape is sexual.

Friedman: Erotic for *whom?*

Paglia: Erotic for the man!

Friedman: Yes, but there are two people having sex. You don't just want it to be erotic for him, and you feel vulnerable as a result of it.

Paglia: From twenty-five years ago, the material that goes into my book is coming from my study of rape as demonstrated in the whole of human cultures, everywhere in literature and art. All ethical men, from the beginning of time on, have protested against rape. This is not just a recent feminist discovery.

Friedman: Okay, now you use an interesting term—"ethical men."

Paglia: All ethical men, yes.

Friedman: Do you agree that a man has some responsibility to have discipline for himself?

Paglia: Correct! Oh, *yes!*

Friedman: Is it that you feel that we are being the enchantress, that we are sending out messages that we deny that we're sending?

Paglia: First let me say that I think that rape cannot be discussed separate from ethics, that we have to consider it as part of all of human behavior. We must begin training people for ethical behavior from earliest childhood. You cannot suddenly focus in on the freshman year and expect to solve the rape problem!—if you have people who are raised without religion, without ethical codes, without morality. Throughout all of history, ethical men have not murdered, have not stolen, have not raped. Feminism's claim that it discovered rape is simply false. Now, yes, I do believe there is an element of provocative behavior. I do feel that women have to realize their sexual power over men. This is part of our power.

Friedman: Okay, let's get this out of the way. A woman wants to wear a see-through blouse, a very short skirt, walk out on the streets at any time of the day and night. She says, "I have a right to feel free to do this. I can dress or undress any way I choose, and a man doesn't have a right to touch me unless I *tell* him that he has that right." What's your position on this?

Paglia: Let me make a parallel, Sonya. We have the *right* to leave our purse on a park bench in Central Park and go play twenty-five feet away and hope the purse is going to be there when we return, okay? Now, this is just simply stupid behavior. If someone steals the purse, we pursue the thief, we put him in jail. We also say to you, "That was really *stupid!*" Now, the same thing here. You may have the *right* to leave your purse there, you may have the *right* to dress in that way, but you are running a *risk!* . . .

Friedman: I think you're going to find a lot of women taking issue with what you say about date rape.

Paglia: Actually, I find that a tremendous number of women agree with me, especially working-class women. Women who are street-smart agree with me. It's the white middle-class women who have problem with it. And also I find that foreigners, people from Europe, know that I'm the one who has the voice of realism in rape. I have to explain to them how absurd the feminist position is today on the question! [A woman from Massachusetts calls: "Her attitude is *condoning rape!*"]

Friedman: It does come across a little bit that way. I don't think you mean to condone rape.

Paglia: Certainly not!

Friedman: But you're really putting the responsibility on women—that if they go out with a man, that whatever happens, they have set themselves up for.

Paglia: I feel that sex is basically combat. I feel that the sexes are at war. . . .

PART THREE

FREE SPEECH, HATE SPEECH, AND CAMPUS SPEECH CODES

GERALD GUNTHER

Good Speech, Bad Speech—No

I am deeply troubled by current efforts—however well-intentioned—to place new limits on freedom of expression at this and other campuses. Such limits are not only incompatible with the mission and meaning of a university; they also send exactly the wrong message from academia to society as a whole. University campuses should exhibit greater, not less, freedom of expression than prevails in society at large.

Proponents of new limits argue that historic First Amendment rights must be balanced against "Stanford's commitment to the diversity of ideas and persons." Clearly, there is ample room and need for vigorous University action to combat racial and other discrimination. But curbing freedom of speech is the wrong way to do so. The proper answer to bad speech is usually more and better speech—not new laws, litigation, and repression.

Lest it be thought that I am insensitive to the pain imposed by expressions of racial or religious hatred, let me say that I have suffered that pain and empathize with others under similar verbal assault. My deep belief in the principles of the First Amendment arises from my own experiences.

I received my elementary education in a public school in a very small town in Nazi Germany. There I was subjected to vehement anti-Semitic remarks from my teacher, classmates and others—"Judensau" (Jew pig) was far from the harshest. I can assure you that they hurt. More generally, I lived in a country where ideological orthodoxy reigned and where the opportunity for dissent was severely limited.

The lesson I have drawn from my childhood in Nazi Germany and my happier adult life in this country is the need to walk the sometimes difficult path of denouncing the bigots' hateful ideas with all my power, yet at the same time challenging any community's attempt to suppress hateful ideas by force of law.

Obviously, given my own experience, I do *not* quarrel with the claim that words *can* do harm. But I firmly deny that a showing of harm suffices to deny First Amendment protection, and I insist on the elementary First Amendment principle that our Constitution usually protects even offensive, harmful expression.

That is why—at the risk of being thought callous or doctrinaire—I feel compelled to speak out against the attempt by some members of the Stanford community to enlarge the area of forbidden speech under the Fundamental Standard. Such proposals, in my view, seriously undervalue the First Amendment and far too readily endanger its precious content. Limitations on free expression beyond those established by law should be eschewed in an institution committed to diversity and the First Amendment.

In explaining my position, I will avoid extensive legal arguments. Instead, I want to speak from the heart, on the basis of my own background and of my understanding of First Amendment principles—principles supported by an even larger number of scholars and Supreme Court justices, especially since the days of the Warren Court.

Among the core principles is that any official effort to suppress expression must be viewed with the greatest skepticism and suspicion. Only in very narrow, urgent circumstances should government or similar institutions be permitted to inhibit speech. True, there are certain categories of speech that may be prohibited; but the number and scope of these categories has steadily shrunk over the last fifty years. Face-to-face insults are one such category; incitement to immediate illegal action is another. But opinions expressed in debates and arguments about a wide range of political and social issues should not be suppressed simply because of disagreement with those views, with the content of the expression.

Similarly, speech should not and cannot be banned simply because it is "offensive" to substantial parts or a majority of a community. The refusal to suppress offensive speech is one of the most difficult obligations the free speech principle imposes upon all of us; yet it is also one of the First Amendment's greatest glories—indeed it is a central test of a community's commitment to free speech.

The Supreme Court's 1989 decision to allow flag-burning as a form of political protest, in *Texas v. Johnson,* warrants careful pondering by all those who continue to advocate campus restraints on "racist speech." As Justice Brennan's majority opinion in *Johnson* reminded, "If there is a bedrock principle underlying the First Amendment, it is that the Government may not prohibit the expression of an idea simply because society finds the idea itself offensive or disagreeable." In refusing to place flag-burning outside the First Amendment, moreover, the *Johnson* majority insisted (in words especially apt for the "racist speech" debate): "The First Amendment does not guarantee that other concepts virtually sacred to our Nation as a whole—*such as the principle that discrimination on the basis of race is odious and destructive*—will go unquestioned in the marketplace of ideas. We decline, therefore, to create for the flag an exception to the joust of principles protected by the First Amendment." (Italics added.)

Campus proponents of restricting offensive speech are currently relying for justification on the Supreme Court's allegedly repeated reiteration that "fighting words" constitute an exception to the First Amendment. Such an exception has indeed been recognized in a number of lower court cases. However, there has only been *one* case in the history of the Supreme Court in which a majority of the Justices has ever found a statement to be a punishable resort to "fighting words." That was *Chaplinsky v. New Hampshire,* a nearly fifty-year-old case involving words which would very likely not be found punishable today.

More significant is what has happened in the nearly half-century since: Despite repeated appeals to the Supreme Court to recognize the applicability of the "fighting words" exception by affirming challenged convictions, the Court has in every instance refused. One must wonder about the strength of an exception that, while theoretically recognized, has for so long not been found apt in practice. (Moreover, the proposed Stanford rules are *not* limited to face-to-face insults to an addressee, and thus go well beyond the traditional, albeit fragile, "fighting words" exception.)

The phenomenon of racist and other offensive speech that Stanford now faces is not a new one in the history of the First Amendment. In recent decades, for example, well-meaning but in my view misguided majorities have sought to suppress not only racist speech but also antiwar and anti-draft speech, civil rights demonstrators, the Nazis and the Ku Klux Klan, and left-wing groups.

Typically, it is people on the extremes of the political spectrum (including those who advocate overthrow of our constitutional system and those who would not protect their opponents' right to dissent were they the majority) who feel the brunt of repression and have found protection in the First Amendment; typically, it is well-meaning people in the majority who believe that their "community standards," their sensibilities, their sense of outrage, justify restraints.

Those in power in a community recurrently seek to repress speech they find abhorrent; and their efforts are understandable human impulses. Yet freedom of expression—and especially the protection of dissident speech, the most important function of the First Amendment—is an anti-majoritarian principle. Is it too much to hope that, especially on a university campus, a majority can be persuaded of the value of freedom of expression and of the resultant need to curb our impulses to repress dissident views?

The principles to which I appeal are not new. They have been expressed, for example, by the most distinguished Supreme Court justices ever since the beginning of the Court's confrontations with First Amendment issues nearly seventy years ago. These principles are reflected in the words of so imperfect a First Amendment defender as Justice Oliver Wendell Holmes: "If there is any principle of the Constitution that more imperatively calls for attachment than any other it is the principle of free thought—not free thought for those who agree with us but freedom for the thought that we hate."

This is the principle most elaborately and eloquently addressed by Justice Louis D. Brandeis, who reminded us that the First Amendment rests on a belief "in the power of reason as applied through public discussion" and therefore bars "silence coerced by law—the argument of force in its worst form."

This theme, first articulated in dissents, has repeatedly been voiced in majority opinions in more recent decades. It underlies Justice Douglas's remark in striking down a conviction under a law banning speech that "stirs the public to anger"; "A function of free speech [is] to invite dispute. . . . Speech is often provocative and challenging. That is why freedom of speech [is ordinarily] protected against censorship or punishment."

It also underlies Justice William J. Brennan's comment about our "profound national commitment to the principle that debate on public issues should be uninhibited, robust and wide-open, and that it may well include vehement, caustic and sometimes unpleasantly sharp attacks"—a comment he followed with a reminder that constitutional protection "does not turn upon the truth, popularity or social utility of the ideas and beliefs which are offered."

These principles underlie as well the repeated insistence by Justice John Marshall Harlan, again in majority opinions, that the mere "inutility or immorality" of a message cannot justify its repression, and that the state may not punish because of "underlying content of the message." Moreover, Justice Harlan, in one of the finest First Amendment opinions on the books, noted, in words that Stanford would ignore at its peril at this time:

> The constitutional right of free expression is powerful medicine in a society
> as diverse and populous as ours. . . . To many, the immediate consequence
> of this freedom may often appear to be only verbal tumult, discord and even
> offensive utterance. These are, however, within established limits, in truth
> necessary side effects of the broader enduring values which the process of
> open debate permits us to achieve. That the air may at times seem filled
> with verbal cacophony is, in this sense, not a sign of weakness but of
> strength.

In this same passage, Justice Harlan warned that a power to ban speech merely because it is offensive is an "inherently boundless" notion, and added that "we think it is largely because governmental officials cannot make principled distinctions in this area that the Constitution leaves matters of taste and style so largely to the individual." (The Justice made these comments while overturning the conviction of an antiwar protestor for "offensive conduct." The defendant had worn, in a courthouse corridor, a jacket bearing the words "Fuck the Draft." It bears noting, in light of the ongoing campus debate, that Justice Harlan's majority opinion also warned that "we cannot indulge in the facile assumption that one can forbid particular words without also running the substantial risk of suppressing ideas in the process.")

I restate these principles and repeat these words for reasons going far beyond the fact that they are familiar to me as a First Amendment scholar. I believe—in my heart as well as my mind—that these principles and ideals are not only established but right. I hope that the entire Stanford community will seriously reflect upon the risks to free expression, lest we weaken hard-won liberties at Stanford and, by example, in this nation.

1. Appreciate his depiction! the struggle between free speech and liberty that which is bad. has a good handle of the various sides of the issue — seems understanding

2. issue: Can free speech do so much negative as to make it necessary to put increased restriction on it?

con. No

reasons — First Amendment we are obligated to uphold it. The market place of ideas is where ideas should be limited, not by gov't.

3. Not at all — I taught same ideas after a rebellion by Christian kids who see the wrongness of an idea + it doesn't seem just to allow it.

Campus Speech Codes:
Doe v. University of Michigan

Some campuses have recently instituted "speech codes" designed to prevent racist, sexist, and other forms of speech. One of the most restrictive of these codes was found at the University of Michigan. The policy outlawed conduct that "stigmatizes or victimizes" students on the basis of "race, ethnicity, religion, sex and sexual orientation." This suit was brought by a graduate student who wished to remain anonymous to protect himself from adverse publicity and is therefore referred to only as "John Doe."—Eds.

1. Introduction

It is an unfortunate fact of our constitutional system that the ideals of freedom and equality are often in conflict. The difficult and sometimes painful task of our political and legal institutions is to mediate the appropriate balance between these two competing values. Recently, the University of Michigan at Ann Arbor (the University), a state-chartered university, . . . adopted a Policy . . . in an attempt to curb what the University's governing Board of Regents (Regents) viewed as a rising tide of racial intolerance and harassment on campus. The Policy prohibited individuals, under the penalty of sanctions, from "stigmatizing or victimizing" individuals or groups on the basis of race, ethnicity, religion, sex, sexual orientation, creed, national origin, ancestry, age, marital status, handicap or Vietnam-era veteran status. . . .

2. Facts Generally

According to the University, in the last three years incidents of racism and racial harassment appeared to become increasingly frequent at the Univer-

---

721 F. Supp. 852 (E.D.Mich. 1989). Some citations omitted. This opinion was written by District Judge Avern Cohen.

sity. For example, on January 27, 1987, unknown persons distributed a flier declaring "open season" on blacks, which it referred to as "saucer lips, porch monkeys, and jigaboos." On February 4, 1987, a student disc jockey at an on-campus radio station allowed racist jokes to be broadcast. At a demonstration protesting these incidents, a Ku Klux Klan uniform was displayed from a dormitory window. . . .

On December 14, 1987, the Acting President circulated a confidential memorandum to the University's executive officers detailing a proposal for an anti-discrimination disciplinary policy. The proposed policy prohibited "[h]arassment of anyone through word or deed or any other behavior which discriminates on the basis of inappropriate criteria." The Acting President recognized at the time that the proposed policy would engender serious First Amendment problems, but reasoned that

> just as an individual cannot shout "Fire!" in a crowded theater and then claim immunity from prosecution for causing a riot on the basis of exercising his rights of free speech, so a great many American universities have taken the position that students at a university cannot by speaking or writing discriminatory remarks which seriously offend many individuals beyond the immediate victim, and which, therefore detract from the necessary educational climate of a campus, claim immunity from a campus disciplinary proceeding. I believe that position to be valid.

The other "American universities" to which the President referred . . . were not identified at any time. Nor was any document presented to the Court in any form which "valid[ates]" this "position." . . .

3. The University of Michigan Policy on Discrimination and Discriminatory Harassment

A. The Terms of the Policy

The Policy established a three-tiered system whereby the degree of regulation was dependent on the location of the conduct at issue. The broadest range of speech and dialogue was "tolerated" in variously described public parts of the campus. Only an act of physical violence or destruction of property was considered sanctionable in these settings. Publications sponsored by the University such as the *Michigan Daily* and the *Michigan Review* were not subject to regulation. The conduct of students living in University housing is primarily governed by the standard provisions of individual leases, however the Policy appeared to apply in this setting as well. The Policy by its terms applied specifically to "[e]ducational and academic centers, such as classroom buildings, libraries, research laboratories, recreation and study centers[.]" In these areas, persons were subject to discipline for:

1. Any behavior, verbal or physical, that stigmatizes or victimizes an individual on the basis of race, ethnicity, religion, sex, sexual orientation, creed, national origin, ancestry, age, marital status, handicap or Vietnam-era veteran status, and that

a. Involves an express or implied threat to an individual's academic efforts, employment, participation in University sponsored extra-curricular activities or personal safety; or

b. Has the purpose or reasonably foreseeable effect of interfering with an individual's academic efforts, employment, participation in University sponsored extra-curricular activities or personal safety; or

c. Creates an intimidating, hostile, or demeaning environment for educational pursuits, employment or participation in University sponsored extra-curricular activities.

2. Sexual advances, requests for sexual favors, and verbal or physical conduct that stigmatizes or victimizes an individual on the basis of sex or sexual orientation where such behavior:

a. Involves an express or implied threat to an individual's academic efforts, employment, participation in University sponsored extra-curricular activities or personal safety; or

b. Has the purpose or reasonably foreseeable effect of interfering with an individual's academic efforts, employment, participation in University sponsored extra-curricular activities or personal safety; or

c. Creates an intimidating, hostile, or demeaning environment for educational pursuits, employment or participation in University sponsored extra-curricular activities. . . .

B. Hearing Procedures

Any member of the University community could initiate the process leading to sanctions by either filing a formal complaint with an appropriate University office or by seeking informal counseling with described University officials and support centers. . . .

C. Sanctions

The Policy provided for progressive discipline based on the severity of the violation. It stated that the University encouraged hearing panels to impose

sanctions that include an educational element in order to sensitize the perpetrator to the harmfulness of his or her conduct. The Policy provided,
however, that compulsory class attendance should not be imposed "in an
attempt to change deeply held religious or moral convictions." Depending
on the intent of the accused student, the effect of the conduct, and whether
the accused student is a repeat offender, one or more of the following sanctions may be imposed: (1) formal reprimand; (2) community service;
(3) class attendance; (4) restitution; (5) removal from University housing;
(6) suspension from specific courses and activities; (7) suspension; (8) expulsion. The sanctions of suspension and expulsion could only be imposed
for violent or dangerous acts, repeated offenses, or a willful failure to comply with a lesser sanction. The University President could set aside or lessen
any sanction.

D. Interpretive Guide

Shortly after the promulgation of the policy in the fall of 1988, the University Office of Affirmative Action issued an interpretive guide (Guide) entitled *What Students Should Know about Discrimination and Discriminatory Harassment by Students in the University Environment*. The Guide
purported to be an authoritative interpretation of the Policy and provided
examples of sanctionable conduct. These included:

A flyer containing racist threats distributed in a residence hall.
Racist graffiti written on the door of an Asian student's study carrel.
A male student makes remarks in class like "Women just aren't as good in
    this field as men," thus creating a hostile learning atmosphere for female
    classmates.
Students in a residence hall have a floor party and invite everyone on their
    floor except one person because they think she might be a lesbian.
A black student is confronted and racially insulted by two white students in
    a cafeteria.
Male students leave pornographic pictures and jokes on the desk of a female
    graduate student.
Two men demand that their roommate in the residence hall move out and
    be tested for AIDS.

In addition, the Guide contained a separate section entitled "You are a ha-
rasser when . . ." which contains the following examples of discriminatory
conduct:

You exclude someone from a study group because that person is of a
    different race, sex, or ethnic origin than you are.
You tell jokes about gay men and lesbians.

Your student organization sponsors entertainment that includes a comedian
who slurs Hispanics.

You display a confederate flag on the door of your room in the residence
hall.

You laugh at a joke about someone in your class who stutters.

You make obscene telephone calls or send racist notes or computer messages.

You comment in a derogatory way about a particular person or group's
physical appearance or sexual orientation, or their cultural origins, or
religious beliefs.

It is not clear whether each of these actions would subject a student to
sanctions, although the title of the section suggests that they would. . . .

4. Standing

Doe is a psychology graduate student. His specialty is the field of biopsy-
chology, which he describes as the interdisciplinary study of the biological
bases of individual differences in personality traits and mental abilities.
Doe said that certain controversial theories positing biologically-based differences between sexes and races might be perceived as "sexist" and "racist" by some students, and he feared that discussion of such theories might
be sanctionable under the Policy. He asserted that his right to freely and
openly discuss these theories was impermissibly chilled, and he requested
that the Policy be declared unconstitutional and enjoined on the grounds of
vagueness and overbreadth. . . .

. . . The Policy prohibited conduct which "stigmatizes or victimizes" students on the basis of "race, ethnicity, religion, sex, sexual orientation" and
other invidious factors. However, the terms "stigmatize" and "victimize"
are not self defining. These words can only be understood with reference to
some exogenous value system. What one individual might find victimizing
or stigmatizing, another individual might not.

. . . The record clearly shows that there existed a realistic and credible
threat that Doe could be sanctioned were he to discuss certain biopsycho-
logical theories.

. . . [T]he University attorney who researched the law and assisted in the
drafting of the Policy, wrote a memorandum in which he conceded that
merely offensive speech was constitutionally protected, but declared that

[w]e cannot be frustrated by the reluctance of the courts and the common
law to recognize the personal damage that is caused by discriminatory
speech, nor should our policy attempt to conform to traditional methods of

identifying harmful speech. Rather the University should identify and prohibit that speech that causes damage to individuals within the community.

The record before the Court thus indicated that the drafters of the policy intended that speech need only be offensive to be sanctionable.

The Guide also suggested that the kinds of ideas Doe wished to discuss would be sanctionable. The Guide was the University's authoritative interpretation of the Policy. It explicitly stated that an example of sanctionable conduct would include:

A male student makes remarks in class like "Women just aren't as good in this field as men," thus creating a hostile learning atmosphere for female classmates.

Doe said in an affidavit that he would like to discuss questions relating to sex and race differences in his capacity as a teaching assistant in Psychology 430, Comparative Animal Behavior. He went on to say:

An appropriate topic for discussion in the discussion groups is sexual differences between male and female mammals, including humans. [One] . . . hypothesis regarding sex differences in mental abilities is that men as a group do better than women in some spatially related mental tasks partly because of a biological difference. This may partly explain, for example, why many more men than women chose to enter the engineering profession.

Doe also said that some students and teachers regarded such theories as "sexist" and he feared that he might be charged with a violation of the Policy if he were to discuss them. In light of the statements in the Guide, such fears could not be dismissed as speculative and conjectural. The ideas discussed in Doe's field of study bear sufficient similarity to ideas denounced as "harassing" in the Guide to constitute a realistic and specific threat of prosecution.

. . . A review of the University's discriminatory harassment complaint files suggested that on at least three separate occasions, students were disciplined or threatened with discipline for comments made in a classroom setting. These are . . . discussed *infra*. At least one student was subject to a formal hearing because he stated in the context of a social work research class that he believed that homosexuality was a disease that could be psychologically treated. As will be discussed below, the Policy was enforced so broadly and indiscriminately, that plaintiff's fears of prosecution were entirely reasonable. Accordingly, the Court found that Doe had standing to challenge the policy.

5. *Vagueness and Overbreadth*

... While the University's power to regulate so-called pure speech is ...
limited, ... certain categories can be generally described as unprotected by
the First Amendment. It is clear that so-called "fighting words" are not
entitled to First Amendment protection. *Chaplinsky v. New Hampshire,*
315 U.S. 568 (1942). These would include "the lewd and obscene, the profane, the libelous, and the insulting or 'fighting words'—those which by
their very utterance inflict injury or tend to incite an immediate breach of
the peace." *Id.* at 572. Under certain circumstances racial and ethnic epithets, slurs, and insults might fall within this description and could constitutionally be prohibited by the University. In addition, such speech may
also be sufficient to state a claim for common law intentional infliction of
emotional distress. Credible threats of violence or property damage made
with the specific intent to harass or intimidate the victim because of his
race, sex, religion, or national origin is punishable both criminally and civ-
illy under state law. Similarly, speech which has the effect of inciting immi-
nent lawless action and which is likely to incite such action may also be
lawfully punished. . . .

What the University could not do, however, was establish an anti-
discrimination policy which had the effect of prohibiting certain speech be-
cause it disagreed with ideas or messages sought to be conveyed. *Texas v.
Johnson* [holding that laws punishing flag burning are unconstitutional].
As the Supreme Court stated in *West Virginia State Board of Education v.
Barnette,* 319 U.S. 624 (1943):

> If there is any star fixed in our constitutional constellation, it is that no
> official, high or petty, can prescribe what shall be orthodox in politics,
> nationalism, religion, or other matters of opinion or force citizens to
> confess by word or act their faith therein.

Nor could the University proscribe speech simply because it was found to
be offensive, even gravely so, by large numbers of people. *Texas v. Johnson,
supra.* . . . These principles acquire a special significance in the university
setting, where the free and unfettered interplay of competing views is essential to the institution's educational mission. . . .

Overbreadth

Doe claimed that the Policy was invalid because it was facially overbroad.
It is fundamental that statutes regulating First Amendment activities must
be narrowly drawn to address only the specific evil at hand. . . .

The Supreme Court has consistently held that statutes punishing speech or conduct solely on the grounds that they are unseemly or offensive are unconstitutionally overbroad. In *Houston v. Hill,* the Supreme Court struck down a City of Houston ordinance which provided that "[i]t shall be unlawful for any person to assault or strike or in any manner oppose, molest, and abuse or interrupt any policeman in the execution of his duty." . . . In *Paplish v. University of Missouri,* (1973), the Supreme Court ordered the reinstatement of a university student expelled for distributing an underground newspaper sporting the headline "Motherfucker acquitted" on the grounds that "the mere dissemination of ideas—no matter how offensive to good taste—on a state university campus may not be shut off in the name alone of conventions of decency." *Id.* at 670. Although the Supreme Court acknowledged that reasonable restrictions on the time, place, and manner of distribution might have been permissible, "the opinions below show clearly that [plaintiff] was dismissed because of the disapproved *content* of the newspaper." *Id.* Most recently, in *Texas v. Johnson, supra,* the Supreme Court invalidated a Texas statute prohibiting burning of the American flag on the grounds that there was no showing that the prohibited conduct was likely to incite a breach of the peace. These cases stand generally for the proposition that the state may not prohibit broad classes of speech, some of which may indeed be legitimately regulable, if in so doing a substantial amount of constitutionally protected conduct is also prohibited. This was the fundamental infirmity of the Policy. . . .

Vagueness

Doe also urges that the policy be struck down on the grounds that it is impermissibly vague. A statute is unconstitutionally vague when "men of common intelligence must necessarily guess at its meaning." A statute must give adequate warning of the conduct which is to be prohibited and must set out explicit standards for those who apply it. . . .

Looking at the plain language of the Policy, it was simply impossible to discern any limitation on its scope or any conceptual distinction between protected and unprotected conduct. . . . The operative words in the cause section required that language must "stigmatize" or "victimize" an individual. However, both of these terms are general and elude precise definition. Moreover, it is clear that the fact that a statement may victimize or stigmatize an individual does not, in and of itself, strip it of protection under the accepted First Amendment tests. . . .

. . . Students of common understanding were necessarily forced to guess at whether a comment about a controversial issue would later be found to be sanctionable under the Policy. The terms of the Policy were so vague that its enforcement would violate the due process clause.

A N D R E W   A L T M A N

Liberalism and Campus Hate Speech

In this article, I develop a liberal argument in favor of certain narrowly drawn rules prohibiting hate speech. The argument steers a middle course between those who reject all forms of campus hate-speech regulation and those who favor relatively sweeping forms of regulation. Like those who reject all regulation, I argue that rules against hate speech are not view-point-neutral. Like those who favor sweeping regulation, I accept the claim that hate speech can cause serious psychological harm to those at whom it is directed. However, I do not believe that such harm can justify regulation, sweeping or otherwise. Instead, I argue that some forms of hate speech inflict on their victims a certain kind of wrong, and it is on the basis of this wrong that regulation can be justified. The kind of wrong in question is one that is inflicted in virtue of the performance of a certain kind of speech-act characteristic of some forms of hate speech, and I argue that rules targeting this speech-act wrong will be relatively narrow in scope.[1]

Hate Speech, Harassment, and Neutrality

Hate-speech regulations typically provide for disciplinary action against students for making racist, sexist, or homophobic utterances or for engaging in behavior that expresses the same kinds of discriminatory attitudes.[2] The stimulus for the regulations has been an apparent upsurge in racist, sexist, and homophobic incidents on college campuses over the past decade. The regulations that have actually been proposed or enacted vary widely in the scope of what they prohibit.

The rules at Stanford University are narrow in scope. They require that speech meet three conditions before it falls into the proscribed zone: the speaker must intend to insult or stigmatize another on the basis of certain characteristics such as race, gender, or sexual orientation; the speech must be addressed directly to those whom it is intended to stigmatize; and the speech must employ epithets or terms that similarly convey "visceral hate or contempt" for the people at whom it is directed.[3]

On the other hand, the rules of the University of Connecticut, in their original form, were relatively sweeping in scope. According to these rules, "Every member of the University is obligated to refrain from actions that intimidate, humiliate or demean persons or groups or that undermine their security or self-esteem." Explicitly mentioned as examples of proscribed speech were "making inconsiderate jokes . . . stereotyping the experiences, background, and skills of individuals, . . . imitating stereotypes in speech or mannerisms [and] attributing objections to any of the above actions to 'hypersensitivity' of the targeted individual or group."

Even the narrower forms of hate-speech regulation, such as we find at Stanford, must be distinguished from a simple prohibition of verbal harassment. As commonly understood, harassment involves a pattern of conduct that is intended to annoy a person so much as to disrupt substantially her activities. No one questions the authority of universities to enact regulations that prohibit such conduct, whether the conduct be verbal or not. There are three principal differences between hate-speech rules and rules against harassment. First, hate-speech rules do not require a pattern of conduct: a single incident is sufficient to incur liability. Second, hate-speech rules describe the offending conduct in ways that refer to the moral and political viewpoint it expresses. The conduct is not simply annoying or disturbing; it is racist, sexist, or homophobic.

The third difference is tied closely to the second and is the most important one: rules against hate speech are not viewpoint-neutral. Such rules rest on the view that racism, sexism, and homophobia are morally wrong. The liberal principle of viewpoint-neutrality holds that those in authority should not be permitted to limit speech on the ground that it expresses a viewpoint that is wrong, evil, or otherwise deficient. Yet, hate-speech rules rest on precisely such a basis. Rules against harassment, on the other hand, are not viewpoint-biased. Anyone in our society could accept the prohibition of harassment because it would not violate their normative political or moral beliefs to do so. The same cannot be said for hate-speech rules because they embody a view of race, gender, and homosexuality contrary to the normative viewpoints held by some people.

If I am correct in claiming that hate-speech regulations are not viewpoint-neutral, this will raise a strong prima facie case against them from a liberal perspective. . . .

Viewpoint-neutrality is not simply a matter of the effects of speech regulation on the liberty of various groups to express their views in the language they prefer. It is also concerned with the kinds of justification that must be offered for speech regulation. The fact is that any plausible justification of hate-speech regulation hinges on the premise that racism, sexism, and homophobia are wrong. Without that premise there would be no basis for arguing that the viewpoint-neutral proscription of verbal harassment is insufficient to protect the rights of minorities and women. The liberal who favors hate-speech regulations, no matter how narrowly drawn, must therefore be prepared to carve out an exception to the principle of view-point-neutrality.

The Harms of Hate Speech

Many of the proponents of campus hate-speech regulation defend their position by arguing that hate speech causes serious harm to those who are the targets of such speech. Among the most basic of these harms are psychological ones. Even when it involves no direct threat of violence, hate speech can cause abiding feelings of fear, anxiety, and insecurity in those at whom it is targeted. As Mari Matsuda has argued, this is in part because many forms of such speech tacitly draw on a history of violence against certain groups.[4] The symbols and language of hate speech call up historical memories of violent persecution and may encourage fears of current violence. Moreover, hate speech can cause a variety of other harms, from feelings of isolation, to a loss of self-confidence, to physical problems associated with serious psychological disturbance.[5]

The question is whether or not the potential for inflicting these harms is sufficient ground for some sort of hate-speech regulation. As powerful as these appeals to the harms of hate speech are, there is a fundamental sticking point in accepting them as justification for regulation, from a liberal point of view. The basic problem is that the proposed justification sweeps too broadly for a liberal to countenance it. Forms of racist, sexist, or homophobic speech that the liberal is committed to protecting may cause precisely the kinds of harm that the proposed justification invokes.

The liberal will not accept the regulation of racist, sexist, or homophobic speech couched in a scientific, religious, philosophical, or political mode of discourse. The regulation of such speech would not merely carve out a minor exception to the principle of viewpoint-neutrality but would, rather, eviscerate it in a way unacceptable to any liberal. Yet, those forms of hate speech can surely cause in minorities the harms that are invoked to justify regulation: insecurity, anxiety, isolation, loss of self-confidence, and so on. Thus, the liberal must invoke something beyond these kinds of harm in order to justify any hate-speech regulation.

Liberals who favor regulation typically add to their argument the contention that the value to society of the hate speech they would proscribe is virtually nil, while scientific, religious, philosophical, and political forms of hate speech have at least some significant value. Thus, Mary Ellen Gale says that the forms she would prohibit "neither advance knowledge, seek truth, expose government abuses, initiate dialogue, encourage participation, further tolerance of divergent views, nor enhance the victim's individual dignity or self respect."[6] As an example of such worthless hate speech Gale cites an incident of white students writing a message on the mirror in the dorm room of blacks: "African monkeys, why don't you go back to the jungle."[7] But she would protect a great deal of racist or sexist speech, such as a meeting of neo-Nazi students at which swastikas are publicly displayed and speeches made that condemn the presence of Jews and blacks on campus.[8]

Although Gale ends up defending relatively narrow regulations, I believe liberals should be very hesitant to accept her argument for distinguishing regulable from nonregulable hate speech. One problem is that she omits from her list of the values that valuable speech serves one which liberals have long considered important, especially for speech that upsets and disturbs others. Such speech, it is argued, enables the speaker to "blow off steam" in a relatively nondestructive and nonviolent way. Calling particular blacks "African monkeys" might serve as a psychological substitute for harming them in a much more serious way, for example, by lynchings or beatings.

Gale could respond that slurring blacks might just as well serve as an encouragement and prelude to the more serious harms. But the same can be said of forms of hate speech that Gale would protect from regulation, for example, the speech at the neo-Nazi student meeting. Moreover, liberals should argue that it is the job of legal rules against assault, battery, conspiracy, rape, and so on to protect people from violence. It is, at best, highly speculative that hate speech on campus contributes to violence against minorities or women. And while the claim about blowing off steam is also a highly speculative one, the liberal tradition clearly puts a substantial burden of proof on those who would silence speech.

There is a more basic problem with any effort to draw the line between regulable and nonregulable hate speech by appealing to the value of speech. Such appeals invariably involve substantial departures from the principle of viewpoint-neutrality. There is no way to make differential judgments about the value of different types of hate speech without taking one or another moral and political viewpoint. Gale's criteria clearly illustrate this as they are heavily tilted against the values of racists and sexists, and yet she does not adequately address the question of how a liberal position can accommodate such substantial departures from viewpoint-neutrality. . . .

I do not assume that the principle of viewpoint-neutrality is an absolute or ultimate one within the liberal framework. Liberals do defend some types of speech regulation that seem to rely on viewpoint-based claims. For example, they would not reject copyright laws, even if it could be shown— as seems plausible—that those laws are biased against the views of people who regard private property as theft.[9] Moreover, the viewpoint-neutrality principle itself rests on deeper liberal concerns which it is thought to serve. Ideally, a liberal argument for the regulation of hate speech would show that regulations can be developed that accommodate these deeper concerns and that simultaneously serve important liberal values. I believe that there is such a liberal argument. In order to show this, however, it is necessary to examine a kind of wrong committed by hate speakers that is quite different from the harmful psychological effects of their speech.

Subordination and Speech Acts

Some proponents of regulation claim that there is an especially close connection between hate speech and the subordination of minorities. Thus, Charles Lawrence contends, "all racist speech constructs the social reality that constrains the liberty of non-whites because of their race."[10] Along the same lines, Mari Matsuda claims, "racist speech is particularly harmful because it is a mechanism of subordination."[11]

The position of Lawrence and Matsuda can be clarified and elaborated using J. L. Austin's distinction between perlocutionary effects and illocutionary force.[12] The perlocutionary effects of an utterance consist of its causal effects on the hearer: infuriating her, persuading her, frightening her, and so on. The illocutionary force of an utterance consists of the kind of speech act one is performing in making the utterance: advising, warning, stating, claiming, arguing, and so on. Lawrence and Matsuda are not simply suggesting that the direct perlocutionary effects of racist speech constitute harm. Nor are they simply suggesting that hate speech can persuade listeners to accept beliefs that then motivate them to commit acts of harm against racial minorities. That again is a matter of the perlocutionary effects of hate speech. Rather, I believe that they are suggesting that hate speech can inflict a wrong in virtue of its illocutionary acts, the very speech acts performed in the utterances of such speech.[13]

What exactly does this speech-act wrong amount to? My suggestion is that it is the wrong of treating a person as having inferior moral standing. In other words, hate speech involves the performance of a certain kind of illocutionary act, namely, the act of treating someone as a moral subordinate.[14]

Treating persons as moral subordinates means treating them in a way that takes their interests to be intrinsically less important, and their lives inherently less valuable, than the interests and lives of those who belong to some reference group. There are many ways of treating people as moral subordinates that are natural as opposed to conventional: the status of these acts as acts of subordination depend solely on universal principles of morality and not on the conventions of a given society. Slavery and genocide, for example, treat people as having inferior moral standing simply in virtue of the affront of such practices to universal moral principles.

Other ways of treating people as moral subordinates have both natural and conventional elements. The practice of racial segregation is an example. It is subordinating because the conditions imposed on blacks by such treatment violate moral principles but also because the act of separation is a convention for putting the minority group in its (supposedly) proper, subordinate place.

I believe that the language of racist, sexist, and homophobic slurs and epithets provides wholly conventional ways of treating people as moral subordinates. Terms such as 'kike', 'faggot', 'spic', and 'nigger' are verbal instruments of subordination. They are used not only to express hatred or contempt for people but also to "put them in their place," that is, to treat them as having inferior moral standing.

It is commonly recognized that through language we can "put people down," to use the vernacular expression. There are many different modes of putting people down: putting them down as less intelligent or less clever or less articulate or less skillful. Putting people down in these ways is not identical to treating them as moral subordinates, and the ordinary put-down does not involve regarding someone as having inferior moral standing. The put-downs that are accomplished with the slurs and epithets of hate speech are different from the ordinary verbal put-down in that respect, even though both sorts of put-down are done through language.

I have contended that the primary verbal instruments for treating people as moral subordinates are the slurs and epithets of hate speech. In order to see this more clearly, consider the difference between derisively calling someone a "faggot" and saying to that person, with equal derision, "You are contemptible for being homosexual." Both utterances can treat the homosexual as a moral subordinate, but the former accomplishes it much more powerfully than the latter. This is, I believe, because the conventional rules of language make the epithet 'faggot' a term whose principal purpose is precisely to treat homosexuals as having inferior moral standing.

I do not believe that a clean and neat line can be drawn around those forms of hate speech that treat their targets as moral subordinates. Slurs and epithets are certainly used that way often, but not always, as is evidenced by the fact that sometimes victimized groups seize on the slurs that historically have subordinated them and seek to "transvalue" the terms. For example, homosexuals have done this with the term 'queer', seeking to turn it into a term of pride rather than one of subordination. . . .

The absence of a neat and clean line around those forms of hate speech that subordinate through speech acts does not entail that it is futile to attempt to formulate regulations that target such hate speech. Rules and regulations rarely have an exact fit with what they aim to prevent: over- and underinclusiveness are pervasive in any system of rules that seeks to regulate conduct. The problem is to develop rules that have a reasonably good fit. Later I argue that there are hate-speech regulations that target subordinating hate speech reasonably well. But first I must argue that such speech commits a wrong that may be legitimately targeted by regulation.

Speech-Act Wrong

I have argued that some forms of hate speech treat their targets as moral subordinates on account of race, gender, or sexual preference. Such treatment runs counter to the central liberal idea of persons as free and equal. To that extent, it constitutes a wrong, a speech-act wrong inflicted on those whom it addresses. However, it does not follow that it is a wrong that may be legitimately targeted by regulation. A liberal republic is not a republic of virtue in which the authorities prohibit every conceivable wrong. The liberal republic protects a substantial zone of liberty around the individual in which she is free from authoritative intrusion even to do some things that are wrong.

Yet, the wrongs of subordination based on such characteristics as race, gender, and sexual preference are not just any old wrongs. Historically, they are among the principal wrongs that have prevented—and continue to prevent—Western liberal democracies from living up to their ideals and principles. As such, these wrongs are especially appropriate targets of regulation in our liberal republic. Liberals recognize the special importance of combating such wrongs in their strong support for laws prohibiting discrimination in employment, housing, and public accommodations. And even if the regulation of speech-act subordination on campus is not regarded as mandatory for universities, it does seem that the choice of an institution to regulate that type of subordination on campus is at least justifiable within a liberal framework.

In opposition, it may be argued that subordination is a serious wrong that should be targeted but that the line should be drawn when it comes to subordination through speech. There, viewpoint-neutrality must govern. But I believe that the principle of viewpoint-neutrality must be understood as resting on deeper liberal concerns. Other things being equal, a departure from viewpoint-neutrality will be justified if it can accommodate these deeper concerns while at the same time serving the liberal principle of the equality of persons.

The concerns fall into three basic categories. First is the Millian idea that speech can promote individual development and contribute to the public political dialogue, even when it is wrong, misguided, or otherwise deficient. Second is the Madisonian reason that the authorities cannot be trusted with formulating and enforcing rules that silence certain views: they will be too tempted to abuse such rules in order to promote their own advantage or their own sectarian viewpoint.[15] Third is the idea that any departures from viewpoint-neutrality might serve as precedents that could be seized upon by would-be censors with antiliberal agendas to further their broad efforts to silence speech and expression.[16]

These concerns that underlie viewpoint-neutrality must be accommodated for hate-speech regulation to be justifiable from a liberal perspective. But that cannot be done in the abstract. It needs to done in the context of a particular set of regulations. In the next section, I argue that there are regulations that target reasonably well those forms of hate speech that subordinate, and in the following section I argue that such regulations accommodate the concerns that underlie the liberal endorsement of the viewpoint-neutrality principle.

Targeting Speech-Act Wrong

If I am right in thinking that the slurs and epithets of hate speech are the principal instruments of the speech-act wrong of treating someone as a moral subordinate and that such a wrong is a legitimate target of regulation, then it will not be difficult to formulate rules that have a reasonably good fit with the wrong they legitimately seek to regulate. In general, what are needed are rules that prohibit speech that (*a*) employs slurs and epithets conventionally used to subordinate persons on account of their race, gender, religion, ethnicity, or sexual preference, (*b*) is addressed to particular persons, and (*c*) is expressed with the intention of degrading such persons on account of their race, gender, religion, ethnicity, or sexual preference. With some modification, this is essentially what one finds in the regulations drafted by Grey for Stanford.[17]

Restricting the prohibition to slurs and epithets addressed to specific persons will capture many speech-act wrongs of subordination. But it will not capture them all. Slurs and epithets are not necessary for such speech acts, as I conceded earlier. In addition, it may be possible to treat someone as a moral subordinate through a speech act, even though the utterance is not addressing that person. However, prohibiting more than slurs and epithets would run a high risk of serious overinclusiveness, capturing much speech that performs legitimate speech acts such as stating and arguing. And prohibiting all use of slurs and epithets, whatever the context, would mandate a degree of intrusiveness into the private lives of students that would be difficult for liberals to license.

The regulations should identify examples of the kinds of terms that count as epithets or slurs conventionally used to perform speech acts of subordination. This is required in order to give people sufficient fair warning. But because the terms of natural languages are not precise, univocal, and unchanging, it is not possible to give an exhaustive list, nor is it mandatory to try. Individuals who innocently use an epithet that conventionally subordinates can plead lack of the requisite intent. . . .

Accommodating Liberal Concerns

I have argued that regulations should target those forms of hate speech that inflict the speech-act wrong of subordination on their victims. This wrong is distinct from the psychological harm that hate speech causes. In targeting speech-act subordination, the aim of regulation is not to prohibit speech that has undesirable psychological effects on individuals but, rather, to prohibit speech that treats people as moral subordinates. To target speech that has undesirable psychological effects is invariably to target certain ideas, since it is through the communication of ideas that the psychological harm occurs. In contrast, targeting speech-act subordination does not target ideas. Any idea would be free from regulation as long as it was expressed through a speech act other than one which subordinates: stating, arguing, claiming, defending, and so on would all be free of regulation.[18]

Because of these differences, regulations that target speech-act subordination can accommodate the liberal concerns underlying viewpoint-neutrality, while regulations that sweep more broadly cannot. Consider the important Millian idea that individual development requires that people be left free to say things that are wrong and to learn from their mistakes. Under the sort of regulation I endorse, people would be perfectly free to make racist, sexist, and homophobic assertions and arguments and to learn of the deficiencies of their views from the counterassertions and counterarguments of others. And the equally important Millian point that public dialogue gains even through the expression of false ideas is accommodated in a similar way. Whatever contribution a racist viewpoint can bring to public discussion can be made under regulations that only target speech-act subordination.

The liberal fear of trusting the authorities is somewhat more worrisome. Some liberals have argued that the authorities cannot be trusted with impartial enforcement of hate-speech regulations. Nadine Strossen, for example, claims that the hate-speech regulations at the University of Michigan have been applied in a biased manner, punishing the racist and homophobic speech of blacks but not of whites.[19] Still, it is not at all clear that the biased application of rules is any more of a problem with rules that are not viewpoint-neutral than with those that are. A neutral rule against harassment can also be enforced in a racially discriminatory manner. There is no reason to think a priori that narrowly drawn hate-speech rules would be any more liable to such abuse. Of course, if it did turn out that there was a pervasive problem with the biased enforcement of hate-speech rules, any sensible liberal would advocate rescinding them. But absent a good reason for thinking that this is likely to happen—not just that it could conceivably happen—the potential for abusive enforcement is no basis for rejecting the kind of regulation I have defended.

Still remaining is the problem of precedent: even narrowly drawn regulations targeting only speech-act subordination could be cited as precedent for more sweeping, antiliberal restrictions by those at other universities or in the community at large who are not committed to liberal values.[20] In response to this concern, it should be argued that narrowly drawn rules will not serve well as precedents for would-be censors with antiliberal agendas. Those who wish to silence socialists, for example, on the ground that socialism is as discredited as racism will find scant precedential support from regulations that allow the expression of racist opinions as long as they are not couched in slurs and epithets directed at specific individuals.

There may be some precedent-setting risk in such narrow regulations. Those who wish to censor the arts, for example, might draw an analogy between the epithets that narrow hate-speech regulations proscribe and the "trash" they would proscribe: both forms of expression are indecent, ugly, and repulsive to the average American, or so the argument might go.

Yet, would-be art censors already have precedents at their disposal providing much closer analogies in antiobscenity laws. Hate-speech regulations are not likely to give would-be censors of the arts any additional ammunition. To this, a liberal opponent of any hate-speech regulation might reply that there is no reason to take the risk. But the response will be that there is a good reason, namely, to prevent the wrong of speech-act subordination that is inflicted by certain forms of hate speech.

Conclusion

There is a defensible liberal middle ground between those who oppose all campus hate-speech regulation and those who favor the sweeping regulation of such speech. But the best defense of this middle ground requires the recognition that speech acts of subordination are at the heart of the hate-speech issue. Some forms of hate speech do wrong to people by treating them as moral subordinates. This is the wrong that can and should be the target of campus hate-speech regulations.

NOTES

1. In a discussion of the strictly legal issues surrounding the regulation of campus hate speech, the distinction between private and public universities would be an important one. The philosophical considerations on which this article focuses, however, apply both to public and private institutions.

2. In this article, I will focus on the restruction of racist (understood broadly to include anti-Semitic), sexist, and homophobic expression. In addition to such expression, regulations typically prohibit discriminatory utterances based on ethnicity, religion, and physical appearance. The argument I develop in favor of regulation applies noncontroversially to ethnicity and religion, as well as to race, gender, and sexual preference. But in a later section I argue against the prohibition of discriminatory remarks based on appearance. I understand 'speech' as whatever has nonnatural meaning according to Grice's account, i.e., any utterances or actions having the following nested intentions behind them: the intention to produce a certain effect in the audience, to have the audience recognize that intention, and to have that recognition be the reason for the prodution of the effect. See Paul Grice, "Meaning," in his *Studies in the Way of Words* (Cambridge, Mass.: Harvard University Press, 1989), pp. 220–21. On this Gricean account, not only verbal utterances but also the display of symbols or flags, gestures, drawings, and more will count as speech. Although some commentators have produced counterexamples to this account of speaker's meaning, I do not believe that they pose insurmountable problems. See Robert Fogelin, "Review of Grice, *Studies in the Way of Words,*" *Journal of Philosophy* 88 (1991): 217.

3. The full text of the Stanford regulations is in Thomas Grey, "Civil Rights v. Civil Liberties: The Case of Discriminatory Verbal Harassment," *Social Philosophy and Policy* 8 91991): 106–7.

4. Mari Matsuda, "Legal Storytelling: Public Response to Racist Speech: Considering the Victim's Story," *Michigan Law Review* 87 (1989): 2329–34, 2352.

5. See Richard Delgado, "Words That Wound: A Tort Action for Racial Insults, Epithets and Name-Calling," *Harvard Civil Rights—Civil Liberties Law Review* 17 (1982): 137, 146.

6. Mary Ellen Gale, "Reimagining the First Amendment: Racist Speech and Equal Liberty," *St. John's Law Review* 65 (1991): 179–80.

7. Ibid., p. 176.

8. Ibid.

9. I think liberals could argue that the deviation of copyright laws from viewpoint-neutrality is both minor and reasonable, given the extreme rarity of the anti-property view in our society and given the great social value that such laws are seen as serving.

10. Charles Lawrence, "If He Hollers Let Him Go: Regulating Racist Speech on Campus," *Duke Law Journal* (1990), p. 444.

11. Matsuda, p. 2357.

12. J. L. Austin, *How to Do Things with Words* (New York: Oxford University Press, 1962), pp. 98 ff. The concept of an illocutionary act has been refined and elaborated by John Searle in a series of works starting with "Austin on Locutionary and Illocutionary Acts," *Philosophical Review* 77 (1968): 420–21. Also see his *Speech Acts* (New York: Cambridge University Press, 1969), p. 31, and *Expression and Meaning* (New York: Cambridge University Press, 1979); and John Searle and D. Vanderveken, *Foundations of Illocutionary Logic* (New York: Cambridge University Press, 1985).

13. Both Lawrence and Matsuda describe racist speech as a unique form of speech in its internal relation to subordination. See Lawrence, p. 440, n. 42; and Matsuda, p. 2356. I do not think that their view is correct. Homophobic and sexist speech, e.g., can also be subordinating. In fact, Lawrence and Matsuda are applying to racist speech essentially the same idea that several feminist writers have applied to pornography. These feminists argue that pornography does not simply depict the subordination of women; it actually subordinates them. See Melinda Vadas, "A First Look at the Pornography/Civil Rights Ordinance: Could Pornography Be the Subordination of Women?" *Journal of Philosophy* 84 (1987): 487–511.

14. Lawrence and Matsuda argue that all racist speech is subordinating. I reject their argument below and claim that the speech act of treating someone as a moral subordinate is not characteristic of all forms of racist speech. They also describe the wrong of speech-act subordination as a "harm." But the wrong does not in itself interfere with a person's formulation and pursuit of her plans and purposes. On that basis, I have been persuaded by my colleague Peter Caws that it is better to avoid the term 'harm' when describing speech-act subordination. Why such speech acts are, from a liberal perspective, wrongs is explained below.

15. See Frederick Schauer, "The Second-Best First Amendment," *William and Mary Law Review* 31 (1989): 1–2.

16. Peter Linzer, "White Liberal Looks at Racist Speech," *St. John's Law Review* 65 (1991): 219.

17. Stanford describes the intent that is needed for a hate speaker to be liable as the intent to insult or stigmatize. My reservations about formulating the requisite intent in terms of 'insult' are given below.

18. A similar argument was made by some supporters of a legal ban on desecrating the American flag through such acts as burning it: to the extent that the ban would prohibit some people from expressing their political viewpoints, it was only a minor departure from viewpoint-neutrality, since those people had an array of other ways to express their views. But the critical difference between the flag-burning case and the hate-speech case is that flag burning is not an act that treats anyone as a moral subordinate.

19. Nadine Strossen, "Regulating Racist Speech on Campus: A Modest Proposal?" *Duke Law Journal* (1990), pp. 557–58. Eric Barendt argues that the British criminal law against racist speech "has often been used to convict militant black spokesmen" (Eric Barendt, *Freedom of Speech* [Oxford: Clarendon, 1985], p. 163).

20. This concern should be distinguished from the idea that any hate-speech regulation is a step down the slippery slope to the totalitarian control of ideas. That idea is difficult to take seriously. Even for nations that have gone much farther in regulating hate speech than anything envisioned by liberal proponents of regulation in the United States, countries such as England, France, and Germany, the idea that they are on the road to totalitarianism is preposterous.

PART FOUR

RACE AND AFFIRMATIVE ACTION ON CAMPUS

Affirmative Action
in Universities:
Regents of the University
of California v. Bakke

Allan Bakke is a white man who applied for admission to the medical school at the University of California at Davis. Only a tiny percentage of doctors are not white. In order to help remedy this situation, Davis had an affirmative action program that set aside 16 out of its 100 entrance places for minority students. If qualified minority students could not be found, those places were not to be filled. In addition to the special admission process, minority students were free to compete through the regular admission process for one of the unrestricted 84 positions. Bakke was refused admission, but he sued the University of California, contending that he had been discriminated against in violation of both the 1964 Civil Rights Act and the equal protection clause of the Constitution. He argued that he would have won admission if those 16 places had not been withdrawn from open competition and reserved for minority students. The University of California did not deny this but contended that its program was legally permissible and socially necessary. [The Court reported that Bakke scored in the 97th percentile on the MCAT while the average of the minority students admitted under the quota system was the 30th; his GPA was 3.44 as opposed to 2.42 for the minority students who were admitted.]—Eds.

Mr. Justice Powell: Although many of the Framers of the Fourteenth Amendment conceived of its primary function as bridging the vast distance between members of the Negro race and the white "majority," the Amendment itself was framed in universal terms, without reference to color, ethnic origin, or condition of prior [servitude.] . . .

Over the past 30 years, this Court has embarked upon the crucial mission of interpreting the Equal Protection Clause with the view of assuring

438 U.S. 265 (1978). Some citations omitted.

to all persons "the protection of equal laws" in a nation confronting a legacy of slavery and racial discrimination. . . .

Petitioner [U. C. Davis] urges us to adopt for the first time a more restrictive view [and] hold that discrimination against members of the white "majority" cannot be suspect if its purpose can be characterized as "benign." [But it] is far too late to argue that the guarantee of equal protection to *all* persons permits the recognition of special wards entitled to a degree of protection greater than that accorded others. . . .

The concepts of "majority" and "minority" necessarily reflect temporary arrangements and political judgments. The white "majority" itself is composed of various minority groups, most of which can lay claim to a history of prior discrimination at the hands of the state and private individuals. Not all of these groups can receive preferential treatment and corresponding judicial tolerance of distinctions drawn in terms of race and nationality, for then the only "majority" left would be a new minority of White Anglo-Saxon Protestants. There is no principled basis for deciding which groups would merit "heightened judicial solicitude" and which would not. . . .

Moreover, there are serious problems of justice connected with the idea of preference itself. . . . Preferential programs may only reinforce common stereotypes holding that certain groups are unable to achieve success without special protection based on a factor having no relationship to individual worth. . . . There is [also] a measure of inequity in forcing innocent persons in respondent's position to bear the burdens of redressing grievances not of their making.

In this case, [there] has been no determination by the legislature or a responsible administrative agency that the University engaged in a discriminatory practice requiring remedial efforts. . . . [When] a classification denies an individual opportunities or benefits enjoyed by others solely because of his race or ethnic background, it must be regarded as suspect.

[The] special admissions program purports to serve the purposes of: (i) "reducing the historic deficit of traditionally disfavored minorities in medical schools and the medical profession"; (ii) countering the effects of societal discrimination; (iii) increasing the number of physicians who will practice in communities currently underserved; and (iv) obtaining the educational benefits that flow from an ethnically diverse student body. It is necessary to decide which, if any, of these purposes is substantial enough to support the use of a suspect classification.

A. If petitioner's purpose is to assure within its student body some specified percentage of a particular group merely because of its race or ethnic origin, such preferential purpose must be rejected not as insubstantial but as facially invalid. Preferring members of any one group for no reason other than race or ethnic origin is discrimination for its own sake. This the Constitution forbids.

B. The State certainly has a legitimate and substantial interest in ameliorating, or eliminating where feasible, the disabling effects of identified discrimination. . . . We have never approved a classification that aids persons perceived as members of relatively victimized groups at the expense of other innocent individuals in the absence of judicial, legislative, or administrative findings of constitutional or statutory violations. . . . Petitioner does not purport to have made, and is in no position to make, such findings. . . .

Hence, the purpose of helping certain groups whom the faculty of the Davis Medical School perceived as victims of "societal discrimination" does not justify a classification that imposes disadvantages upon persons like respondent, who bear no responsibility for whatever harm the beneficiaries of the special admissions program are thought to have suffered. . . .

C. Petitioner identifies, as another purpose of its program, improving the delivery of health care services to communities currently undeserved. . . . It may be correct to assume that some of them will carry out this intention, and that it is more likely they will practice in minority communities than the average white doctor. . . . An applicant of whatever race who has demonstrated his concern for disadvantaged minorities in the past and who declares that practice in such a community is his primary professional goal would be more likely to contribute to alleviation of the medical shortage than one who is chosen entirely on the basis of race and disadvantage. . . .

D. The fourth goal asserted by petitioner is the attainment of a diverse student body. . . . Physicians serve a heterogeneous population. An otherwise qualified medical student with a particular background—whether it be ethnic, geographic, culturally advantaged or disadvantaged—may bring to a professional school of medicine experiences, outlooks and ideas that enrich the training of its student body and better equip its graduates to render with understanding their vital service to humanity.

Ethnic diversity, however, is only one element in a range of factors a university properly may consider in attaining the goal of a heterogeneous student body. . . . [The] diversity that furthers a compelling state interest encompasses a far broader array of qualifications and characteristics of which racial or ethnic origin is but a single though important element. Petitioner's special admissions program, focused *solely* on ethnic diversity, would hinder rather than further attainment of genuine diversity. . . .

The experience of other university admissions programs, which take race into account in achieving the educational diversity valued by the First Amendment, demonstrates that the assignment of a fixed number of places to a minority group is not a necessary means toward that end. An illuminating example is found in the Harvard College program.

In such an admissions program, race or ethnic background may be deemed a "plus" in a particular applicant's file, yet it does not insulate the individual from comparison with all [others]. . . . This kind of program treats each applicant as an individual in the admissions process. The applicant who loses out [to] another candidate receiving a "plus" on the basis of ethnic background will not have been foreclosed from all consideration [simply] because he was not the right color or had the wrong surname. . . .

It has been suggested that an admissions program which considers race only as one factor is simply a subtle and more sophisticated—but no less effective—means of according racial preference than the Davis program. A facial intent to discriminate, however, is evident [in] this case. No such facial infirmity exists in an admissions program where race or ethnic background is simply one element—to be weighed fairly against other elements—in the selection process. . . .

[W]hen a State's distribution of benefits or imposition of burden hinges on the color of a person's skin or ancestry, that individual is entitled to a demonstration that the challenged classification is necessary to promote a substantial state interest. Petitioner has failed to carry this burden. . . .

In enjoining petitioner from ever considering the race of any applicant, however, the courts below failed to recognize that the State has a substantial interest that legitimately may be served by a properly devised admissions program involving the competitive consideration of race and ethnic origin. For this reason, so much of the California court's judgment as enjoins petitioner from any consideration of the race of any applicant must be reversed.

Mr. Justice Brennan, concurring in the judgment and dissenting in part: Since we conclude that the [program] is constitutional, we would reverse the judgment below in all respects. Mr. Justice Powell agrees that some uses of race in university admissions are permissible and, therefore, he joins with us to make five votes reversing the judgment below insofar as it prohibits the University from establishing race-conscious programs in the future. . . .

[E]ven today officially sanctioned discrimination is not a thing of the past. Against this background, claims that law must be "colorblind" or that the datum of race is no longer relevant to public policy must be seen as aspiration rather than as description of reality. This is not to denigrate aspiration; for reality rebukes us that race has too often been used by those who would stigmatize and oppress minorities. Yet we cannot [let] color blindness become myopia which masks the reality that many "created equal" have been treated within our lifetimes as inferior both by the law and by their fellow citizens. . . .

[A] government practice or statute which restricts "fundamental rights" or which contain "suspect classifications" is to be subjected to "strict scrutiny." . . . But no fundamental right is involved here. . . . Nor do whites as a class have any of the "traditional indicia of suspectedness: the class is not saddled with such disabilities, or subjected to such a history of purposeful unequal treatment, or relegated to such a position of political powerlessness as to command extraordinary protection from the majoritarian political process." . . .

Moreover, [this] is not a case where racial classifications are "irrelevant and therefore prohibited." Nor has anyone suggested that the University's purposes contravene the cardinal principle that racial classifications that stigmatize—because they are drawn on the presumption that one race is inferior to another or because they put the weight of government behind racial hatred and separatism—are invalid without more. . . .

Davis had a sound basis for believing that the problem of underrepresentation of minorities was substantial and chronic and that the problem was attributable to handicaps imposed on minority applicants by past and present racial discrimination. Until at least 1973, the practice of medicine in this country [was] largely the prerogative of whites. . . .

Davis clearly could conclude that the serious and persistent underrepresentation [is] the result of handicaps under which minority applicants labor as a consequence of a background of deliberate, purposeful discrimination against minorities in education and in society generally, as well as in the medical profession. . . .

The habit of discrimination and the cultural tradition of race prejudice [were] not immediately dissipated [by *Brown I*]. Rather, massive official and private resistance prevented, and to a lesser extent still prevents, attainment of equal opportunity in education at all levels and in the professions. The generation of minority students applying to Davis Medical School since it opened in 1968—most of whom were born before or about the time *Brown I* was decided—clearly have been victims of this discrimination. Judicial decrees recognizing discrimination in public education in California testify to the fact of widespread discrimination suffered by California-born minority applicants; many minority group members living in California, moreover, were born and reared in school districts in southern States segregated by law. [T]he conclusion is inescapable that applicants to medical school must be few indeed who endured the effects of de jure segregation, the resistance to *Brown I*, or the equally debilitating pervasive private discrimination fostered by our long history of official discrimination, and yet come to the starting line with an education equal to whites.

It is not even claimed that Davis' program in any way operates to stigmatize or single out any discrete and insular, or even any identifiable, nonminority group. Nor will harm comparable to that imposed upon racial minorities by exclusion or separation on grounds of race be the likely result of the program. It does not, for example, establish an exclusive preserve for minority [students]. Rather, its purpose is to overcome the effects ofsegregation by bringing the races together. True, whites are excluded from participation in the special admissions program, but this fact only operates to reduce the number of whites to be admitted in the regular admissions program in order to permit admission of a reasonable percentage—less than their proportion of the California population—of otherwise underrepresented qualified minority applicants.

Nor was Bakke in any sense stamped as inferior by [rejection].

Unlike discrimination against racial minorities, the use of racial preferences for remedial purposes does not inflict a pervasive injury upon individual whites in the sense that wherever they go or whatever they do there is a significant likelihood that they will be treated as second-class citizens because of their color. This distinction does not mean that the exclusion of a white resulting from the preferential use of race is not sufficiently serious to require justification; but it does mean that the injury inflicted by such a policy is not distinguishable from disadvantages caused by a wide range of government actions, none of which has ever been thought impermissible for that reason alone.

In addition, there is simply no evidence that the Davis program discriminates intentionally or unintentionally against any minority group which it purports to benefit. The program does not establish a quota in the invidious sense of a ceiling on the number of minority applicants to be admitted. Nor can the program reasonably be regarded as stigmatizing the program's beneficiaries or their race as inferior. The Davis program does not simply advance less qualified applicants; rather, it compensates applicants, whom it is uncontested are fully qualified to study medicine, for educational disadvantage which it was reasonable to conclude was a product of state-fostered discrimination. Once admitted, these students must satisfy the same degree [requirements]; they are taught by the same faculty in the same classes; and their performance is evaluated by the same standards by which regularly admitted students are judged. . . . We disagree with the lower courts' conclusion that the Davis program's use of race was unreasonable in light of its objectives. First, as petitioner argues, there are no practical means by which it could achieve its ends in the foreseeable future without the use of race-conscious measures. . . .

Second, [the] program does not simply equate minority status with disadvantage. Rather, Davis considers [each] applicant's personal history to determine whether he or she has likely been disadvantaged by racial discrimination. The record makes clear that only minority applicants likely to have been isolated from the mainstream of American life are considered in the special [program].

Finally, Davis' special admissions program cannot be said to violate the Constitution simply because it has set aside a predetermined number of places for qualified minority applicants rather than using minority status as a positive factor to be considered in evaluating the applications of disadvantaged minority applicants. For purposes of constitutional adjudication, there is no difference between the two approaches.

LINO A. GRAGLIA

Affirmative Discrimination

The *Brown* decision in 1954, and a companion case, *Bolling v. Sharpe,* prohibited legally required racial segregation in schools and, it quickly appeared, in any government-run facility—e.g., public beaches and bath-houses, municipal golf courses, city buses. The power and appeal of the *Brown* non-discrimination principle proved irresistible and led to the great-est civil-rights advance in our history, the enactment of the 1964 Civil Rights Act, soon supplemented by the 1965 Voting Rights Act and the 1968 Fair Housing Act. Racial discrimination was at last effectively prohibited.

It is not to be expected, however, that so great a moral crusade would be permitted to come to an end merely because its objective had been accomplished. On the contrary, total success more easily serves as a spur to still greater accomplishments.

Racial discrimination had been prohibited and largely ended, but equal-ity of condition between blacks and whites obviously would not quickly be the result. The time had therefore come to move to equality of condition by fiat. The crucial move was made by the Supreme Court in *Green v. County School Board* in 1968, in which the Court changed the *Brown* prohibition of segregation and all racial discrimination by government into a require-ment of integration and racial discrimination by government.

It was not politically feasible in 1968 for the Court candidly to state its new position. The Court avoided this by insisting that although assignment to schools by race was indeed now required, it was not required for its own sake, but only as a "remedy" for past unconstitutional segregation. As Justice Blackmun wrote, concurring in the *Bakke* case ten years later. "In order to get beyond racism, we must first take race into account. There is no other way." . . .

The term "affirmative action" had perhaps first been used in Executive Order 10925, issued by the Kennedy Administration in March 1961, di-rected at eliminating racial discrimination by government contractors. It originally meant the taking of positive steps—for example, the widespread advertising of job openings—to equalize opportunity. But with the passing of time its meaning changed. . . .

Title VI prohibits racial discrimination by institutions that receive federal funds. Yet in 1978, in *Regents of the University of California* v. *Bakke,* the Court held that Title VI also did not apply to discrimination against whites. There was no evidence in any of the cases that the preferred blacks had been discriminated against by the employer or educational institution or that the rejected whites had caused or benefited from any such discrimination. Despite the remedy rationale, the absence of a showing of actual racial injury and racial benefit was simply irrelevant.

Group Benefits, Group Costs

The basis of the rationale is the assumption that members of all racial groups can be expected to appear in all institutions and activities more or less proportionately to their numbers in the general population. The "underrepresentation" of any racial group, it is therefore argued, can be taken as evidence of discrimination. The argument necessarily invites a search for alternative explanations, and alternative explanations are not difficult to find.

The fact is that there is a very large, long-standing, and apparently unyielding difference between blacks as a group and whites as a group—despite, of course, large areas of overlap—in academic ability as measured by standard aptitude and achievement tests, such as the Scholastic Aptitude Test (SAT), Law School Admissions Test (LSAT), Medical College Admission Test (MCAT), and Graduate Record Examination, Quantitative (GREQ). Robert Klitgaard, a former admissions officer at Harvard, reports that of those who took the GREQ in the 1978–79 school year, only 143 blacks had scores above 650, compared to 27,470 whites, and only 50 blacks had scores above 700, compared to 14,450 whites. Among law-school entrants in the fall of 1976, the total number of blacks with LSAT scores above 600 (old scale) and an undergraduate Grade Point Average (GPA) above 3.25 (B+) was 39; the number of whites with such scores was 13,151.

Any messenger who brings news this bad will, of course, have to be attacked. In the early days of "affirmative action" (the late 1960s and early 1970s) a principal claim of its proponents was that the standard tests were biased against members of racial minorities. If this were true, then the admission of members of such groups with lower scores than are required for whites would not constitute the use of racial preferences but merely an attempt to make prediction more accurate; no "affirmative action" is involved in adjusting measuring devices to measure more accurately.

The claim, however, is not true. By test bias is meant, presumably, that the test generally underpredicts the actual performance of members of some group. There is now general agreement that the ability and achievement tests are not biased by this standard. Indeed, investigations have shown that the tests very substantially *overpredict* the actual performance of blacks.

Even leaving overprediction out of account, the number of blacks meeting the ordinary admission criteria for even moderately selective institutions is extremely low. Most elite schools of all types, however, now strive to obtain an entering class that is at least 5 percent black. To obtain this percentage requires, not that blacks be preferred to whites when all other things are more or less equal—a common understanding of "affirmative action"—or even that the ordinary admission standards be bent or shaded; it requires that ordinary standards be largely abandoned.

A frequently noted effect is virtually to guarantee that the preferentially admitted students are placed in schools for which they are greatly underqualified. It is as if professional baseball decided to "advantage" an identifiable group of players at the beginning of their professional careers by placing them in a league at least one level above the one in which they could be expected to compete effectively.

Equality by Stealth

The admission of an identifiable group of greatly underqualified students is a prescription for frustration, resentment, loss of self-esteem, and racial animosity. Forces powerful enough to institute so radical and unpromising a program will, however, be powerful enough to respond to its disastrous consequences with something other than a confession that they have made a terrible mistake. If the racially admitted prove unable to do the work, that will indicate that the curriculum has to be changed. If racial preferences generate racial resentments, that will indicate that whites require specialized instruction in the moral shortcomings of their race. If "affirmative action" is then even more strongly protested, that will indicate that protest must be disallowed.

Thus are born demands for black studies and multiculturalism, which perform the twin functions of reducing the need for ordinary academic work and providing support for the view that the academic difficulties of the black students are the result, not of substantially lower qualifications, but of racial antipathy.

And thus the current insistence on "political correctness," sanctioned by ostracism, vilification, or worse, and the suddenly discovered need for "anti-harassment" and "hate speech" codes. Nothing is more politically incorrect than to point out that a school's "affirmative action" policy is actually a policy of racially preferential admissions, unless it is to specify the actual disparity in the admissions standards being applied to persons from different racial groups. Proponents of anti-harassment codes are correct that it is extremely humiliating to racially preferred students to have a public discussion of the school's admission policy. Instead of concluding that the policy is, for this reason alone, very unlikely to prove beneficial, they conclude that such discussions must be banned.

"Affirmative action" is a fungus that can survive only underground in the dark. If "affirmative action" is a morally defensible policy, why are its proponents loath to have it known just how moral they have been? Because, of course, no one wants it known that he is, as black Yale law professor Stephen Carter puts it, "an affirmative action baby." Or as Thomas Sowell puts it: "What all the arguments and campaigns for quotas are really saying, loud and clear, is that *black people just don't have it,* and that they will have to be given something in order to have something. . . . Those black people who are already competent . . . will be completely undermined, as black becomes synonymous—in the minds of black and white alike—with incompetence, and black achievement becomes synonymous with charity or payoffs."

A recent typically ludicrous illustration of the deceit inherent in "affirmative action" was proved when Georgetown law student Timothy Maguire disclosed in a student newspaper his discovery that his black classmates were admitted with much lower LSAT scores and GPAs than those required of whites. The result was outraged protest by the black students and indignant disavowal, in effect, of "affirmative action" by those who were most responsible for its adoption. Although known as ardent proponent of racially preferential admissions, Dean Judith Areen flatly denied that any racially preferential admissions took place at the school she led. Those who mistakenly thought otherwise failed to understand that many factors—e.g., a required essay—are considered in determining admission.

We are to understand, apparently, that there is an inverse correlation between high LSAT scores and GPAs an ability to write an essay on why one wants to be a law student at Georgetown. This peculiarity also manifests itself disproportionately in the case of black applicants. This explanation made sense to the editorial writers of the *New York Times,* who repeated it in an editorial severely chastising Maguire for his "obsession with numbers" and total misunderstanding of the Georgetown admission process.

The American Association of Law Schools (AALS), the Law School Admission Council, and the American Bar Association (ABA), Section of Legal Education and Admission to the Bar, felt called upon to comment on the Georgetown incident. Like Dean Areen, the highest officials of the legal-education establishment asserted that the critics failed to understand the complexities of the law-school admission process. "Besides the LSAT and undergraduate GPA," a joint press release explained, "several other considerations are taken into account." These considerations include "personal statements from applicants, letters of recommendation, work experience, and the applicant's prior success in overcoming personal disadvantage." The list included no mention of race. Small wonder that innocent newspapers like the *New York Times* are bewildered as to how strange notions about the use of racial preferences in law-school admissions could possibly have arisen.

To law schools, however, the press release did more than provide a demonstration of lawyerly skill and example of lawyerly integrity. The AALS and ABA are accrediting institutions. Their stated accreditation standards make clear—and their visiting accreditation committees, usually nicely balanced by race and sex, make even clearer—that a substantial number of black students is an accreditation consideration.

Disadvantage and Diversity

The various arguments offered for "affirmative action" have grown almost too threadbare with use to require further refutation. By far the most important, that racial preferences can be justified as compensation for past unfair disadvantages, is obviously invalid, because preferences truly meant to compensate for disadvantage would be applied on the basis of disadvantage, not on the basis of race. Persons who have been unfairly disadvantaged should undoubtedly be made whole to the extent feasible, but race is neither an accurate nor an appropriate proxy for such disadvantage. It is inaccurate because not all and only blacks have suffered from disadvantage. Indeed, racially preferential admissions to institutions of higher education ordinary help, not those most in need of help, but middle-class and upper-middle-class blacks. The argument from disadvantage has potency only because, as Glenn Loury has put it, "The suffering of the poorest blacks creates, if you will, a fund of political capital upon which all members of the group can draw when pressing racially based claims."

Racially preferential admission is also an inappropriate means of compensation for several reasons. First, our historic assimilationist national policy has been to insist upon the general irrelevancy of one's membership in a particular racial group as a basis for government action. Second, lack of qualification for a course study can rationally addressed only by taking steps to remove the lack, not by overlooking it and proceeding as if it did not exist. Finally, it is plainly unjust that the cost of racially preferential admissions should be largely borne by the particular individuals whom the racially preferred replace, even though they bear no particular responsibility for the disadvantage for which compensation is supposedly being made.

The newest buzzword for racial discrimination—which after more than two decades of official sanction still may not speak its proper name—is "diversity," a word that is largely replacing the term "affirmative action" (as it becomes less a euphemism than a pejorative) and providing an alternative to the remedy rationale. Just as the remedy argument uses race as a proxy for disadvantage, the diversity argument uses race as a proxy for unusual characteristics. But just as disadvantage, not race, would the criterion if the objective were compensation, so unusual characteristics or experiences would be the criterion if the objective were educational diversity. In practice, the blacks who are preferentially admitted are frequently the children of teachers or other professionals and have a social, economic, and educational background virtually indistinguishable from that of the average middle-class white applicant. "Affirmative action" enforcers do not check schools for diversity of views or experience in the student body; they check only for the presence of blacks and—to a much lesser extent—members of other preferred groups.

The diversity argument was made popular by Justice Powell's opinion in the *Bakke* case, the Court's first decision upholding explicit discrimination against whites. Justice Powell was an inveterate seeker of the middle way, which usually meant, as in *Bakke,* evading the problem by attempting to have it both ways. For example, he found the use of racial quotas unconstitutional because it violates an excluded applicant's "right to individual consideration without regard to his race" and "involves the use of an explicit racial classification." He then, however, approved of the use of an applicant's ("minority") race as a "plus factor," even though it violates the same right and uses the same classification. Expressing views that were his alone, Powell announced that discrimination against whites is every bit as constitutionally disfavored as discrimination against blacks, to be subjected to the strictest judicial scrutiny and permitted only when found to serve a "compelling interest" that could not be served in any other way. He then held that discrimination against whites in admission to medical school is constitutionally permissible nonetheless, because it serves the school's interest—protected by the First Amendment, he said—in a student body with a diversity of views. Powell's attempt to find a middle way between protecting and not protecting whites equally with blacks failed, but it made "diversity" a term of art and rallying cry in the fight for racially preferential admissions.

Perverse Incentives

Among the defects serious enough to be disqualifying of both the remedy and the diversity rationales is that they create perverse and destructive incentives. The remedy rationale requires insistence, not only upon America's racist past, but, even more important, upon the assumption that racism continues largely unabated, although, perhaps, in more subtle and less overt forms. If blacks disproportionately fail to obtain desirable positions because of a lack of the usual qualifications, then the appropriate remedy, even if the lack is due to past racial discrimination, is to attempt to upgrade their qualifications. If the failure is due to present discrimination, however, the only corrective may be racial preferences and quotas.

Proponents of "affirmative action" must, therefore, continually assert that white Americans are implacably opposed to black advance. Professor Derrick Bell of the Harvard Law School claims, for example, that if a magic pill were discovered to make blacks exceptionally law-abiding, whites would destroy it to prevent that from happening. Black crime, he tells us, is actually in the interest of whites because much of the country's economic activity—for example, the production of prison uniforms—is dependent upon it.

In fact, there is every indication that most whites are intensely interested in black progress and derive an extra measure of satisfaction from every example of black success. Basketball games and boxing matches seem only to have gained in appeal and marketability as they became increasingly dominated by blacks. The highest incomes in the entertainment industry in recent years have been earned by blacks. The only noticeable expressions of discontent with the fact that Colin Powell is the nation's highest national security officer have been by black proponents of "affirmative action."

The corollary to insistence that whites are opposed to black advance is the essential futility of hopes for progress by blacks through their own efforts. But the notion that academic success and hard work are pointless for blacks is debilitating, almost certainly the last message that it is in their interest to hear.

As the remedy rationale requires insistence on pervasive white racism, the diversity rationale requires insistence on the existence of important racial differences. Preference for blacks will not produce any significant benefits of diversity unless there are in fact important differences between blacks and whites, and unless the preferred blacks can be relied upon to manifest them. It is thus in the interest of blacks in general—and perhaps, indeed, the duty of the preferred black in particular—to "act black" as much as possible. In the school context this usually means, unfortunately, displaying an exceptional sensitivity to possible racial slights and an ability to see malignant racism as the explanation of most historical events and social phenomena.

Other Agendas

The drive for "affirmative action" is a phenomenon in need of further and more candid explanation than it has so far received. How can adoption of a policy that is virtually a formula for escalating racial consciousness and tension be thought a desirable course of action?

A more plausible explanation for at least some of the demand for "affirmative action" is that it supports an extensive "civil rights" bureaucracy that grew up in the long fight to end racial discrimination and that is now prospering and expanding in the movement to reinstate it. Every college and school, if not every department, must now have an "affirmative action" officer and specialists in racial- and ethnic-group liaison. The more racial tension increases on campus and generally, the greater will be the need for their services.

Further, it remains true that a large proportion of blacks live in the desperate social conditions of an "underclass." It is argued by many that improvement of these conditions requires that the issue of race not be permitted to recede from public attention. "Affirmative action" serves to keep the issue very much alive.

Racial issues seem also to be for some people part of a larger agenda. There are, particularly in our colleges and universities, earnest seekers for a more just and equal society who find themselves thoroughly alienated from their present society and its institutions. The worldwide waning of the appeal of socialism has reduced the potential of economic class differences as the basis of hope for "fundamental social change." Race and sex differences are the most likely substitutes. The pursuit of perfect economic equality, it has turned out, may not be such a good idea, but surely no one today can be so insensitive to the demands of justice as to oppose equality in terms of race and sex. Proponents of any proposal advanced in the name of increasing such equality will enjoy a huge advantage over opponents.

The most important basis for the continuing support of "affirmative action" is indicated perhaps by the arguments made for it by a law professor at a major public university in two debates held about ten years apart. In the first debate, ten or twelve years ago, he supported "affirmative action" with a long list of the then standard arguments: biased tests, compensation, role models, services to deprived groups, and so on. His enthusiasm for "affirmative action" because of the many good effects he expected it to have seemed unbounded. Indeed, "affirmative action" was working so well at his school that the school decided to drop Japanese-Americans as specially preferred group because substantial numbers of Japanese-American applicants had been found to meet the ordinary standards. He confidently foresaw the day when the same would be true, first of Mexican-Americans and then of blacks.

In another debate about two years ago, this professor's enthusiasm was gone and his argument much changed. He still supported "affirmative action," but his reasons had been reduced to a single one: "We simply must have blacks in this institution." The problem is undoubtedly a severe one: if a stable multiracial society requires that all racial groups be more or less proportionately represented in all important institutions and activities, it requires what no multiracial society has ever achieved.

A more promising approach to social stability, surely, is to maintain a system of law, government, and public policy that uniformly insists on the total irrelevance, at least for official or public purposes, of claimed membership in any particular racial group. It may be naïve idealism to believe that racial peace can be achieved through official inculcation of the view that racial distinctions are odious and pointless, but it is at least an ideal worth pursuing. We can be certain, on the other hand, that racial peace will not be found through policies that enhance racial consciousness, presume the existence of widespread and near-ineradicable racial animosity, and insist that racial distinctions are of central importance.

DUNCAN KENNEDY

A Cultural Pluralist Case
for Affirmative Action

Duncan Kennedy argues against a position he terms "color-blind meritocratic fundamentalism." Earlier in the essay, he characterized it as emphasizing the idea that knowledge is produced by individual effort whose value
depends on individual talent rather than on the experience out of which it
was formed, that prejudice and discrimination are opposed to individual
merit, and that institutions should strive to produce knowledge in accord
with individual merit and should therefore ignore race, sex, class and other
"irrelevant" features in assessing it.—Eds.

I begin with a color-blind meritocratic fundamentalism, a system of ideas
about race, merit, and the proper organization of academic institutions.
Fundamentalism is a critique of race-conscious decision making in academia. The second part of the essay presents the political and cultural cases
for large-scale affirmative action. The political case is based on the idea
that the intelligentsias of subordinated cultural communities should have
access to the resources that are necessary for groups to exercise effective
political power. The cultural case is based on the idea that a large increase
in the number of minority legal scholars would improve the quality and
increase the social value of legal scholarship, without being unfair to those
displaced.

The third section presents a "cultural pluralist" understanding of American life, one that recognizes that there are dominant and subordinate communities competing in markets and bureaucracies. It proposes that the political and cultural good effect to be anticipated from affirmative action is
the development within legal scholarship of the ideological debates that
minority intelligentsias have pursued in other fields. I conclude that we can
judge scholarship without regard to culture and ideology only if we are
willing to use criteria of judgment that leave out the most important aspects of legal academic accomplishment. . . .

My attitude toward meritocracy derives from my experience as a white
male ruling-class child who got good grades, gained admission to one elite

institution after another, and then landed a job and eventually tenure at Harvard Law School. I belong to a group (only partly generationally defined) that since some point in childhood has felt alienated within this lived experience of working for success according to the criteria of merit that these elite institutions administer.

This alienation had and has two facets. First is a pervasive skepticism about the "standards" according to which we have achieved success. Always subject to the charge that we are simultaneously biting the hand that feeds us and soiling the nest, we just don't believe that it is real "merit" that institutions measure, anywhere in the system. Success is a function of particular knacks, some socially desirable (being "smart") and some not (sucking up)—and of nothing more grandiose. This is not rejection of the idea that some work is better than other work. It is rejection of the institutional mechanisms that currently produce such judgments, of the individuals who manage the institutions, and of the substantive outcomes.

The second facet is a sense of shame and guilt at living in unjust, segregated racial privilege, combined with a sense of loss stemming from the way we have been diminished by isolation from what the subordinated cultural communities of the United States might have contributed to our lives, intellectual, political and personal. I might add that the members of this wholly hypothetical group have not done much (but not nothing, either) about the situation. . . .

The Political and Cultural Arguments for Affirmative Action

The Political Case

I favor large-scale race-based affirmative action, using quotas if they are necessary to produce results. The first basis for this view is that law school teaching positions are a small but significant part of the wealth of the United States. They are also a small but significant part of the political apparatus of the United States, by which I mean that the knowledge law teachers produce is intrinsically political and actually effective in our political system. In short, legal knowledge is ideological. A second basic idea is that we should be a culturally pluralist society that deliberately structures institutions so that communities and social classes share wealth and power. The sharing of wealth and power that occur automatically, so to speak, through the melting pot, the market, and meritocracy are not enough, according to this notion. At a minimum, cultural pluralism means that we should structure the competition of racial and ethnic communities and social classes in markets and bureaucracies, and in the political system, in such a way that no community or class is systematically subordinated.

From these two ideas I draw the conclusion that, completely independently of "merit" as we currently determine it, there should be a substantial representation of all numerically significant minority communities on American law faculties. The analogy is to the right to vote, which we refuse to distribute on the basis of merit, and to the right of free speech, which we refuse to limit to those who deserve to speak or whose speech has merit. The value at stake is community rather than individual empowerment. In the case of affirmative action, as in those of voting and free speech, the goal is political, and *prior to* the achievement of enlightenment or the reward of "merit" as determined by existing institutions.

Race is, at present, a rough but adequate proxy for connection to a subordinated community, one the avoids institutional judgments about the cultural identity of particular candidates. I would use it for this reason only, not because race is itself an index of merit, and in spite of its culturally constructed character and the arbitrariness involved in using it as a predictor of the traits of any particular individual. My argument is thus addressed to only one of the multiple forms of group subordination, though it could be extended to gender, sexual preference, social class, and ethnicity within the "white community."

The political argument includes the idea that minority communities can't compete effectively for wealth and power without intelligentsias that produce the kinds of knowledge, especially political or ideological knowledge, that will help them get what they want. To do this, they need or at least could use some number of legal academic jobs. It also includes the idea that cultural diversity and cultural development are good in themselves, even when they do not lead to increased power for subordinated communities in markets and political systems. . . .

Affirmative Action and the Quality of Work

The standards that law schools apply in deciding whom to hire and whom to promote function to exclude scholars from cultural communities with a history of subordination. Because we exclude them, we get contributions to legal knowledge from only a small number of people with ties to those communities. I believe that if there were a lot more such people, they would make contributions that, taken as a whole, would have a culturally specific character. Judging by my own culturally and ideologically contingent standards, I think they would produce outstanding work not otherwise available. Law schools would do better to invest resources in evoking this contribution than in the fungible white male candidates at the margin who get jobs under the existing selection systems (though quite a few who appear marginal turn out to be terrific).

I don't mean that there would be a minority "line." But there would be a variety of positions, debates, and styles of legal academic writing that everyone would identify as resulting from the rise of minority legal culture. Some of these debates, positions, and styles would be produced by whites, but would be no less a product of change in the racial makeup of the academy. Some of the new work would certainly look wrong or mediocre to me. But some would knock our socks off, in unexpected ways and in ways already presaged by Critical Race Theory. I have no doubt that in terms of the social and intellectual value of scholarly output, legal academia would be better off than it is now. We have lost a lot by preventing minorities from making this contribution. We can't get it unless we give them the resources, in the form of legal academic jobs, to make it.

Second, some legal scholarship is exciting and enriching and stimulating, but not very much. People seem to produce the good stuff through neurotic, often dramatic processes, full of twists and turns and surprises. Most legal scholarship seems to be done pretty much by the numbers, and it's hard to make any sharp quality differential between articles. This stuff is useful. Writing it is hard work. But it doesn't require deep scholarship or reflect high ability. A great many people who are excluded by the "standards" from teaching law could do it as well or as mediocrely as those who do it in fact. I think we would lose little in the way of quality even if massive affirmative action failed to produce the rich harvest of new ideas and approaches that I anticipate.

The possibility of dramatically improving legal scholarship provides a second strong reason for a massive affirmative action program. It is not just that there is no tradeoff between quality and affirmative action. The existing system denies us a benefit. Even in the absence of the political justification, I would favor a new system on this ground. . . .

Affirmative Action and White Entitlements

Are the excluded whites "entitled" to prevent this improvement in scholarship? I would say they are not. Even if all the color-blind criteria of academic promise that we can think of favor a white candidate, he or she lacks something we want in some substantial number of those we will hire. He or she has less promise of doing work with the particular strengths likely to derive from connection to a subordinated cultural community.

The white male law teaching applicant whose résumé and interviews would get him the job were it not for affirmative action has indeed accomplished something, and will not be rewarded for it with the job. But if he understands in advance that the terms of the competition are that he is competing against other white males, for the limited number of slots that a politically just system makes available to people who have had his advantages, then I don't think he has any reason to complain when a job he would have gotten under a different (less just) system goes to a minority applicant. But the excluded white candidates do not have as strong a claim as assumed above.

First, those who win out in the existing system have no claim to be "the best," even according to the color-blind criteria, because the underlying systems of race and class, and the system of testing, exclude so many potential competitors from the very beginning. The competition in which our teaching applicants and tenure candidates win out is restricted, with only a tiny number of notable exceptions, to people born within a certain race-class distance of those positions. At every step, the differences in educational resources and the testing process screen out millions of people who might be able to do the job of law professor better than those who end up getting it. As against those excluded from the competition by race and class and the vagaries of the testing system, those who win out have only a very limited claim of entitlement.

Second, the "standards" that law schools apply in hiring assistant professors and promoting them to tenure are at best very rough proxies for accomplishment as we assess it after the fact. People who get good grades and have prestigious clerkships often turn out to be duds as legal scholars and teachers by the standards of those who appointed them. People with less impressive résumés often turn out to be exciting scholars and teachers. . . .

There is no tradeoff between racial justice and legal academic quality. Indeed, both goals point in the same direction. There is no claim of entitlement against these goals even for candidates who are plausibly the best by every color-blind criterion. The claims of actual candidates likely to be rejected are weakened by the exclusion of competitors, especially competitors from the groups that would gain by affirmative action. Their claims are further weakened by the fact that their accomplishments are mere proxies for legal academic merit, and by the low cultural quality and arbitrary subjectivism of the screening system that would otherwise have delivered them the goods.

Destabilizing Attitudes About Race and Merit

It would be a beneficial side effect of massive, politically and culturally grounded affirmative action if it upset or destabilized the way most law teachers experience the whole issue of merit, and especially its relationship to race. . . . We are generally dependent on the stream of pellets of meritocratic praise and blame, addicted to the continual reward of being told that we are better, and that our law schools are better, according to an objective merit scale, than other teachers and other schools. And as a group we are excessively susceptible to injury by judgments that we fall below others.

One resulting vice is resentment, intense preoccupation with the ways in which one has been unjustly denied the praise or job or honor that one's "merit" "entitles" one to, and with the ways in which others have received more than their due. A second vice is careerism or opportunism, in which an interest in climbing the ladder or maximizing one's academic capital comes to dominate attachment to any set of ideas or any set of autonomous judgments about others. . . .

Affirmative action has already somewhat destabilized these patterns. They might be further jarred by an explicitly political and culturally based increase, because everyone involved in the enterprise would be forced to recognize a degree of relativity to the idea of merit. Dissociating some hiring and promotion decisions from any particular set of credentials undermines everyone's sense that one's true being is one's academic capital.

A political move to large-scale affirmative action would say to minorities, "Here is a part of the resources. Do what you can with it." It would free whites from some of the political obligation that comes of unjust treatment of minorities. It would reduce the nagging sense that our ability to assess merit is consciously or unconsciously corrupted because we now accomplish limited power and wealth sharing through academic decisions on hiring and promotion.

It would reduce the sense that we coerce minorities who want the rewards we have to offer into "being like us." It would also increase integration, the chance for more relations with minorities in our own workplaces. But it would do this without presupposing that our "merit" joins us together in a way that is "more important than" or "independent of" cultural community. In short, it might promote integration while undermining the ideology of colorblindness.

There are obvious dangers. The proposal might increase the stereotyping of minorities as intellectually inferior. It might lead to protracted, destructive racial conflict between majority and minority groups on faculties, and within those groups. It might be impossible to design a scheme of wealth and power sharing that would be easy to administer so as to avoid endless conflict about how to define it in practice. I don't deny these dangers. I just think them worth risking, given the possible benefits. . . .

The Cultural Subordination Thesis

The issue is whether there is enough cultural distinctiveness, and enough subordination and exclusion, so that we must treat representation in academia as a political question, and so that we can expect major intellectual gains from doing so. The argument thus far has been largely hypothetical. Even if one accepted the value of the notions of culture and ideology, one might deny that, in the actual conditions of the United States today, cultural and ideological differences are significant. Or one might merely deny that they are large enough so that we need to structure law schools to take them into account.

The cultural pluralist position to the contrary rests on a whole complex of ideas about American society. I introduce them below in highly schematic form. Together they define a variant of the "nationalist" ideology.

Premises of Cultural Pluralism

Groups exist in a sense that goes beyond individuals' having similar traits. People in groups act together, working out common goals and then engaging in a cooperative process of trying to achieve them. Just as important, they engage in discussion and mutual criticism both about the goals and about what members are doing (or not doing) to achieve them. This is true of small task-oriented groups (family members getting the car packed for a trip) and also of large, diffuse ones, like "the black community" or a law faculty.

An important human reality is the experience of defining oneself as "a member of a group" in this strong sense of sharing goals and a discursive practice. Another important experience is being treated by others as a group member. One's interlocutor interprets what one says and does as derived from a shared project. We all constantly identify groups and their members, assuming that we need to in order to understand other people and predict what they will do.

Communities are more than mere statistical groupings of individuals with particular traits, but less than self-organized groups. Membership presupposes interaction, but the interaction may be sporadic, routine, alienated. A community is a historically specific collection of people with a common past, and a future that will take place on the basis of what has gone before. That basis can be reinterpreted but not obliterated. We are stuck, at any given moment, in the communities we started or ended in, and that is never "just anywhere." Wherever it is, it is both more inert than a self-organized group and less demanding. The crucial idea is that communities are made up of living individuals, but they have an element of transindividual stability and particularity; to be a member is to be *situated,* and we can be situated only in one or two places at a time. Membership is limiting as well as empowering.

Communities have cultures. This means that individuals have traits that are neither genetically determined nor voluntarily chosen, but rather consciously and unconsciously taught through community life. Community life forms customs and habits, capacities to produce linguistic and other performances, and individual understandings of good and bad, true and false, worthy and unworthy. Culture is first of all a product of community. People living in different groups possess different understandings of value as well as exhibiting different capacities and behavior traits (kinship, cooking, dress). But as I am using it, culture is a characteristic of an individual as well. You can break all your ties to a community yet remain a person with that community's cultural identity.

A large part of the population of the United States lives in racial and ethnic communities that have a measure of cultural distinctiveness. The distinctiveness comes in part from the origins in Africa, Asia, Europe, and Latin America of the different groups that live here. But the cultures of particular communities have been dramatically transformed by the experience of immigration, forced transportation, or annexation and by the heterogeneous cultural life of this country. Each group has put its culture of origin together with its peculiar circumstances in the United States to produce a distinct set of behaviors, attitudes, beliefs, and values.

The racial and ethnic communities of the United States are in constant contact with one another. This contact is asymmetrical. There is a dominant cultural community that is less influenced by and less conscious of the subordinated groups than they are influenced by and conscious of it. As a result, it is hard to identify any aspect of the cultures of subordinated groups that might be relevant to academic production and that has not been influenced by contact with the dominant culture.

The boundaries of cultural communities are blurred by the presence of large numbers of people who can trace their family history back into a subordinated community, but who now regard themselves and are regarded by others as situated in a culturally intermediate space, or as assimilated to the dominant culture. There are millions of people for whom the "authenticity" of having always belonged to a relatively homogeneous community with an unselfconsciously shared ethos is simply impossible. Most of those likely to benefit by a program of culturally conscious distribution of academic power and opportunity come from these intermediate, multicultural positions. (The existence of this group may make it more likely that we could actually succeed in implementing cultural diversity.)

Though communities are different in some ways that are best understood through the neutral idea of culture (some groups do things one way, value one set of things; other groups do it in different ways), other differences are not like that. Americans pursue their collective and individual projects in a situation of group domination and group subordination; that is, we can compare "how well" different groups have done with regard to income, housing, health, education, local and national political power, and access to cultural resources. The groups are not so different that they define these things in radically different ways, or that some groups are just not interested in them. With respect to those common measures of equality and inequality, we all recognize that some groups are enormously better off than others.

The experiences of youth in a particular community, or on the border between communities, equip individuals with resources for competition in markets and bureaucracies. Different communities have different access to wealth and power with which to endow their members. Even if the rules of competition were neutral with respect to cultural identity, differences in resources would produce predictable differences in rewards.

In fact, the rules of competition in markets and bureaucracies are structured in ways (both formal and informal) that advantage people from dominant communities regardless of the resources they bring as individuals to the completion. Historically, the white community imposed systematic race-based discrimination, outright job and housing segregation, and rules that excluded racial minorities and women from directly exercising political power. In the current situation, particular cultural groups control or dominate some markets and bureaucracies, and these groups exercise their inevitably enormous range of discretion in ways that favor dominant over subordinated communities. Racial and gender discrimination still direct the flow of opportunities and thereby affect the shares groups achieve.

The notion of domination and subordination is meant to indicate that we cannot understand what happens according to a model in which all people in the society have innate or individual qualities and individual preferences that they bring into a neutrally structured competitive process that correlates their rewards with their social contributions. There are patterns to the characteristics of the individuals society produces—they are identifiably members of the particular communities they grew up in, and their fortunes depend on that fact.

Differences of fortune result from themselves in a circular process. To speak of domination is to say that the group and individual exercise of power given by resources occurs in a competitive struggle in which the better-off communities manage over time to reproduce their advantage by winning enough in each game to reconstitute their stakes. Even the rules of the game are produced by the game, in the sense that power to compete is also power to modify the rules. The dominant communities are those that have the most resources and rewards, those that manage to influence the rules that define the game to their advantage, and those that through time manage to reproduce or improve their top-dog position through competitive struggle.

The game is cooperative as well as competitive. In order to gain rewards, the members of the different communities have to cooperate across ethnic lines in producing goods and services. There are all kinds of influences and concrete alliances formed, and there are areas in which and moments when community identity is actually pretty much submerged in the collective aspects of tasks. Within the communities, there are divisions that are best understood in class terms, and other crosscutting divisions that represent the community's participation in national life (region, gender, religion, and so forth). Both power and resistance to power pervade the structure.

Though there is a self-conscious ruling class at the top, neither the class nor the structure fully controls the outcomes and impacts of the game for the communities whose members play it. All the players are functions of the game, as well as vice versa. There is no "outside position." Communities themselves change internally and through collision with other communities, but the process has as much fate, drift, and chance mutation to it as it does mechanical necessity or self-organized group will. Communities can disperse or assimilate and then reform, and they can die out or be killed.

The American racial and ethnic communities have intelligentsias, linked in overlapping patterns to a national intelligentsia and to each other. By an intelligentsia, I mean a "knowledge class" working in education, the arts, social work, the law, religion, the media, therapy, consulting, and myriad spinoffs like charitable foundations, or for-profit research ventures. Intelligentsia members perform multiple functions beyond their formal job descriptions. In self-organizing groups or individually, some of them work at defining their community's identity (its cultural distinctiveness) or lack thereof, its interests in competition and cooperation with other communities, and its possible strategies.

The national, racial, and ethnic intelligentsias are internally divided along ideological lines. One national ideological axis is radical-liberal-moderate-conservative-rightist. Another is traditional-modern-postmodern. Another is science-social science-humanities-arts. There is also a wide range of ideological debates within particular intelligentsias, for example about their relationship to the national community.

An ideology in the sense in which I am using it is a set of contested ideas that provides a "partisan" interpretation (descriptive and normative) of a field of social conflict. The social conflict could be between capital and labor, farmers and banks, men and women, gay and straight, North and South, native-born and foreign-born, export industries and import industries, or whatever. The concepts that describe and justify the positions of the conflicting groups can be drawn from almost anywhere, from philosophy to economics to religion to biology. Ideologies reflect and at the same time influence social conflict.

Ideologists choose their ideas, in the sense that there is no consensus either in their favor or against them. Many people may think a particular system is objectively right and many others that it is objectively wrong, or it may be seen as posing a question that one can resolve only by a leap of faith. The most basic criticism of ideologists is that they choose their ideas to fit their partisan allegiance, and therefore lack allegiance to "truth." In the conception of ideology I am using, it must always be recognized that people sometimes distort their intellectual work to serve causes or interests they adhere to. At the same time we have to recognize that where there is social conflict, and contested interpretations of that conflict, there is no intellectual space outside ideology. Intelligentsia virtue consists not in maintaining "objectively" or "neutrality," which is impossible once there is ideological division, but in attempting to empower an audience to judge for itself.

It follows that being an ideologist doesn't mean being closed-minded, uninterested in questioning fundamental assumptions, or blind to evidence that contradicts those assumptions. In this sense of the term, one is in the position of the ideologist just by virtue of having, at any given moment, made choices between contested views that influence (and are influenced by) the intellectual work one does. "Moderates" are ideologists because when they call themselves that they implicitly appeal to a controversial critique of "ideologues." (This is the ideology of moderation.) . . .

What Might Be Gained Through Large-Scale Affirmative Action

In light of the above, I would deny the existence of a "black point of view" or a "black voice" in any essentialist (or racialist) sense. But that denial doesn't answer the particular questions that are relevant to the political and cultural arguments for large-scale affirmative action. The first of these is whether minority communities would get, from a much larger minority legal intelligentsia, a scholarly output that would better serve their diverse political, social, and economic interests than what they get from an overwhelmingly white legal intelligentsia. The second is whether the legal academic community as a whole would get a more valuable corpus of scholarship.

I see two likely changes in this regard. A much larger minority intelligentsia should produce more scholarship about the legal issues that have impact on minority communities. The subject matter of scholarship is determined at present by the unregulated "interest" of academics. What we decide to write about just "flows naturally" from our backgrounds, education, and individual peculiarities. It is obvious that some significant proportion of minority intellectuals would be led in this way to write about minority legal issues.

The precedent for this is the creation of modern civil rights law by black lawyers who devised the litigation strategy of the National Association for the Advancement of Colored People. It would be farfetched to argue that the race of these lawyers was irrelevant to their choice of subject matter, or that the black civil rights cause would have evolved in the same way had all the lawyers involved been white.

Along with more scholarship on minority issues, there should be more scholarship on the implications for minorities of *any* issue currently under debate. In other words, Hispanic scholars working on the purest of corporate law questions within the most unquestionably Anglo scholarly paradigm are still, I think, more likely than white scholars to devote, over the long run, some time to thinking about the implications of law in their chosen technical area for the Hispanic communities.

The second anticipated change is crucial to my argument. Along with a quantitative change in focus, it seems likely that an increase in minority scholarship would change the framework of ideological conflict within which issues concerning not only race but also other matters are discussed. I do not mean by this that there is a black (or other minority) ideology. The point is rather that there are historic, already established *debates* within the minority intelligentsias that are obviously relevant to law but have been largely absent from legal scholarship.

In the black intellectual community, debates that have only begun to get played out and transformed in law include those between nationalists and integrationists, between progressives and conservatives, between those who see current racism as a more or less important determinant of current black social conditions, and between black feminists and traditionalists. The nationalist versus integrationist and gender debates are now for the first time beginning to get a hearing as a result of the presence of more minorities in the legal academy. There are similar debates in the other minority communities.

The Cultural Case in the Context of Cultural Subordination

It comes down to a question of value. I have come (belatedly) to the view that American culture and politics are rendered radically more intelligible when viewed through the lens that intellectuals of color have constructed over the years. There is more in this general literature than any one person can assimilate. But there is nowhere near as much legal scholarship as there ought to be. Scholars with ties to subordinated communities are uniquely situated in respect to these ideological resources, and more likely than white scholars to mobilize them to contribute to our understanding of law-in-society.

They are uniquely situated because, in Randall Kennedy's words, "even taking into account class, gender, and other divisions," there does indeed remain "an irreducible link of commonality in the experience of people of color: rich or poor, male or female, learned or ignorant, *all* people of color are to some degree 'outsiders' in a society that is intensely color-conscious and in which the hegemony of whites is overwhelming."[1] The ideological literature of subordinate communities comes out of this experience, in all its variants, and is addressed to it. The flowering in legal scholarship of this literature combined with these experiences is just not something we can plausibly expect from white scholars.

Again, the resources are not Truths to which only people of color have access (though, who knows, such truths may exist), but debates involving all the complexity of incompatible conceptual frameworks and flatly contradictory conclusions. They relate the internal dialectics of subordinated communities, and the dialectic of their interaction with the United States at large. They are open to multiple interpretations, including specifically white interpretations. For this reason, a substantial increase in the number of minority scholars should also improve white scholarship.

An increase in scholarship that takes seriously the issues that have been raised by the black intelligentsia would have relevance to the debates in legal scholarship about gender, sexual orientation, and class. Indeed, I find it hard to think about, say, the separatist or culturalist strand in modern feminism without relating it to the debate about racial identity with which it is intertwined. The historical influence of black liberation thought on all other forms of late twentieth-century American theory about subordinated groups has been enormous. But the influence has been indirect in legal thought, in part because of the small size of minority legal intelligentsias. Wherever groups are in question, whether in corporate or family law, or in the law of federalism or local government law, the historic minority debates and their contemporary extensions should have an impact on sophisticated mainstream thinking.

The issue is not whether there should be a cultural bias in judging actual work. When we have the work before us, there is no reason not to consult it and decide for ourselves, individually, who has produced knowledge of value to us. In judging value to us, the cultural status of the producer is irrelevant, and so is the "merit" of the producer. In and of themselves they neither add nor subtract value, though knowing the author's status and accomplishment can change our understanding of a work and allow us to find value in it that we would otherwise have missed. This knowledge can also mislead us. There is no way to eliminate this risk, since, as I will argue in the next section, we can understand and assess the work only as a text situated in *some* presupposed cultural and ideological context, and assess it only from our own particular cultural and ideological situation.

There is nothing that *precludes* white scholars from making the contributions anticipated from scholars of color. An outsider may learn about a culture and its debates and produce work about or even "within" them that is "better" than anything an insider has produced. There are advantages as well as disadvantages to outsider status, and everyone in a multicultural society is simultaneously inside and outside. And there is nothing to guarantee that minority scholars will choose to or be able to make those contributions. They may squander their resources or decide to do work that is indistinguishable in subject matter and approach from that of white scholars. But their track record, with and without affirmative action, has been good enough, easily, even as tokens, to sustain a prediction of excellence to come.

The Political Case in the Context of Cultural Subordination

Through scholarship focusing on their own concerns and through ideological debate played out in the legal arena, minority communities (through their intelligentsias) develop themselves internally, assimilate for their own purposes the resources of the cultural at large, and build power for the competitive struggle with other groups. The power to create this kind of knowledge is political power. Therefore, it should be shared by all groups within the community affected.

This argument has two levels. First, both the choice and the application of academic standards have strikingly contingent cultural and ideological dimensions. Law faculties distribute political resources (jobs) through a process that is political in fact, if not in name. One group (white males of the dominant culture) largely monopolizes this distribution process and, perhaps not so surprisingly, also largely monopolizes the benefits (jobs). This outcome is politically illegitimate. Second, anybody who disagrees with what I have just said, and maintains instead that standards are and should be apolitical, holds a position that is itself ideological. Law faculties shouldn't make the ideological choice between color-blind meritocracy and some form of race-conscious power-sharing without a substantial participation of minorities in the decision.

Cultural and Ideological Dimensions of Academic Standards.   There are different questions we ask when assessing an academic work. There is the question of truth or falsity, understood to be a question susceptible of answers that when argued out will produce a broad consensus. Then there are questions of "originality" and questions of "interest" or "value."

My experience has been that work in law (like, I assume, some work in physics) is sometimes wrong or untrue in a quite strong sense. I am convinced that when the error is pointed out just about everyone will agree that it was an error. I don't think the kinds of cultural differences that can plausibly be asserted to characterize American society have much impact on these judgments. This is *sometimes* true as well of questions of originality, interest, and value.

Judgments of originality are obviously more contested. And judgments about whether the problem addressed was "interesting" or "valuable" seem to be strongly influenced by the politics of academic life. Different people in a field often have very different ideas about which true, original work is interesting. Though the judges have a strong sense that they know what they mean by interest, and that they are not making "merely" subjective judgments, they also concede that the standard is difficult to apply.

More important for our purposes, they will generally concede that interest or value can be judged only by reference to a particular research tradition or scholarly paradigm, usually one among many that might have won dominance in the field. Yet conclusions at the level of what is valuable or interesting are very often dispositive in deciding which of two articles is better.

Once we acknowledge the possible existence of different research traditions, or collective scholarly projects, we have to acknowledge that the white male occupants of faculty positions have more than the power to decide which performances are better. They have also had the power to create the traditions or projects within which they will make these judgments. It seems obvious that these traditions or projects are culturally and ideologically specific products.

The projects themselves, as well as the judgments of originality, interest, and value they ground (not the narrow judgments of truth and falsity) would almost certainly change if people of excluded cultures and excluded ideologies were allocated power and opportunity to create research traditions and scholarly projects of their own, or to participate in those ongoing. If this were done, there would be a gradual reevaluation of existing legal scholarship. Some currently low-ranked work would gain esteem, and some high-ranked work would lose it. There are no metacriteria of merit that determine which among culturally and ideologically specific research traditions or scholarly paradigms is "better" or "truer." Judgments of merit are inevitably culturally and ideologically contingent because they are inevitably paradigm-dependent.

The choice of standards of originality, interest, and value in judging academic work has profound consequences for what a society knows about itself and its values, and for who the members of society *are* in consequence of their existence within the particular known universe that the knowledge-licensers have promoted. Who they are in turn reacts back through their powers and weaknesses onto the knowledge-licensing process that has created its own author.

At a much more mundane level, the choice of standards controls the choice of personnel in the enterprise of knowledge production, which in turn affects the relative power of the cultural communities that compete in civil society. Excluded communities compete in the legislative process, for example, on the basis of social science data assembled in research projects whose funding and direction is under the control of the dominant community. They compete for favorable rulings from courts on the basis of economic theories about the relative importance of distributional equity and efficiency that are unmistakably tied to the white conservative and white moderate research agendas of law and economics scholars.

The fundamentalist has to deal with the claim that choices to allocate scholarly opportunity are grounded in power rather than in merit, and function to reproduce the very distribution of power they reflect. The power is that of white, mainly male academics, mainly of "moderate" ideology, to impose their standards. They hold, and have held for many generations, the positions to which society has allocated authority to distribute this kind of opportunity. And they have distributed it to themselves.

As with the cultural case, there is nothing to guarantee that a larger minority legal intelligentsia would use the resources of law schools in ways that I would find politically constructive. More jobs might just widen the gap between scholars of color and their communities, and the hiring process might select those least likely, for class and ideological reasons, to pursue the project of empowerment. If that happened, those for whom empowerment is the goal would have to think of something else.

Who Gets to Decide Whether or Not to Share Power?   The decision-making process is decentralized, and largely depoliticized, in the sense of not understood as political. The main decision-makers are faculty members of law schools. My (ideological) position is that the depoliticization is bad, the decentralization good. If depoliticization would lead to centralization within the state sector, then these positions conflict. But assume for the moment that they are not in conflict—that faculties so inclined could go a long way toward power-sharing with subordinated cultural communities (and social classes) without losing their autonomy through conflict with other political institutions (such as state legislatures) committed to color-blind fundamentalism. . . .

The question is whether law faculties as presently constituted are the proper people to make these ideological decisions. Our selection processes, combined with our historic selection *practice,* fail to guarantee adequately that the whole community will be represented in these decisions. That is, they are democratically inadequate. Some measure of democracy is required in decision making that will affect the very being of the community.

At this point the argument does a kind of backflip. Suppose that the fundamentalist responds to the claim of inclusion, based on the political nature of knowledge production, that the premise is wrong. Knowledge is true or false, not left or right. The goal is to produce as much of it as possible, without regard to the politics of the producers. This goal is inherently apolitical or suprapolitical.

The second-level argument is that the question whether these decisions are necessarily ideological is itself ideological. Even if you think knowledge production can be, is, and ought to be nonpolitical, you still have to decide whether that view is one you should be authorized to implement institutionally without having to argue and contend with people who disagree.

Color-blind meritocratic fundamentalism is itself an ideology. The very concepts of race, culture, merit, and knowledge are intensely contested both within and between groups. . . . The question whether knowledge production is political is itself political. Is the community's process for resolving the contest—its political process, in short—a good one?

The current procedure is inadequate because it involves neither the normal democratic procedure of majority vote nor any of the more complex procedures that often seem adequate to guarantee representation of all interests. Recognition of the political character of the decisions being made need mean neither merger into the central state apparatuses nor local "home rule" through elections. But it does mean that the licensers have to do *something* to bring about accountability for their choices between and within the competing ideologies. That something should be affirmative action sufficiently extensive that minorities have enough representation on faculties to be players in the decision about whether to adopt race conscious decision making.

Do Race-Based Criteria of Scholarly Judgment "Derogate Individuality"?

. . . [The claim that race-conscious decision making "derogates from individuality"] is typical of fundamentalist thinking as it might apply to a culturally and politically based affirmative action program. . . . I recognize that this is a danger, but I think its degree has to be assessed case by case. In most situations, it is easy to distinguish between racist and antiracist use of racial categories. Facially neutral categories can accomplish almost anything a confirmed racist would want. Whether we do better on balance by using race explicitly in institutional decision making, or by finding other ways to achieve racial objectives, isn't a question to which we will ever find a decisive empirical answer. I advocate pervasive use of race-conscious decision making because we can't deal with the problem of subordination without confronting it directly, we can't fully achieve the value of cultural pluralism without self-consciously designing our institutions with that in mind. . . .

Culture, Ideology, and Individuality

Culture.   The category of culture fits neither the color-blind meritocratic view, emphasizing individual freedom to succeed or fail under universally agreed standards, nor the racialist view that biology has the power to determine people as meritorious or meritless. Its significance for fundamentalism is that membership in a culture looks somewhat like a status attribute of the individual rather than like something "earned" or "achieved." Culture is reproduced through child rearing and through life in a habitually closed discursive system.

It is also true that people can "change cultures" or "assimilate" to a culture other than their own. People are often "bicultural" or even "tricultural." As with class, there seem to be no inherent limits on what a person can achieve in an adopted culture. On the other hand, assimilation is hard work, a talent in itself. At moments of cultural crisis, or as a matter of course, depending on the culture's self-understanding, the assimilated person's "authenticity" may be questioned, and the mere existence of this possibility makes for a distinctive relationship to the community in question.

Introducing the notion of culture blurs the distinction between judging on the basis of "mere" status, assumed to have no connection with capacities or other qualities of individuals, and judging on "achievement of the individual," assumed to be independent of status. Culture is both deeply ingrained (not changeable at will, even if changeable over the long run) and strongly differentiating; my ability to produce artifacts with meaning is therefore tied to my status.

This concept of culture makes the notion of "inert" experience transformed into something of value by the "individual" seem pretty crude. The individual is "made" by a whole body of experiences, shaped into a particular cultural being. When he or she sets out to produce an artifact out of a particular experience, what gets made is a product of all these other experiences that are collective, group, consciously and unconsciously cultural experiences. These collective things influence everything from the way the particular "raw material" is experienced to the way it is translated into whatever artifactual medium the "individual" chooses.

Culture is an attribute of an individual that is "inherited" (though not biological), both in the sense of "coming from the past" and in the sense of being, in any particular case, partially ineradicable through individual will. And it is an attribute that produces a heavy collective influence on all the performances and capacities of the individual. The fundamentalist cannot level against cultural claims the charge of "irrelevance" or "irrationality" that is enough to dismiss claims based on race per se.

At the same time, there is the experience of freedom within culture (indeed, where else could one experience it, since there is no extracultural space), and the experience of individual accomplishment. A given culture may be more or less committed to the "cultural fluidity, intellectual freedom, and individual autonomy" Kennedy's article defends. People self-consciously make their own selection from among the positions or attitudes available within a culture, and they choose positions and attitudes *toward* the very culture that constitutes their being. A person's action can change the culture that defines the possibilities of action. Recognizing culture doesn't *annihilate* the individual. But recognizing it does blur the boundary between self and social context, and problematizes the assertion that a capacity or an artifact can be divided up into one part that is the inert matter and another part that is reflective of "will," "accomplishment," or "achievement."

Ideology. Once you choose an ideology, you have "rejected one path in favor of another," and what you see and do as you travel that path will be different from what you would have seen and done going the other way. Ideology is commitment. It is the decision to work on this line of inquiry rather than that one, to assume away these issues rather than those, in a situation in which you cannot say that there was no other course available. You may be able to say that given your good faith belief in the rightness of your path, you obviously had no choice. But if other people believed equally in good faith that your path was wrong, and theirs right, then your choice was ideological. Once you've made, explicitly or implicitly, choices of this kind, there are kinds of work you don't find yourself doing and kinds of problems you find yourself just ignoring. . . .

One's ideology is more a matter of choice than one's cultural identity, but it poses similar difficulties for the fundamentalist understanding of individual merit. When you choose one among the possible ideological paths, you lose, as you travel along it, access to the data and the perspective you might have had along another possible path. Of course, it is not as though the view from another ideological vantage point is just unimaginable. And it is always possible to go back and start again or to set off through the underbrush. But whenever you stop and decide to write something, you do it from a particular position on the ideological map. You are enlightened but also limited, "situated" in ideological space much as you are situated in a community and in a cultural identity. There is no no-position position.

Further, ideologies are collective projects created over time. Individuals discover them, in the sense of coming upon them, but do not invent them, any more than an individual can invent a culture. Once you discover an ideology, you explore it, grapple with its great figures or its everyday clichés, assimilate to it little by little or undergo conversion. You adapt it to your purposes and perhaps try to change it, even radically, but it has a transindividual continuity. Someone else will reinterpret your reinterpretation.

Finally, the "you" who pursues preideological purposes is never in a purely instrumental relation to the ideology that consciously or unconsciously provides your framework and conceptual vocabulary. The frame remakes you through and through even as "you" "use" "it." ... [T]he "slant" that each person's ideological formation gives his or her work and his or her judgments of other people's work is neither an idiosyncratic individual matter, irrelevant in the same way that hair or eye or skin color is irrelevant, nor a distortion that one could purge if one tried hard enough.

Individuality. Individuality, against this background, is a problematic as well as an indispensable idea. There are many possible interpretations, but two seem to me to emerge tempered rather than consumed by critical fire. Both start from the notion that culture and ideology provide a vocabulary from which "individuals" pick and choose, constrained by their situation in time and space but with plenty available, even in the most apparently "disadvantaged" position, from which to produce their "selves."

In the first interpretation, individuality is something we read into behavior, from the most mundane to the most exalted, behavior that may seem at first glance nothing more than a jumble of familiar elements culled from the stockpiles of culture, ideology, and psychology. Everyone has a race, a sex, a class, a culture, ideological presuppositions, even a more or less immutable neurotic style. But no one is only these things, because each person's production of self at any given moment, in any given law review article, is a particular selection and combination from an inexhaustible universe of possibilities. "Individuality" is an effect produced on, an experience of, "readers," brought about by the juxtaposition of elements in a way that is neither logically compelled nor arbitrary, but recognizably designed to say something to someone.

In this way of looking at it, my individuality is something you have access to only through my behavior, my tone of voice, or my tome on hardy perennials. I exist, even for myself, only embedded in materials—some of my choosing, some not—materials produced by others for purposes other than those I now pursue.

In the second interpretation of individuality we try to get at the producer of these shows, to sneak behind the curtain and confront the Wizard of Oz. But there is an infinite regress. Who is the wizard producing the modest humbug who produced the Wizard? The condition of meeting up with another "individual," in this second view, is accepting that he or she will just appear on your wave length, in moments of intersubjective zap. There is no assurance that he or she will be there, in contact, at the next moment, or that when he or she reappears it will be as "the same person." There is no way to fix the other through understanding (through an image of what he or she is really like, or a theory of his or her personality, or whatever). Both the other and the self are unitary in the moment but multiple over time—intelligible in the moment but contradictory taken all together. The individual, in this view, is what is not embedded, and therefore what is ineffable, unjudgeable, ungraspable with the apparatus of thought.

I subscribe to both views (they do not seem to me incompatible), and so am happy to be called an "individualist." But neither view allows the operation of meritocratic judgment of a person or a work, without regard to cultural and ideological context, that is so important in fundamentalism. . . .

Because you know that I am a white American intellectual writing in the 1990s, there are a million things I can say in this article without saying them, because you will infer them from this cultural context. And there are a million things you will read in that I didn't mean to be there. I see the interdependence, the inseparability, of my individuality and my context as inevitable and also something to be embraced. Likewise my simultaneous limitation and empowerment by the fact of working in a context. My individuality is not "derogated" when I am judged and when I communicate in a context, though there is bitter with the sweet. The same is true of ideology.

Rational Meritocratic Judgment Cannot Be Culturally and Ideologically Neutral

The flip side is that there is no evaluation aimed at getting at what I value in my own work that won't be contingent on your cultural identity. What I am trying to achieve in my work is a contribution to a cultural situation in which I am implicated, culturally specific. This is equally true of the people whose judgment I most value. I can't be judged outside of my context, they can't judge me outside of their context. No matter how favorable the judgment, I can't take it as "objective." But I can criticize critiques and reject their condemnation as "distorted." I don't have to claim or to abandon either universality or context-dependence. I can switch back and forth between the two perspectives, though without any "metalevel" assurance that I'm ever getting it right. All of the above applies to my ideological as well as to my cultural context. . . .

The argument may involve racism. I see racism as more than inaccurate stereotyping. It is "neurotic" in the same sense that the fetishizing of merit is. It is insisting on the stereotype's truth because you want or need it to be true, in the absence of evidence, or in the face of evidence that the group or a particular member is completely different from what you expected. The racist, whether white or black, won't let you be other than what he or she wants you to be, and that is something bad. But if you accept that you have a cultural identity, the attack on it can't be dismissed as "just" irrational, in the way it could if all cultural communities were the same, or if the differences between them made no difference.

It might be true that the racist is making a correct negative judgment about something that really is a part of you but that there is little or nothing you can do about. It might be true because cultural communities are different and you have characteristics that are derived from your cultural community. The hatred you encounter is wrong or crazy, as hatred. But there might be, somewhere mixed in with it, a valid negative judgment on your group identity. If you don't think that's so, then even after you have rejected and condemned the crazy hatred dimension, you have to defend the communal aspect of your being on the "merits."

Against this background, it seems legitimate and useful . . . to attempt an explicitly race-conscious assessment of the white liberal constitutional law scholarship. . . .

I don't agree . . . that we can't try to figure out whether, for example, a distaste for the "reparations" argument for affirmative action is characteristic trait of a particular white liberal mode of constitutional law analysis. And I see nothing wrong with trying to connect such a trait to the unconscious motives of white liberal scholars as a culturally and ideologically distinct group, or with condemning it as a "defect." It is not, for me, a question of the legitimacy of a type of analysis, but of the plausibility of a particular interpretation. . . .

In order to achieve [an] ideal meritocratic academy, we [would] have to imagine that both the bitter and the sweet of cultural and ideological differences are eliminated or reduced to such an extent that it no longer seems important to take them into account in structuring hiring and promotion. So long as they exist, there will be an element of cultural and ideological contingency to judgments of merit, or an element of arbitrariness in substituting "objective" but nonsubstantive criteria. I see the differences and the process of self-consciously negotiating to take the element of contingency into account as valuable in themselves. So the fundamentalist utopia seems to me impoverished. We could have color-blind meritocracy only in a society less desirable than ours would be, if we could preserve class, cultural, community, and ideological differences but consciously mitigate their bad effects.

Conclusion

If there is a conceptual theme to this essay, it is that of "positionality," or "situatedness." The individual in his or her culture, the individual as a practitioner of an ideology, the individual in relation to his or her own neurotic structures is always somewhere, has always just been somewhere else, and is empowered and limited by being in that spot on the way from some other spot. Communities are like that too, though in a complicated way. One of the things that define a community's position—its situation, and the specific possibilities that go with it—is its history of collective accomplishment. Another is its history of crimes against humanity. It seems unlikely that there are communities without such histories.

The crime of slavery is deep in the past of white America. But ever since slavery, in each succeeding decade after the Emancipation Proclamation, we have added new crimes until it sometimes seems that the weight of commission and omission lies so heavily on nonwhite America that there just isn't anything that anyone can do about it. All anyone can hope is to be out of the way of the whirlwind, the big one and all the little ones played out in day-to-day life.

The bad history also creates opportunities that other communities don't have, or have in different ways. It would be quite something to build a multicultural society on the basis of what has happened here, where we have neither a consensual foundation in history nor a myth of human benevolence to make it all seem natural. An American multicultural society will arise out of guilt, anger, mistrust, cynicism, bitter conflict, and a great deal of confusion and contradiction, if it arises at all, and would be, to my mind, the more wonderful for it.

The specific proposal put forth above, for a kind of cultural proportional representation in the exercise of ideological power through legal academia, would be a very small step in that direction. As is true of any very specific proposal that can be implemented right now by small numbers of people holding local power, it is a drop in the bucket. But the minute we imagine it as a government policy applied in a consistent way across the whole range of situations to which it is arguably applicable, it loses most of its appeal. First, none of us local powerholders could do much to bring it about, and, second, taking the proposal seriously as state policy might lead to all kinds of disastrous unintended side-effects.

This has been a proposal for drops in the bucket, not for the reorganization of state power. If it made a trivial contribution at vast social cost, we could abandon it as we adopted it, faculty by faculty, decision by decision. If it worked, the "kerplunk" of drops falling in nearly empty buckets might cause others to prick up their ears. And in any case legal academics can, and so should, exercise their power to govern themselves in accord with the ideals of democracy and intellectual integrity—ideals that white supremacy compromises all around us.

NOTES

1. Randall Kennedy, "Racial Critiques of Legal Academia," 102 *Harvard Law Review*, 1745 (1989), p. 1784. Kennedy says that there "might" be a link of commonality among people of color.

SHELBY STEELE

The Recoloring of Campus Life: Student Racism, Academic Pluralism, and the End of a Dream

Today's undergraduates were born after the passage of the 1964 Civil Rights Act. They grew up in an age when racial equality was for the first time enforceable by law. This too was a time when blacks suddenly appeared on television, as mayors of big cities, as icons of popular culture, as teachers, and in some cases even as neighbors. Today's black and white college students, veterans of "Sesame Street" and often of integrated grammar and high schools, have had more opportunities to know each other than any previous generation in American history. Not enough opportunities perhaps, but enough to make the notion of racial tension on campus something of a mystery, at least to me.

To look at this mystery, I left my own campus with its burden of familiarity and talked with black and white students at California schools where racial incidents had occurred. Stanford, UCLA, and Berkeley. I spoke with black and white students—not with Asians and Hispanics—because, as always, blacks and whites represent the deepest lines of division, and because I hesitate to wander onto the complex territory of other minority groups. A phrase by William H. Gass—"the hidden internality of thing"—describes, with maybe a little too much grandeur, what I hoped to find. But it is what I wanted to find, for this is the kind of problem that makes a black person nervous, which is not to say that it doesn't unnerve whites as well. Once every six months or so someone yells "nigger" at me from a passing car. I don't like to think that these solo artists might soon make up a chorus, or worse, that this chorus might one day soon sing to me from the paths of my own campus.

I have long believed that the trouble between the races is seldom what it appears to be. It was not hard to see after my first talks with students that

176

racial tension on campus is a problem that misrepresents itself. It has the same look, the archetypal pattern, of America's timeless racial conflict—white racism and black protest. And I think part of our concern over it comes from the fact that it has the feel of a relapse, illness gone and come again. But if we are seeing the same symptoms, I don't believe we are dealing with the same illness. For one thing, I think racial tension on campus is more the result of racial equality than inequality.

How to live with racial difference has been America's profound social problem. For the first hundred years or so following emancipation it was controlled by a legally sanctioned inequality that kept the races from each other. No longer is this the case. On campuses today, as throughout society, blacks enjoy equality under the law—a profound social advancement. No student may be kept out of a class or a dormitory or an extracurricular activity because of his or her race. But there is paradox here: on a campus where members of all races are gathered, mixed together in the classroom as well as socially, differences are more exposed than ever. And this is where the trouble starts. For members of each race—young adults coming into their own, often away from home for the first time—bring to this site of freedom, exploration, and (now, today) equality, very deep fears, anxieties, inchoate feelings of racial shame, anger, and guilt. These feelings could lie dormant in the home, in familiar neighborhoods, in simpler days of childhood. But the college campus, with its structures of interaction and adult-level competition—the big exam, the dorm, the mixer—is another matter. I think campus racism is born of the rub between racial difference and a setting, the campus itself, devoted to interaction and equality. On our campuses, such concentrated micro-societies, all that remains unresolved between blacks and whites, all the old wounds and shames that have never been addressed, present themselves for attention—and present our youth with pressures they cannot always handle.

I have mentioned one paradox: racial fears and anxieties among blacks and whites, bubbling up in an era of racial equality under the law, in settings that are among the freest and fairest in society. But there is another, related paradox, stemming from the notion of—and practice of—affirmative action. Under the provisions of the Equal Employment Opportunity Act of 1972, all state governments and institutions (including universities) were forced to initiate plans to increase the proportion of minority and women employees and, in the case of universities, of students too. Affirmative action plans that establish racial quotas were ruled unconstitutional more than ten years ago in *University of California v. Bakke,* but such plans are still thought by some to secretly exist, and lawsuits having to do with alleged quotas are still very much with us. But quotas are only the most controversial aspect of affirmative action; the principle of affirmative action is reflected in various university programs aimed at redressing and overcoming past patterns of discrimination. Of course, to be conscious of past patterns of discriminations—the fact, say, that public schools in the black inner cities are more crowded and employ fewer top-notch teachers than a white suburban public school, and that this is a factor in student performance—is only reasonable. But in doing this we also call attention quite obviously to difference: in the case of blacks and whites, racial difference. What has emerged on campus in recent years—as a result of the new equality and of affirmative action and, in a sense, as a result of progress—is a *politics of difference,* a troubling, volatile politics in which each group justifies itself, its sense of worth and its pursuit of power, through difference alone.

In this context, racial, ethnic, and gender differences become forms of sovereignty, campuses become balkanized, and each group fights with whatever means are available. No doubt there are many factors that have contributed to the rise of racial tension on campus: What has been the role of fraternities, which have returned to campus with their inclusions and exclusions? What role has the heightened notion of college as some first step to personal, financial success played in increasing competition, and thus tension? But mostly, what I sense is that in interactive settings, fighting the fights of "difference," old ghosts are stirred and haunt again. Black and white Americans simply have the power to make each other feel shame and guilt. In most situations, we may be able to deny these feelings, keep them at bay. But these feelings are likely to surface on college campuses, where young people are groping for identity and power, and where difference is made to matter so greatly. In a way, racial tension on campus in the eighties might have been inevitable.

I would like, first, to discuss black students, their anxieties and vulnerabilities. The accusation black Americans have always lived with is that they are inferior—inferior simply because they are black. And this accusation has been too uniform, too ingrained in cultural imagery, too enforced by law, custom, and every form of power not to have left a mark. Black inferiority was a precept accepted by the founders of this nation; it was a principle of social organization that relegated blacks to the sidelines of American life. So when young black students find themselves on white campuses surrounded by those who have historically claimed superiority, they are also surrounded by the myth of their inferiority.

Of course, it is true that many young people come to college with some anxiety about not being good enough. But only blacks come wearing a color that is still, in the minds of some, a sign of inferiority. Poles, Jews, Hispanics, and other groups also endure degrading stereotypes. But two things make the myth of black inferiority a far heavier burden—the broadness of its scope and its incarnation in color. There are not only more stereotypes of blacks than of other groups, but these stereotypes are also more dehumanizing, more focused on the most despised human traits: stupidity, laziness, sexual immorality, dirtiness, and so on. In America's racial and ethnic hierarchy, blacks have clearly been relegated to the lowest level— have been burdened with an ambiguous, animalistic humanity. Moreover, this is made unavoidable for blacks by sheer visibility of black skin, a skin that evokes the myth of inferiority on sight. Today this myth is sadly reinforced for many black students by affirmative action programs, under which blacks may often enter college with lower test scores and high school grade point averages than whites. "They see me as an affirmative action case," one black student told me at UCLA. This reinforces the myth of inferiority by implying that blacks are not good enough to make it into college on their own.

So when a black student enters college, the myth of inferiority compounds the normal anxiousness over whether he or she will be good enough. This anxiety is not only personal but also racial. The families of these students will have pounded into them the fact that blacks are not inferior. And probably more than anything it is this pounding that finally leaves the mark. If I am not interior, why the need to say so?

This myth of inferiority constitutes a very sharp and ongoing anxiety for young blacks, the nature of which is very precise: it is the terror that somehow, through one's actions or by virtue of some "proof" (a poor grade, a flubbed response in class), one's fear of inferiority—inculcated in ways large and small by society—will be confirmed as real. On a university campus where intelligence itself is the ultimate measure, this anxiety is bound to be triggered.

A black student I met at UCLA was disturbed a little when I asked him if he ever felt vulnerable—anxious about "black inferiority"—as a black student. But after a long pause, he finally said, "I think I do." The example he gave was of a large lecture class he'd taken with over three hundred students. Fifty or so black students sat in the back of the lecture hall and "acted out every stereotype in the book." They were loud, ate food, came in late—and generally got lower grades than whites in the class. "I knew I would be seen like them, and I didn't like it. I never sat by them." Seen like what, I asked, though we both knew the answer. "As lazy, ignorant, and stupid," he said sadly.

Had the group at the back been white fraternity brothers, they would not have been seen as dumb whites, of course. And a frat brother who worried about his grades would not worry that he be seen "like them." The terror in this situation for the black student I spoke with was that his own deeply buried anxiety would be given credence, that the myth would be verified, and that he would feel shame and humiliation not because of who he was but simply because he was black. In this lecture hall his race, quite apart from his performance, might subject him to four unendurable feelings—

diminishment, accountability to the preconceptions of whites, a powerlessness to change those preconceptions, and finally, shame. These are the feelings that make up his racial anxiety, and that of all blacks on any campus. On a white campus a black is never far from these feelings, and even his unconscious knowledge that he is subject to them can undermine his self-esteem. There are blacks on any campus who are not up to doing good college-level work. Certain black students may not be happy or motivated or in the appropriate field of study—*just like whites*. (Let us not forget that many white students get poor grades, fail, drop out.) Moreover, many more blacks than whites are not quite prepared for college, may have to catch up, owing to factors beyond their control: poor previous schooling, for example. But the white who has to catch up will not be anxious that his being behind is a matter of his whiteness, of his being racially inferior. The black student may well have such fear.

This, I believe, is one reason why black colleges in America turn out 37 percent of all black college graduates though they enroll only 16 percent of black college students. Without whites around on campus, the myth of inferiority is in abeyance and, along with it, a great reservoir of culturally imposed self-doubt. On black campuses, feelings of inferiority are personal; on campuses with a white majority, a black's problems have a way of becoming a "black" problem.

But this feeling of vulnerability a black may feel, in itself, is not as serious a problem as what he or she does with it. To admit that one is made anxious in integrated situations about the myth of racial inferiority is difficult for young blacks. It seems like admitting that one is racially inferior. And so, most often, the student will deny harboring the feelings. This is where some of the pangs of racial tension begin, because denial always involves distortion.

In order to deny a problem we must tell ourselves that the problem is something different from what it really is. A black student at Berkeley told me that he felt defensive every time he walked into a classroom of white faces. When I asked why, he said, "Because I know they're all racists. They think blacks are stupid." Of course it may be true that some whites feel this way, but the singular focus on white racism allows this student to obscure his own underlying racial anxiety. He can now say that his problem—facing a classroom of white faces, *fearing* that they think he is dumb—is entirely the result of certifiable white racism and has nothing to do with his own anxieties, or even that this particular academic subject may not be his best. Now all the terror of his anxiety, its powerful energy, is devoted to simply *seeing* racism. Whatever evidence of racism he finds—and looking this hard, he will no doubt find some—can be brought in to buttress his distorted view of the problem while his actual deep-seated anxiety goes unseen.

Denial, and the distortion that results, places the problem *outside* the self and in the world. It is not that I have any inferiority anxiety because of my race; it is that I am going to school with people who don't like blacks. This is the shift in thinking that allows black students to reenact the protest pattern of the sixties. *Denied racial anxiety-distortion-reenactment* is the process by which feelings of inferiority are transformed into an exaggerated white menace—which is then protested against with the techniques of the past. Under the sway of this process, black students believe that history is repeating itself, that it's just like the sixties, or fifties. In fact, it is not-yet-healed wounds from the past, rather than the inequality that created the wounds, that is the real problem.

This process generates an unconscious need to exaggerate the level of racism on campus—to make it a matter of the system, not just a handful of students. Racism is the avenue away from the true inner anxiety. How many students demonstrating for black theme dorms—demonstrating in the style of the sixties, when the battle was to win for blacks a place on campus—might be better off spending their time reading and studying? Black students have the highest dropout rate and the lowest grade point average of any group in American universities. This need not be so. And it is not the result of not having black theme dorms.

It was my very good fortune to go to college in 1964, when the question of black "inferiority" was openly talked about among blacks. The summer before I left for college, I heard Martin Luther King speak in Chicago, and he laid it on the line for black students everywhere: "When you are behind in a footrace, the only way to get ahead is to run faster than the man in front of you. So when your white roommate says he's tired and goes to sleep, you stay up and burn the midnight oil." His statement that we were "behind in a footrace" acknowledged that, because of history, of few opportunities, of racism, we were, in a sense, "inferior." But this had to do with what had been done to our parents and their parents, not with inherent inferiority. And because it was acknowledged, it was presented to us as a challenge rather than a mark of shame.

Of the eighteen black students (in a student body of one thousand) who were on campus in my freshman year, all graduated, though a number of us were not from the middle class. At the university where I currently teach, the dropout rate for black students is 72 percent, despite the presence of several academic support programs, a counseling center with black counselors, an Afro-American studies department, black faculty, administrators, and staff, a general education curriculum that emphasizes "cultural pluralism," an Educational Opportunities Program, a mentor program, a black faculty and staff association, and an administration and faculty that often announce the need to do more for black students.

It may be unfair to compare my generation with the current one. Parents do this compulsively and to little end but self-congratulation. But I don't congratulate my generation. I think we were advantaged. We came along at a time when racial integration was held in high esteem. And integration was a very challenging social concept for both blacks and whites. We were remaking ourselves—that's what one did at college—and making history. We had something to prove. This was a profound advantage; it gave us clarity and a challenge. Achievement in the American mainstream was the goal of integration, and the best thing about this challenge was its secondary message—that we *could* achieve.

There is much irony in the fact that black power would come along in the late sixties and change all this. Black power was a movement of uplift and pride, and yet it also delivered the weight of pride—a weight that would burden black students from then on. Black power "nationalized" the black identity, made blackness itself an object of celebration, an allegiance. But if it transformed a mark of shame into a mark of pride, it also, in the name of pride, required the denial of racial anxiety. Without a frank account of one's anxieties, there is no clear direction, no concrete challenge. Black students today do not get as clear a message from their racial identity as my generation got. They are not filled with the same urgency to prove themselves because black pride has said, *You're already proven, already equal, as good as anybody.*

The "black identity" shaped by black power most forcefully contributes to racial tensions on campuses by basing entitlement more on race than on constitutional rights and standards of merit. With integration, black entitlement derived from constitutional principles of fairness. Black power changed this by skewing the formula from rights to color—if you were black, you were entitled. Thus the United Coalition Against Racism (UCAR) at the University of Michigan could "demand" two years ago that all black professors be given immediate tenure, that there be a special pay incentive for black professors, and that money be provided for an all-black student union. In this formula, black becomes the very color of entitlement, an extra right in itself, and a very dangerous grandiosity is promoted in which blackness amounts to specialness.

Race is, by any standard, an unprincipled source of power. And on campuses the use of racial power by one group makes racial, ethnic, or gender difference a currency of power for all groups. When I make my *difference* into power, other groups must seize upon their difference to contain my power and maintain their position relative to me. Very quickly a kind of politics of difference emerges in which racial, ethnic, and gender groups are forced to assert their entitlement and vie for power based on the single quality that makes them different from one another.

On many campuses today academic departments and programs are established on the basis of difference—black studies, women's studies, Asian studies, and so on—despite the fact that there is nothing in these "difference" departments that cannot be studied within traditional academic disciplines. If their rationale is truly past exclusion from the mainstream curriculum, shouldn't the goal now be complete inclusion rather than separateness? I think this logic is overlooked because those groups are too interested in the power their difference can bring, and they insist on separate departments and programs as tribute to that power.

This politics of difference makes everyone on campus a member of a minority group. It also makes racial tension inevitable. To highlight one's difference as a source of advantage is also, indirectly, to inspire the enemies of that difference. When blackness (and femaleness) become power, then white maleness is also sanctioned as power. A white male student I spoke with at Stanford said, "One of my friends said the other day that we should get together and start a white student union and come up with a list of demands."

It is certainly true that white maleness has long been an unfair source of power. But the sin of white male power is precisely its use of race and gender as a source of entitlement. When minorities and women use their race, ethnicity, and gender in the same way, they not only commit the same sin but also, indirectly, sanction the very form of power that oppressed them in the first place. The politics of difference is based on a tit-for-tat sort of logic in which every victory only calls one's enemies to arms.

This elevation of difference undermines the communal impulse by making each group foreign and inaccessible to others. When difference is celebrated rather than remarked, people must think in terms of difference, they must find meaning in difference, and this meaning comes from an endless process of contrasting one's group with other groups. Blacks use whites to define themselves as different, women use men, Hispanics use whites and blacks, and on it goes. And in the process each group mythologizes and mystifies difference, puts it beyond the full comprehension of outsiders. Difference becomes inaccessible preciousness toward which outsiders are expected to be simply and uncomprehendingly reverential. But beware: in this world, even the insulated world of the college campus, preciousness is a balloon asking for a needle. At Smith College graffiti appears: "Niggers, spics, and chinks. Quit complaining or get out."

I think that those who run our colleges and universities are every bit as responsible for the politics of difference as are minority students. To correct the exclusions once caused by race and gender, universities—under the banner of affirmative action—have relied too heavily on race and gender as criteria. So rather than break the link between difference and power, they have reinforced it. On most campuses today, a well-to-do black student with two professional parents is qualified by his race for scholarship monies that are not available to a lower-middle-class white student. A white female with a private school education and every form of cultural advantage comes under the affirmative action umbrella. This kind of inequity is an invitation to backlash.

What universities are quite rightly trying to do is compensate people for past discrimination and the deprivations that followed from it. But race and gender alone offer only the grossest measure of this. And the failure of universities has been their backing away from the challenge of identifying principles of fairness and merit that make finer and more equitable distinctions. The real challenge is not simply to include a certain number of blacks, but to end discrimination against all blacks and to offer special help to those with talent who have also been economically deprived.

With regard to black students, affirmative action has led universities to correlate color with poverty and disadvantage in so absolute a way as to encourage the politics of difference. But why have they gone along with this? My belief is that it is due to the specific form of racial anxiety to which whites are most subject.

Most of the white students I talked with spoke as if under a faint cloud of accusation. There was always a ring of defensiveness in their complaints about blacks. A white student I spoke to at UCLA told me: "Most white students on this campus think the black student leadership here is made up of oversensitive crybabies who spend all their time looking for things to kick up a ruckus about." A white student at Stanford said, "Blacks do nothing but complain and ask for sympathy when everyone really knows that they don't do well because they don't try. If they worked harder, they could do as well as everyone else."

That these students felt accused was most obvious in their compulsion to assure me that they were not racist. Oblique versions of some-of-my-best-friends-are stories came ritualistically before or after critiques of black students. Some said flatly, "I am not a racist, but . . ." Of course, we all deny being racist, but we only do this compulsively, I think, when we are working against an accusation of bias. I think it was the color of my skin itself that accused them.

This was the meta-message that surrounded these conversations like an aura, and it is, I believe, the core of American racial anxiety. My skin not only accused them; it judged them. And this judgment was a sad gift of history that brought them to account whether they deserved such accountability or not. It said that wherever and whenever blacks were concerned, they had reason to feel guilt. And whether it was earned or unearned, I think it was guilt that set off the compulsion in these students to disclaim. I believe it is true that, in America, black people make white people feel guilty.

Guilt is the essence of white anxiety just as inferiority is the essence of black anxiety. And the terror that it carries for whites is the terror of discovering that one has reason to feel guilt where blacks are concerned—not so much because of what blacks might think but because of what guilt can say about oneself. If the darkest fear of blacks is inferiority, the darkest fear of whites is that their better lot in life is at least partially the result of their capacity for evil—their capacity to dehumanize an entire people for their own benefit and then to be indifferent to the devastation their dehumanization has wrought on successive generations of their victims. This is the terror that whites are vulnerable to regarding blacks. And the mere fact of being white is sufficient to feel it, since even whites with hearts clean of racism benefit from being white—benefit at the expense of blacks. This is a conditional guilt having nothing to do with individual intentions or actions. And it makes for a very powerful anxiety because it threatens whites with a view of themselves as inhuman, just as inferiority threatens blacks with a similar view of themselves. At the dark core of both anxieties is a suspicion of incomplete humanity.

So, the white students I met were not just meeting me; they were also meeting the possibility of their own inhumanity. And this, I think, is what explains how some young white college students in the late eighties could so frankly take part in racially insensitive and outright racist acts. They were expected to be cleaner of racism than any previous generation—they were born into the Great Society. But this expectation overlooks the fact that, for them, color is still an accusation and judgment. In black faces there is a discomforting reflection of white collective shame. Blacks remind them that their racial innocence is questionable, that they are the beneficiaries of past and present racism, and the sins of the father may well have been visited on the children.

And yet young whites tell themselves that they had nothing to do with the oppression of black people. They have a stronger belief in their racial innocence than any previous generation of whites and a natural hostility toward anyone who would challenge that innocence. So (with a great deal of individual variation) they can end up in the paradoxical position of being hostile to blacks as a way of defending their own racial innocence.

I think this is what the young white editors of the *Dartmouth Review* were doing when they harassed black music professor William Cole. Weren't they saying, in effect, I am so free of racial guilt that I can afford to attack blacks ruthlessly and still be racially innocent? The ruthlessness of these attacks was a form of denial, a badge of innocence. The more they were charged with racism, the more ugly and confrontational their harassment became (an escalation unexplained even by the serious charges against Professor Cole). Racism became a means of rejecting racial guilt, a way of showing that they were not, ultimately, racists.

The politics of difference sets up a struggle for innocence among all groups. When difference is the currency of power, each group must fight for the innocence that entitles it to power. To gain this innocence, blacks sting whites with guilt, remind them of their racial past, accuse them of new more subtle forms of racism. One way whites retrieve their innocence is to discredit blacks and deny their difficulties, for in this denial is the denial of their own guilt. To blacks this denial looks like racism, a racism that feeds black innocence and encourages them to throw more guilt at whites. And so the cycle continues. The politics of difference leads each group to pick at the vulnerabilities of the other.

Men and women who run universities—whites, mostly—participate in the politics of difference because they handle their guilt differently than do many of their students. They don't deny it, but still they don't want to *feel* it. And to avoid this feeling of guilt they have tended to go along with whatever blacks put on the table rather than work with them to assess their real needs. University administrators have too often been afraid of guilt and have relied on negotiation and capitulation more to appease their own guilt than to help blacks and other minorities. Administrators would never give white students racial theme dorm where they could be "more comfortable with people of their own kind," yet more and more universities are doing this for black students, thus fostering a kind of voluntary segregation. To avoid the anxieties of integrated situations blacks ask for theme dorms; to avoid guilt, white administrators give theme dorms.

When everyone is on the run from their anxieties about race, race relations on campus can be reduced to the negotiation of avoidances. A pattern of demand and concession develops in which both sides use the other to escape themselves. Black studies departments, black deans of student affairs, black counseling programs, Afro houses, black theme dorms, black homecoming dances and graduation ceremonies—black students and white administrators have slowly engineered a machinery of separatism that, in the name of sacred difference, redraws the ugly lines of segregation.

Black students have not sufficiently helped themselves, and universities, despite all their concessions, have not really done much for blacks. If both faced their anxieties, I think they would see the same thing: academic parity with all other groups should be the overriding mission of black students, and it should also be the first goal that universities have for their black students. Blacks can only *know* they are as good as others when they are, in fact, as good—when their grades are higher and their dropout rate lower. Nothing under the sun will substitute for this, and no amount of concessions will bring it about.

Universities can never be free of guilt until they truly help black students, which means leading and challenging them rather than negotiating and capitulating. It means inspiring them to achieve academic parity, nothing less, and helping them to see their own weaknesses as their greatest challenge. It also means dismantling the machinery of separatism, breaking the link between difference and power, and skewing the formula for entitlement away from race and gender and back to constitutional rights.

As for the young white students who have rediscovered swastikas and the word "nigger," I think that they suffer from an exaggerated sense of their own innocence, as if they were incapable of evil and beyond the reach of guilt. But it is also true that the politics of difference creates an environment that threatens their innocence and makes them defensive. White students are not invited to the negotiating table from which they see blacks and others walk away with concessions. The presumption is that they do not deserve to be there because they are white. So they can only be defensive, and the less mature among them will be aggressive. Guerrilla activity will ensue. Of course this is wrong, but it is also a reflection of an environment where difference carries power and where whites have the wrong "difference."

I think universities should emphasize commonality as a higher value than "diversity" and "pluralism"—buzzwords for the politics of difference. Difference that does not rest on a clearly delineated foundation of commonality is not only inaccessible to those who are not part of the ethnic or racial group, but also antagonistic to them. Difference can enrich only the common ground.

Integration has become an abstract term today, having to do with little more than numbers and racial balances. But it once stood for a high and admirable set of values. It made difference second to commonality, and it asked members of all races to face whatever fears they inspired in each other. I doubt the word will have a new vogue, but the values, under whatever name, are worth working for. . . .

PART FIVE

IDENTITY, ASSIMILATION, AND POLITICS

1 or 3

Age, Race, Class, and Sex: Women Redefining Difference

Much of Western European history conditions us to see human differences in simplistic opposition to each other: dominant/subordinate, good/bad, up/down, superior/inferior. In a society where the good is defined in terms of profit rather than in terms of human need, there must always be some group of people who, through systematized oppression, can be made to feel surplus, to occupy the place of the dehumanized inferior. Within this society, that group is made up of Black and Third World people, working-class people, older people, and women.

As a forty-nine-year-old Black lesbian feminist socialist mother of two, including one boy, and a member of an interracial couple, I usually find myself a part of some group defined as other, deviant, inferior, or just plain wrong. Traditionally, in american society, it is the members of oppressed, objectified groups who are expected to stretch out and bridge the gap between the actualities of our lives and the consciousness of our oppressor. For in order to survive, those of us for whom oppression is as american as apple pie have always had to be watchers, to become familiar with the language and manners of the oppressor, even sometimes adopting them for some illusion of protection. Whenever the need for some pretense of communication arises, those who profit from our oppression call upon us to share our knowledge with them. In other words, it is the responsibility of the oppressed to teach the oppressors their mistakes. I am responsible for educating teachers who dismiss my children's culture in school. Black and Third World people are expected to educate white people as to our humanity. Women are expected to educate men. Lesbians and gay men are expected to educate the heterosexual world. The oppressors maintain their position and evade responsibility for their own actions. There is a constant drain of energy which might be better used in redefining ourselves and devising realistic scenarios for altering the present and constructing the future.

191

Institutionalized rejection of difference is an absolute necessity in a profit economy which needs outsiders as surplus people. As members of such an economy, we have *all* been programmed to respond to the human differences between us with fear and loathing and to handle that difference in one of three ways: ignore it, and if that is not possible, copy it if we think it is dominant, or destroy it if we think it is subordinate. But we have no patterns for relating across our human differences as equals. As a result, those differences have been misnamed and misused in the service of separation and confusion.

Certainly there are very real differences between us of race, age, and sex. But it is not those differences between us that are separating us. It is rather our refusal to recognize those differences, and to examine the distortions which result from our misnaming them and their effects upon human behavior and expectation.

Racism, the belief in the inherent superiority of one race over all others and thereby the right to dominance. Sexism, the belief in the inherent superiority of one sex over the other and thereby the right to dominance. Ageism. Heterosexism. Elitism. Classism.

It is a lifetime pursuit for each one of us to extract these distortions from our living at the same time as we recognize, reclaim, and define those differences upon which they are imposed. For we have all been raised in a society where those distortions were endemic within our living. Too often, we pour the energy needed for recognizing and exploring difference into pretending those differences are insurmountable barriers, or that they do not exist at all. This results in a voluntary isolation, or false and treacherous connections. Either way, we do not develop tools for using human difference as a springboard for creative change within our lives. We speak not of human difference, but of human deviance.

Somewhere, on the edge of consciousness, there is what I call a *mythical norm,* which each one of us within our hearts knows "that is not me." In america, this norm is usually defined as white, thin, male, young, heterosexual, christian, and financially secure. It is with this mythical norm that the trappings of power reside within this society. Those of us who stand outside that power often identify one way in which we are different, and we assume that to be the primary cause of all oppression, forgetting other distortions around difference, some of which we ourselves may be practicing. By and large within the women's movement today, white women focus upon their oppression as women and ignore differences of race, sexual preference, class, and age. There is a pretense to a homogeneity of experience covered by the word *sisterhood* that does not in fact exist.

Unacknowledged class differences rob women of each others' energy and creative insight. Recently a women's magazine collective made the decision for one issue to print only prose, saying poetry was a less "rigorous" or "serious" art form. Yet even the form our creativity takes is often a class issue. Of all the art forms, poetry is the most economical. It is the one which is the most secret, which requires the least physical labor, the least material, and the one which can be done between shifts, in the hospital pantry, on the subway, and on scraps of surplus paper. Over the last few years, writing a novel on tight finances, I came to appreciate the enormous differences in the material demands between poetry and prose. As we reclaim our literature, poetry has been the major voice of poor, working class, and Colored women. A room of one's own may be a necessity for writing prose, but so are reams of paper, a typewriter, and plenty of time. The actual requirements to produce the visual arts also help determine, along class lines, whose art is whose. In this day of inflated prices for material, who are our sculptors, our painters, our photographers? When we speak of a broadly based women's culture, we need to be aware of the effect of class and economic differences on the supplies available for producing art.

As we move toward creating a society within which we can each flourish, ageism is another distortion of relationship which interferes without vision. By ignoring the past, we are encouraged to repeat its mistakes. The "generation gap" is an important social tool for any repressive society. If the younger members of a community view the older members as contemptible or suspect or excess, they will never be able to join hands and examine the living memories of the community, nor ask the all important question, "Why?" This gives rise to a historical amnesia that keeps us working to invent the wheel every time we have to go to the store for bread.

We find ourselves having to repeat and relearn the same old lessons over and over that our mothers did because we do not pass on what we have learned, or because we are unable to listen. For instance, how many times has this all been said before? For another, who would have believed that once again our daughters are allowing their bodies to be hampered and purgatoried by girdles and high heels and hobble skirts?

Ignoring the differences of race between women and the implications of those differences presents the most serious threat to the mobilization of women's joint power.

As white women ignore their built-in privilege of whiteness and define *woman* in terms of their own experience alone, then women of Color become "other," the outsider whose experience and tradition is too "alien" to comprehend. An example of this is the signal absence of the experience of women of Color as a resource for women's studies courses. The literature of women of Color is seldom included in women's literature courses and almost never in other literature courses, nor in women's studies as a whole. All too often, the excuse given is that the literatures of women of Color can

only be taught by Colored women, or that they are too difficult to understand, or that classes cannot "get into" them because they come out of
experiences that are "too different." I have heard this argument presented
by white women of otherwise quite clear intelligence, women who seem to
have no trouble at all teaching and reviewing work that comes out of the
vastly different experiences of Shakespeare, Molière, Dostoyefsky, and
Aristophanes. Surely there must be some other explanation.

This is a very complex question, but I believe one of the reasons white
women have such difficulty reading Black women's work is because of
their reluctance to see Black women as women and different from themselves. To examine Black women's literature effectively requires that we be
seen as whole people in our actual complexities—as individuals, as women,
as human—rather than as one of those problematic but familiar stereotypes
provided in this society in place of genuine images of Black women. And I
believe this holds true for the literatures of other women of Color who are
not Black.

The literatures of all women of Color recreate the textures of our lives,
and many white women are heavily invested in ignoring the real differences. For as long as any difference between us means one of us must be
inferior, then the recognition of any difference must be fraught with guilt.
To allow women of Color to step out of stereotypes is too guilt provoking,
for it threatens the complacency of those women who view oppression only
in terms of sex.

Refusing to recognize difference makes it impossible to see the different
problems and pitfalls facing us as women.

Thus, in a patriarchal power system where whiteskin privilege is a major
prop, the entrapments used to neutralize Black women and white women
are not the same. For example, it is easy for Black women to be used by the
power structure against Black men, not because they are men, but because
they are Black. Therefore, for Black women, it is necessary at all times
to separate the needs of the oppressor from our own legitimate conflicts
within our communities. This same problem does not exist for white
women. Black women and men have shared racist oppression and still
share it, although in different ways. Out of that shared oppression we have
developed joint defenses and joint vulnerabilities to each other that are not
duplicated in the white community, with the exception of the relationship
between Jewish women and Jewish men.

On the other hand, white women face the pitfall of being seduced into
joining the oppressor under the pretense of sharing power. This possibility
does not exist in the same way for women of Color. The tokenism that is
sometimes extended to us is not an invitation to join power; our racial
"otherness" is a visible reality that makes that quite clear. For white

women there is a wider range of pretended choices and rewards for identifying with patriarchal power and its tools.

Today, with the defeat of ERA, the tightening economy, and increased conservatism, it is easier once again for white women to believe the dangerous fantasy that if you are good enough, pretty enough, sweet enough, quiet enough, teach the children to behave, hate the right people, and marry the right men, then you will be allowed to co-exist with patriarchy in relative peace, at least until a man needs your job or the neighborhood rapist happens along. And true, unless one lives and loves in the trenches it is difficult to remember that the war against dehumanization is ceaseless.

But Black women and our children know the fabric of our lives is stitched with violence and with hatred, that there is no rest. We do not deal with it only on the picket lines, or in dark midnight alleys, or in the places where we dare to verbalize our resistance. For us, increasingly, violence weaves through the daily tissues of our living—in the supermarket, in the classroom, in the elevator, in the clinic and the schoolyard, from the plumber, the baker, the saleswoman, the bus driver, the bank teller, the waitress who does not serve us.

Some problems we share as women, some we do not. You fear your children will grow up to join the patriarchy and testify against you, we fear our children will be dragged from a car and shot down in the street, and you will turn your backs upon the reasons they are dying.

The threat of difference has been no less blinding to people of Color. Those of us who are Black must see that the reality of our lives and our struggle does not make us immune to the errors of ignoring and misnaming difference. Within Black communities where racism is a living reality, differences among us often seem dangerous and suspect. The need for unity is often misnamed as a need for homogeneity, and a Black feminist vision mistaken for betrayal of our common interests as a people. Because of the continuous battle against racial erasure that Black women and Black men share, some Black women still refuse to recognize that we are also oppressed as women, and that sexual hostility against Black women is practiced not only by the white racist society, but implemented within our Black communities as well. It is a disease striking the heart of Black nationhood, and silence will not make it disappear. Exacerbated by racism and the pressures of powerlessness, violence against Black women and children often becomes a standard within our communities, one by which manliness can be measured. But these women-hating acts are rarely discussed as crimes against Black women.

As a group, women of Color are the lowest paid wage earners in america. We are the primary targets of abortion and sterilization abuse, here and abroad. In certain parts of Africa, small girls are still being sewed shut between their legs to keep them docile and for men's pleasure. This is known as female circumcision, and it is not a cultural affair as the late Jomo Kenyatta insisted, it is a crime against Black women.

Black women's literature is full of the pain of frequent assault, not only by a racist patriarchy, but also by Black men. Yet the necessity for and history of shared battle have made us, Black women, particularly vulnerable to the false accusation that anti-sexist is anti-Black. Meanwhile, womanhating as a recourse of the powerless is sapping strength from Black communities, and our very lives. Rape is on the increase, reported and unreported, and rape is not aggressive sexuality, it is sexualized aggression. As Kalamu ya Salaam, a Black male writer points out, "As long as male domination exists, rape will exist. Only women revolting and men made conscious of their responsibility to fight sexism can collectively stop rape."[1]

Differences between ourselves as Black women are also being misnamed and used to separate us from one another. As a Black lesbian feminist comfortable with the many different ingredients of my identity, and a woman committed to racial and sexual freedom from oppression, I find I am constantly being encouraged to pluck out some one aspect of myself and present this as the meaningful whole, eclipsing or denying the other parts of self. But this is a destructive and fragmenting way to live. My fullest concentration of energy is available to me only when I integrate all the parts of who I am, openly, allowing power from particular sources of my living to flow back and forth freely through all my different selves, without the restrictions of externally imposed definition. Only then can I bring myself and my energies as a whole to the service of those struggles which I embrace as part of my living.

A fear of lesbians, or of being accused of being a lesbian, has led many Black women into testifying against themselves. It has led some of us into destructive alliances, and others into despair and isolation. In the white women's communities, heterosexism is sometimes a result of identifying with the white patriarchy, a rejection of that interdependence between women-identified women which allows the self to be, rather than to be used in the service of men. Sometimes it reflects a die-hard belief in the protective coloration of heterosexual relationships, sometimes a self-hate which all women have to fight against, taught us from birth.

Although elements of these attitudes exist for all women, there are particular resonances of heterosexism and homophobia among Black women. Despite the fact that woman-bonding has a long and honorable history in the African and African-american communities, and despite the knowledge and accomplishments of many strong and creative women-identified Black women in the political, social and cultural fields, heterosexual Black women often tend to ignore or discount the existence and work of Black lesbians. Part of this attitude has come from an understandable terror of

Black male attack within the close confines of Black society, where the punishment for any female self-assertion is still to be accused of being a lesbian and therefore unworthy of the attention or support of the scarce Black male. But part of this need to misname and ignore Black lesbians comes from a very real fear that openly women-identified Black women who are no longer dependent upon men for their self-definition may well reorder our whole concept of social relationships.

Black women who once insisted that lesbianism was a white woman's problem now insist that Black lesbians are a threat to Black nationhood, are consorting with the enemy, are basically un-Black. These accusations, coming from the very women to whom we look for deep and real understanding, have served to keep many Black lesbians in hiding, caught between the racism of white women and the homophobia of their sisters. Often, their work has been ignored, trivialized, or misnamed, as with the work of Angelina Grimke, Alice Dunbar-Nelson, Lorraine Hansberry. Yet women-bonded women have always been some part of the power of Black communities, from our unmarried aunts to the amazons of Dahomey.

And it is certainly not Black lesbians who are assaulting women and raping children and grandmothers on the streets of our communities.

Across this country, as in Boston during the spring of 1979 following the unsolved murders of twelve Black women, Black lesbians are spearheading movements against violence against Black women.

What are the particular details within each of our lives that can be scrutinized and altered to help bring about change? How do we redefine difference for all women? It is not our differences which separate women, but our reluctance to recognize those differences and to deal effectively with the distortions which have resulted from the ignoring and misnaming of those differences.

As a tool of social control, women have been encouraged to recognize only one area of human difference as legitimate, those differences which exist between women and men. And we have learned to deal across those differences with the urgency of all oppressed subordinates. All of us have had to learn to live or work or coexist with men, from our fathers on. We have recognized and negotiated these differences, even when this recognition only continued the old dominant/subordinate mode of human relationship, where the oppressed must recognize the masters' difference in order to survive.

But our future survival is predicated upon our ability to relate within equality. As women, we must root our internalized patterns of oppression within ourselves if we are to move beyond the most superficial aspects of social change. Now we must recognize differences among women who are our equals, neither inferior nor superior, and devise ways to use each others' difference to enrich our visions and our joint struggles.

The future of our earth may depend upon the ability of all women to identify and develop new definitions of power and new patterns of relating across difference. The old definitions have not served us, nor the earth that supports us. The old patterns, no matter how cleverly rearranged to imitate progress, still condemn us to cosmetically altered repetitions of the same old exchanges, the same old guilt, hatred, recrimination, lamentation, and suspicion.

For we have, built into all of us, old blueprints of expectation and response, old structures of oppression, and these must be altered at the same time as we alter the living conditions which are a result of those structures. For the master's tools will never dismantle the master's house.

As Paulo Freire shows so well in *The Pedagogy of the Oppressed*,[2] the true focus of revolutionary change is never merely the oppressive situations which we seek to escape, but that piece of the oppressor which is planted deep within each of us, and which knows only the oppressors' tactics, the oppressors' relationships.

Change means growth, and growth can be painful. But we sharpen self-definition by exposing the self in work and struggle together with those whom we define as different from ourselves, although sharing the same goals. For Black and white, old and young, lesbian and heterosexual women alike, this can mean new paths to our survival.

> We have chosen each other
> and the edge of each others battles
> the war is the same
> if we lose
> someday women's blood will congeal
> upon a dead planet
> if we win
> there is no telling
> we seek beyond history
> for a new and more possible meaning.[3]

NOTES

1. From "Rape: A Radical Analysis, An African-American Perspective" by Kalamu ya Salaam in *Black Books Bulletin,* vol. 6, no. 4 (1980).

2. Seabury Press, New York, 1970.

3. From "Outlines," unpublished poem.

Social Movements and the Politics of Difference

In this chapter I criticize an ideal of justice that defines liberation as the transcendence of group difference, which I refer to as an ideal of assimilation. This ideal usually promotes equal treatment as a primary principle of justice. Recent social movements of oppressed groups challenge this ideal. Many in these movements argue that a positive self-definition of group difference is in fact more liberatory.

I endorse this politics of difference, and argue that at stake is the meaning of social difference itself. Traditional politics that excludes or devalues some persons on account of their group attributes assumes an essentialist meaning of difference; it defines groups as having different natures. An egalitarian politics of difference, on the other hand, defines difference more fluidly and relationally as the product of social processes.

An emancipatory politics that affirms group difference involves a reconception of the meaning of equality. The assimilationist ideal assumes that equal social status for all persons requires treating everyone according to the same principles, rules, and standards. A politics of difference argues, on the other hand, that equality as the participation and inclusion of all groups sometimes requires different treatment for oppressed or disadvantaged groups. To promote social justice, I argue, social policy should sometimes accord special treatment to groups. . . .

Competing Paradigms of Liberation

In "On Racism and Sexism," Richard Wasserstrom (1980) develops a classic statement of the ideal of liberation from group-based oppression as involving the elimination of group-based difference itself. A truly nonracist, nonsexist society, he suggests, would be one in which the race or sex of an individual would be the functional equivalent of eye color in our society today. While physiological differences in skin color or genitals would remain, they would have no significance for a person's sense of identity or how others regard him or her. No political rights or obligations would be connected to race or sex, and no important institutional benefits would be associated with either. People would see no reason to consider race or gender in policy or everyday interactions. In such a society, social group differences would have ceased to exist.

Wasserstrom contrasts this ideal of assimilation with an ideal of diversity much like the one I will argue for, which he agrees is compelling. He offers three primary reasons, however, for choosing the assimilationist ideal of liberation over the ideal of diversity. First, the assimilationist ideal exposes the arbitrariness of group-based social distinctions which are thought natural and necessary. By imagining a society in which race and sex have no social significance, one sees more clearly how pervasively these group categories unnecessarily limit possibilities for some in existing society. Second, the assimilationist ideal presents a clear and unambiguous standard of equality and justice. According to such a standard, any group-related differentiation or discrimination is suspect. Whenever laws or rules, the division of labor, or other social practices allocate benefits differently according to group membership, this is a sign of injustice. The principle of justice is simple: treat everyone according to the same principles, rules, and standards. Third, the assimilationist ideal maximizes choice. In a society where differences make no social difference people can develop themselves as individuals, unconstrained by group norms and expectations.

There is no question that the ideal of liberation as the elimination of group difference has been enormously important in the history of emancipatory politics. The ideal of universal humanity that denies natural differences has been a crucial historical development in the struggle against exclusion and status differentiation. It has made possible the assertion of the equal moral worth of all persons, and thus the right of all to participate and be included in all institutions and positions of power and privilege. The assimilationist ideal retains significant rhetorical power in the face of continued beliefs in the essentially different and inferior natures of women, Blacks, and other groups.

The power of this assimilationist ideal has inspired the struggle of oppressed groups and the supporters against the exclusion and denigration of these groups, and continues to inspire many. Periodically in American history, however, movements of the oppressed have questioned and rejected this "path to belonging." . . . Instead they have seen self-organization and the assertion of a positive group cultural identity as a better strategy for achieving power and participation in dominant institutions. Recent decades have witnessed a resurgence of this "politics of difference" not only among racial and ethnic groups, but also among women, gay men and lesbians, old people, and the disabled. . . .

None of the social movements asserting positive group specificity is in fact a unity. All have group differences within them. The Black movement, for example, includes middle-class Blacks and working-class Blacks, gays and straight people, men and women, and so it is with any other group. The implications of group differences within a social group have been most systematically discussed in the women's movement. Feminist conferences and publications have generated particularly fruitful, though often emotionally wrenching, discussions of the oppression of racial and ethnic blindness and importance of attending to group differences among women. . . . From such discussions emerged principled efforts to provide autonomously organized forums for Black women, Latinas, Jewish women, lesbians, differently abled women, old women, and any other women who see reason for claiming that they have as a group a distinctive voice that might be silenced in a general feminist discourse. Those discussions, along with the practices feminists instituted structure discussion and interaction among differently identifying groups of women, offer some beginning models for the development of a heterogeneous public. Each of the other social movements has also generated discussion of group differences that cut across their identities, leading to other possibilities of coalition and alliance.

Emancipation Through the Politics of Difference

Implicit in emancipatory movements asserting a positive sense of group difference is a different ideal of liberation, which might be called democratic cultural pluralism (cf. Laclau and Mouffe, 1985, pp. 166–71; Cunningham, 1987, pp. 186–99; Nickel, 1987). In this vision the good society does not eliminate or transcend group difference. Rather, there is equality among socially and culturally differentiated groups, who mutually respect one another and affirm one another in their differences. What are the reasons for rejecting the assimilationist ideal and promoting a politics of difference?

. . . Some deny the reality of social groups. For them, group difference is an invidious fiction produced and perpetuated in order to preserve the privilege of the few. Others, such as Wasserstrom, may agree that social groups do now exist and have real social consequences for the way people identify themselves and one another, but assert that such social group differences are undesirable. The assimilationist ideal involves denying either the reality or the desirability of social groups.

Those promoting a politics of difference doubt that a society without group differences is either possible or desirable. Contrary to the assumption of modernization theory, increased urbanization and the extension of equal formal rights to all groups has not led to a decline in particularist affiliations. If anything, the urban concentration and interactions among groups that modernizing social processes introduce tend to reinforce group solidarity and differentiation. Attachment to specific traditions, practices, languages, and other culturally specific forms is a crucial aspect of social existence. People do not usually give up their social group identifications, even when they are oppressed.

Whether eliminating social group difference is possible or desirable in the long run, however, is an academic issue. Today and for the foreseeable future societies are certainly structured by groups, and some are privileged while others are oppressed. New social movements of group specificity do not deny the official story's claim that the ideal of liberation as eliminating difference and treating everyone the same has brought significant improvement in the status of excluded groups. Its main quarrel is with the story's conclusion, namely, that since we have achieved formal equality, only vestiges and holdovers of differential privilege remain, which will die out with the continued persistent assertion of an ideal of social relations that make differences irrelevant to a person's life prospects. The achievement of formal equality does not eliminate social differences, and rhetorical commitment to the sameness of persons makes it impossible even to name how those differences presently structure privilege and oppression.

Though in many respects the law is now blind to group differences, some groups continue to be marked as deviant, as the Other. In everyday interactions, images, and decisions, assumptions about women, Blacks, Hispanics, gay men and lesbians, old people, and other marked groups continue to justify exclusion, avoidance, paternalism, and authoritarian treatment. Continued racist, sexist, homophobic, ageist, and ableist institutions and behavior create particular circumstances for these groups, usually disadvantaging them in their opportunity to develop their capacities. Finally, in part because they have been segregated from one another, and in part because they have particular histories and traditions, there are cultural differences among social groups—differences in language, style of living, body comportment and gestures, values, and perspectives on society.

Today in American society, as in many other societies, there is widespread agreement that no person should be excluded from political and economic activities because of ascribed characteristics. Group differences nevertheless continue to exist, and certain groups continue to be privileged. Under these circumstances, insisting that equality and liberation entail ignoring difference has oppressive consequences in three respects.

First, blindness to difference disadvantages groups whose experience, culture, and socialized capacities differ from those of privileged groups. The strategy of assimilation aims to bring formerly excluded groups into the mainstream. So assimilation always implies coming into the game after it is already begun, after the rules and standards have already been set, and having to prove oneself according to those rules and standards. In the assimilationist strategy, the privileged groups implicitly define the standards according to which all will be measured. Because their privilege involves not recognizing these standards as culturally and experientially specific, the ideal of a common humanity in which all can participate without regard to race, gender, religion, or sexuality poses as neutral and universal. The real differences between oppressed groups and the dominant norm, however, tend to put them at a disadvantage in measuring up to these standards, and for that reason assimilationist policies perpetuate their disadvantage....

Second, the ideal of a universal humanity without social group differences allows privileged groups to ignore their own group specificity. Blindness to difference perpetuates cultural imperialism by allowing norms expressing the point of view and experience of privileged groups to appear neutral and universal. The assimilationist ideal presumes that there is a humanity in general, an unsituated group-neutral human capacity for self-making that left to itself would make individuality flower, thus guaranteeing that each individual will be different.... Because there is no such unsituated group-neutral point of view, the situation and experience of dominant groups tend to define the norms of such a humanity in general. Against such a supposedly neutral humanist ideal, only the oppressed groups come to be marked with particularity; they, and not the privileged groups, are marked, objectified as the Others.

Thus, third, this denigration of groups that deviate from an allegedly neutral standard often produces an internalized devaluation by members of those groups themselves. When there is an ideal of general human standards according to which everyone should be evaluated equally, then Puerto Ricans or Chinese Americans are ashamed of their accents or their parents, Black children despise the female-dominated kith and kin networks of their neighborhoods, and feminists seek to root out their tendency to cry, or to feel compassion for a frustrated stranger. The aspiration to assimilate helps produce the self-loathing and double consciousness characteristic of oppression. The goal of assimilation holds up to people a demand that they "fit," be like the mainstream, in behavior, values, and goals. At the same time, as long as group differences exist, group members will be marked as different—as Black, Jewish, gay—and thus as unable simply to fit. When participation is taken to imply assimilation the oppressed person is caught in an irresolvable dilemma: to participate means to accept and adopt an identity one is not, and to try to participate means to be reminded by oneself and others of the identity one is.

A more subtle analysis of the assimilationist ideal might distinguish between a conformist and a transformational ideal of assimilation. In the conformist ideal, status quo institutions and norms are assumed as given, and disadvantaged groups who differ from those norms are expected to conform to them. A transformational ideal of assimilation, on the other hand, recognizes that institutions as given express the interests and perspective of the dominant groups. Achieving assimilation therefore requires altering many institutions and practices in accordance with neutral rules that truly do not disadvantage or stigmatize any person, so that group membership really is irrelevant to how persons are treated. Wasserstrom's ideal fits a transformational assimilation, as does the group-neutral ideal advocated by some feminists (Taub and Williams, 1987). Unlike the conformist assimilationist, the transformational assimilationist may allow that group-specific policies, such as affirmative action, are necessary and appropriate means for transforming institutions to fit the assimilationist ideal. Whether conformist or transformational, however, the assimilationist ideal still denies that group difference can be positive and desirable; thus any form of the ideal of assimilation constructs group difference as a liability or disadvantage.

Under these circumstances, a politics that asserts the positivity of group difference is liberating and empowering. In the act of reclaiming the identity the dominant culture has taught them to despise and affirming it as an identity to celebrate, the oppressed remove double consciousness. I am just what they say I am—a Jewboy, a colored girl, a fag, a dyke, or a hag—and proud of it. No longer does one have the impossible project of trying to become something one is not under circumstances where the very trying reminds one of who one is. This politics asserts that oppressed groups have distinct cultures, experiences, and perspectives on social life with humanly positive meaning, some of which may even be superior to the culture and perspectives of mainstream society. The rejection and devaluation of one's culture and perspective should not be a condition of full participation in social life.

Asserting the value and specificity of the culture and attributes of oppressed groups, moreover, results in a relativizing of the dominant culture. When feminists assert the validity of feminine sensitivity and the positive value of nurturing behavior, when gays describe the prejudice of heterosexuals as homophobic and their own sexuality as positive and self-developing, when Blacks affirm a distinct Afro-American tradition, then the dominant culture is forced to discover itself for the first time as specific: as Anglo, European, Christian, masculine, straight. In a political struggle where oppressed groups insist on the positive value of their specific culture and experience, it becomes increasingly difficult for dominant groups to parade their norms as neutral and universal, and to construct the values and behavior of the oppressed as deviant, perverted, or inferior. By puncturing the universalist claim to unity that expels some groups and turns them into the Other, the assertion of positive group specificity introduces the possibility of understanding the relation between groups as merely difference, instead of exclusion, opposition, or dominance.

The politics of difference also promotes a notion of group solidarity against the individualism of liberal humanism. Liberal humanism treats each person as an individual, ignoring differences of race, sex, religion, and ethnicity. Each person should be evaluated only according to her or his individual efforts and achievements. With the institutionalization of formal equality some members of formerly excluded groups have indeed succeeded, by mainstream standards. Structural patterns of group privilege and oppression nevertheless remain. When political leaders of oppressed groups reject assimilation they are often affirming group solidarity. Where the dominant culture refuses to see anything but the achievement of autonomous individuals, the oppressed assert that we shall not separate from the people with whom we identify in order to "make it" in a white Anglo male world. The politics of difference insists on liberation of the whole group of Blacks, women, American Indians, and that this can be accomplished only through basic institutional changes. These changes must include group representation in policymaking and an elimination of the hierarchy of rewards that forces everyone to compete for scarce positions at the top.

Thus the assertion of a positive sense of group difference provides a standpoint from which to criticize prevailing institutions and norms. Black Americans find in their traditional communities, which refer to their members as "brother" and "sister," a sense of solidarity absent from the calculating individualism of white professional capitalist society. Feminists find in the traditional female values of nurturing a challenge to a militarist world-view, and lesbians find in their relationships a confrontation with the assumption of complementary gender roles in sexual relationships. From their experience of a culture tied to the land American Indians formulate a critique of the instrumental rationality of European culture that results in pollution and ecological destruction. Having revealed the specificity of the dominant norms which claim universality and neutrality, social movements of the oppressed are in a position to inquire how the dominant institutions must be changed so that they will no longer reproduce the patterns of privilege and oppression.

From the assertion of positive difference the self-organization of oppressed groups follows. Both liberal humanist and leftist political organizations and movements have found it difficult to accept this principle of group autonomy. In a humanist emancipatory politics, if a group is subject to injustice, then all those interested in a just society should unite to combat the powers that perpetuate that injustice. If many groups are subject to injustice, moreover, then they should unite to work for a just society. The politics of difference is certainly not against coalition, nor does it hold that, for example, whites should not work against racial injustice or men against sexist injustice. This politics of group assertion, however, takes as a basic principle that members of oppressed groups need separate organizations that exclude others, especially those from more privileged groups. Separate organization is probably necessary in order for these groups to discover and reinforce the positivity of their specific experience, to collapse and eliminate double consciousness. In discussions within autonomous organizations, group members can determine their specific needs and interests. Separation and self-organization risk creating pressures toward homogenization of the groups themselves, creating new privileges and exclusions. . . . But contemporary emancipatory social movements have found group autonomy an important vehicle for empowerment and the development of a group-specific voice and perspective.

Integration into the full life of the society should not have to imply assimilation to dominant norms and abandonment of group affiliation and culture. If the only alternative to the oppressive exclusion of some groups defined as Other by dominant ideologies is the assertion that they are the same as everybody else, then they will continue to be excluded because they are not the same.

Some might object to the way I have drawn the distinction between an assimilationist ideal of liberation and a radical democratic pluralism. They might claim that I have not painted the ideal of a society that transcends group differences fairly, representing it as homogeneous and conformist. The free society envisaged by liberalism, they might say, is certainly pluralistic. In it persons can affiliate with whomever they choose; liberty encourages a proliferation of life styles, activities, and associations. While I have no quarrel with social diversity in this sense, this vision of liberal pluralism does not touch on the primary issues that give rise to the politics of difference. The vision of liberation as the transcendence of group difference seeks to abolish the public and political significance of group difference, while retaining and promoting both individual and group diversity in private, or nonpolitical, social contexts. . . . This way of distinguishing public and private spheres, where the public represents universal citizenship and the private individual differences, tends to result in group exclusion from the public. Radical democratic pluralism acknowledges and affirms the public and political significance of social group differences as a means of ensuring the participation and inclusion of everyone in social and political institutions.

Reclaiming the Meaning of Difference

Many people inside and outside the movements I have discussed find the rejection of the liberal humanist ideal and the assertion of a positive sense of group difference both confusing and controversial. They fear that any admission by oppressed groups that they are different from the dominant groups risks justifying anew the subordination, special marking, and exclusion of those groups. Since calls for a return of women to the kitchen, Blacks to servant roles and separate schools, and disabled people to nursing homes are not absent from contemporary politics, the danger is real.

It may be true that the assimilationist ideal that treats everyone the same and applies the same standards to all perpetuates disadvantage because real group differences remain that make it unfair to compare the unequals. But this is far preferable to a reestablishment of separate and unequal spheres for different groups justified on the basis of group difference.

Since those asserting group specificity certainly wish to affirm the liberal humanist principle that all persons are of equal moral worth, they appear to be faced with a dilemma. Analyzing W.E.B. Du Bois's arguments for cultural pluralism, Bernard Boxill poses the dilemma this way: "On the one hand, we must overcome segregation because it denies the idea of human brotherhood; on the other hand, to overcome segregation we must self-segregate and therefore also deny the idea of human brotherhood" (Boxill, 1984, p. 174). . . .

These dilemmas are genuine, and exhibit the risks of collective life, where the consequences of one's claims, actions, and policies may not turn out as one intended because others have understood them differently or turned them to different ends. Since ignoring group differences in public policy does not mean that people ignore them in everyday life and inter-action, however, oppression continues even when law and policy declare that all are equal. Thus I think for many groups and in many circumstances it is more empowering to affirm and acknowledge in political life the group differences that already exist in social life. One is more likely to avoid the dilemma of difference in doing this if the meaning of difference itself be-comes a terrain of political struggle. Social movements asserting the posi-tivity of group difference have established this terrain, offering an emanci-patory meaning of difference to replace the old exclusionary meaning.

The oppressive meaning of group difference defines it as absolute other-ness, mutual exclusion, categorical opposition. This essentialist meaning of difference submits to the logic of identity. One group occupies the position of a norm, against which all others are measured. The attempt to reduce all persons to the unity of a common measure constructs as deviant those whose attributes differ from the group-specific attributes implicitly pre-sumed in the norm. The drive to unify the particularity and multiplicity of practices, cultural symbols, and ways of relating in clear and distinct cate-gories turns difference into exclusion. . . .

The attempt to measure all against some universal standard generates a logic of difference as hierarchical dichotomy—masculine/feminine, civilized/savage, and so on. The second term is defined negatively as a lack of the truly human qualities; at the same time it is defined as the comple-ment to the valued term, the object correlating with its subject, that which brings it to completion, wholeness, and identity. By loving and affirming him, a woman serves as a mirror to a man, holding up his virtues for him to see. By carrying the white man's burden to tame and educate the savage peoples, the civilized will realize universal humanity. The exotic orientals are there to know and master, to be the completion of reason's progress in history, which seeks the unity of the world. In every case the valued term achieves its value by its determinately negative relation to the Other.

In the objectifying ideologies of racism, sexism, anti-Semitism, and homophobia, only the oppressed and excluded groups are defined as different. Whereas the privileged groups are neutral and exhibit free and malleable subjectivity, the excluded groups are marked with an essence, imprisoned in a given set of possibilities. By virtue of the characteristics the group is alleged to have by nature, the ideologies allege that group members have specific dispositions that suit them for some activities and not others. Difference in these ideologies always means exclusionary opposition to a norm. There are rational men, and then there are women; there are civilized men, and then there are wild and savage peoples. The marking of difference always implies a good/bad opposition; it is always a devaluation, the naming of an inferiority in relation to a superior standard of humanity.

Difference here always means absolute otherness; the group marked as different has no common nature with the normal or neutral ones. The categorical opposition of groups essentializes them, repressing the differences within groups. In this way the definition of difference as exclusion and opposition actually denies difference. This essentializing categorization also denies difference in that its universalizing norms preclude recognizing and affirming a group's specificity in its own terms.

Essentializing difference expresses a fear of specificity, and a fear of making permeable the categorical border between oneself and the others.... The politics of difference confronts this fear, and aims for an understanding of group difference as indeed ambiguous, relational, shifting, without clear borders that keep people straight—as entailing neither amorphous unity nor pure individuality. By asserting a positive meaning for their own identity, oppressed groups seek to seize the power of naming difference itself, and explode the implicit definition of difference as deviance in relation to a norm, which freezes some groups into a self-enclosed nature. Difference now comes to mean not otherness, exclusive opposition, but specificity, variation, heterogeneity. Difference names relations of similarity and dissimilarity that can be reduced to neither coextensive identity nor nonoverlapping otherness.

The alternative to an essentializing, stigmatizing meaning of difference as opposition is an understanding of difference as ... relational rather than defined by substantive categories and attributes. A relational understanding of difference relativizes the previously universal position of privileged groups, which allows only the oppressed to be marked as different. When group difference appears as a function of comparison between groups, whites are just as specific as Blacks or Latinos, men just as specific as women, able-bodied people just as specific as disabled people. Difference thus emerges not as a description of the attributes of a group, but as a function of the relations between groups and the interaction of groups with institutions.

In this relational understanding, the meaning of difference also becomes contextualized. Group differences will be more or less salient depending on the groups compared, the purposes of the comparison, and the point of view of the comparers. Such contextualized understandings of difference undermine essentialist assumptions. For example, in the context of athletics, health care, social service support, and so on, wheelchair-bound people are different from others, but they are not different in many other respects. Traditional treatment of the disabled entailed exclusion and segregation because the differences between the disabled and the able-bodied were conceptualized as extending to all or most capacities.

In general, then, a relational understanding of group difference rejects exclusion. Difference no longer implies that groups lie outside one another. To say that there are differences among groups does not imply that there are not overlapping experiences, or that two groups have nothing in common. The assumption that real differences in affinity, culture, or privilege imply oppositional categorization must be challenged. Different groups are always similar in some respects, and always potentially share some attributes, experiences, and goals.

Such a relational understanding of difference entails revising the meaning of group identity as well. In asserting the positive difference of their experience, culture, and social perspective, social movements of groups that have experienced cultural imperialism deny that they have a common identity, a set of fixed attributes that clearly mark who belongs and who doesn't. Rather, what makes a group a group is a social process of interaction and differentiation in which some people come to have a particular *affinity* for others. My "affinity group" in a given social situation comprises those people with whom I feel the most comfortable, who are more familiar. Affinity names the manner of sharing assumptions, affective bonding, and networking that recognizably differentiates groups from one another, but not according to some common nature. The salience of a particular person's group affinities may shift according to the social situation or according to changes in her or his life. Membership in a social group is a function not of satisfying some objective criteria, but of a subjective affirmation of affinity with that group, the affirmation of that affinity by other members of the group, and the attribution of membership in that group by persons identifying with other groups. Group identity is constructed from a flowing process in which individuals identify themselves and others in terms of groups, and thus group identity itself flows and shifts with changes in social process.

Groups experiencing cultural imperialism have found themselves objectified and marked with a devalued essence from the outside, by a dominant culture they are excluded from making. The assertion of a positive sense of group difference by these groups is emancipatory because it reclaims the definition of the group by the group, as a creation and construction, rather than a given essence. To be sure, it is difficult to articulate positive elements of group affinity without essentializing them, and these movements do not always succeed in doing so. But they are developing a language to describe their similar social situation and relations to one another, and their similar perceptions and perspectives on social life. These movements engage in the project of cultural revolution, . . . insofar as they take culture as in part a matter of collective choice. While their ideas of women's culture, Afro-American culture, and American Indian culture rely on past cultural expressions, to a significant degree these movements have self-consciously constructed the culture that they claim defines the distinctiveness of their groups.

Contextualizing both the meaning of difference and identity thus allows the acknowledgment of difference within affinity groups. In our complex, plural society, every social group has group differences cutting across it, which are potential sources of wisdom, excitement, conflict, and oppression. Gay men, for example, may be Black, rich, homeless, or old, and these differences produce different identifications and potential conflicts among gay men, as well as affinities with some straight men.

Respecting Difference in Policy

A goal of social justice, I will assume, is social equality. Equality refers not primarily to the distribution of social goods, though distributions are certainly entailed by social equality. It refers primarily to the full participation and inclusion of everyone in a society's major institutions, and the socially supported substantive opportunity for all to develop and exercise their capacities and realize their choices. American society has enacted formal legal equality for members of all groups, with the important and shameful exception of gay men and lesbians. But for many groups social equality is barely on the horizon. Those seeking social equality disagree about whether group-neutral or group-conscious policies best suit that goal, and their disagreement often turns on whether they hold an assimilationist or culturally pluralist ideal. . . .

The issue of formally equal versus group-conscious policies arises primarily in the context of workplace relations and access to political power. I have already discussed one of the primary reasons for preferring group-conscious to neutral policies: policies that are universally formulated and thus blind to differences of race, culture, gender, age, or disability often perpetuate rather than undermine oppression. Universally formulated standards or norms, for example, according to which all competitors for social positions are evaluated, often presume as the norm capacities, values, and cognitive and behavioral styles typical of dominant groups, thus disadvantaging others. Racist, sexist, homophobic, ageist, and ableist aversions and stereotypes, moreover, continue to devalue or render invisible some people, often disadvantaging them in economic and political interactions. Policies that take notice of the specific situation of oppressed groups can offset these disadvantages.

It might be objected that when facially neutral standards or policies disadvantage a group, the standards or policies should simply be restructured so as to be genuinely neutral, rather than replaced by group-conscious policies. For some situations this may be appropriate, but in many the group-related differences allow no neutral formulation. . . .

More important, however, some of the disadvantages that oppressed groups suffer can be remedied in policy only by an affirmative acknowledgment of the group's specificity. . . . Group-conscious polices are sometimes necessary in order to affirm the solidarity of groups, to allow them to affirm their group affinities without suffering disadvantage in the wider society.

Some group-conscious policies are consistent with an assimilationist ideal in which group difference has no social significance, as long as such policies are understood as means to that end, and thus as temporary divergences from group-neutral norms. . . . A culturally pluralist democratic ideal . . . supports group-conscious policies not only as means to the end of equality, but also as intrinsic to the ideal of social equality itself. Groups cannot be socially equal unless their specific experience, culture, and social contributions are publicly affirmed and recognized.

The dilemma of difference exposes the risks involved both in attending to and in ignoring differences. The danger in affirming difference is that the implementation of group-conscious policies will reinstate stigma and exclusion. In the past, group-conscious policies were used to separate those defined as different and exclude them from access to the rights and privileges enjoyed by dominant groups. A crucial principle of democratic cultural pluralism, then, is that group-specific rights and policies should stand together with general civic and political rights of participation and inclusion. Group-conscious policies cannot be used to justify exclusion of or discrimination against members of a group in the exercise of general political and civil rights. A democratic cultural pluralism thus requires a dual system of rights: a general system of rights which are the same for all, and a more specific system of group-conscious policies and rights. . . . In the words of Kenneth Karst:

> When the promise of equal citizenship is fulfilled, the paths to belonging are opened in two directions for members of cultural minorities. As full members of larger society, they have the option to participate to whatever degree they choose. They also may look inward, seeking solidarity within their cultural group, without being penalized for that choice. (Karst, 1986, p. 337)

If "cultural minority" is interpreted to mean any group subject to cultural imperialism, then this statement applies to women, old people, disabled people, gay men and lesbians, and working-class people as much as it applies to ethnic or national groups. I will now briefly consider three cases in which group-specific policies are necessary to support social equality: women, Latinos, and American Indians.

(1) Are women's interests best promoted through gender-neutral or group-conscious rules and policies? This question has been fiercely debated by feminists in recent years. The resulting literature raises crucial questions about dominant models of law and policy that take equality to mean sameness, and offers some subtle analyses of the meaning of equality that do not assume identity (see Vogel, 1990). Most of this discussion has focused on the question of pregnancy and childbirth rights in the workplace.

Advocates of an equal treatment approach to pregnancy argue that women's interests are best served by vigorously pressing for the inclusion of pregnancy leaves and benefits within gender-neutral leave and benefit policies relevant to any physical condition that renders men or women unable to work. The history of protective legislation shows that women cannot trust employers and courts not to use special classification as an excuse for excluding and disadvantaging women, and we are best protected from such exclusion by neutral policies (Williams, 1983). Even such proponents of equal treatment, however, agree that gender-neutral policies that take male lives as the norm will disadvantage women. The answer, according to Nadine Taub and Wendy Williams, is a model of equality in the workplace that recognizes and accommodates the specific needs of all workers; such a model requires significant restructuring of most workplace policy (Taub and Williams, 1986).

In my view an equal treatment approach to pregnancy and childbirth is inadequate because it either implies that women do not have any right to leave and job security when having babies, or assimilates such guarantees under the supposedly gender-neutral category of "disability." Such assimilation is unacceptable because pregnancy and childbirth are usually normal conditions of normal women, because pregnancy and childbirth themselves count as socially necessary work, and because they have unique and variable characteristics and needs (Scales, 1981; Littleton, 1987). Assimilating pregnancy and childbirth to disability tends to stigmatize these processes as "unhealthy." It suggests, moreover, that the primary or only reason that a woman has a right to leave and job security is that she is physically unable to work at her job, or that doing so would be more difficult that when she is not pregnant and recovering from childbirth. While these are important considerations, another reason is that she ought to have the time to establish breast-feeding and develop a relationship and routine with her child, if she chooses. At issue is more than eliminating the disadvantage women suffer because of male models of uninterrupted work. It is also a question of establishing and confirming positive public recognition of the social contribution of childbearing. Such recognition can and should be given without either reducing women to childbearers or suggesting that all women ought to bear children and are lacking if they do not.

Feminists who depart from a gender-neutral model of women's rights generally restrict this departure to the biological situation of childbirth. Most demand that parental leave from a job, for example, should be gender-neutral, in order not to perpetuate the connection of women with the care of children, and in order not to penalize those men who choose more than average childrearing responsibilities. I myself agree with gender-neutral policy on this issue.

Restricting the issue of group-conscious policies for women to childbirth, however, avoids some of the hardest questions involved in promoting women's equality in the workplace. Women suffer workplace disadvantage not only or even primarily because of their birthing capacity, but because their gender socialization and identity orients the desires, temperaments, and capacities of many women toward certain activities and away from others, because many men regard women in inappropriately sexual terms, and because women's clothes, comportment, voices, and so on sometimes disrupt the disembodied ideal of masculinist bureaucracy. Differences between women and men are not only biological, but also socially gendered. Such gender differences are multiple, variable, and do not reduce men and women to segregating essences. Perhaps such differences should not exist, but without doubt they do now. Ignoring these differences sometimes disadvantages women in public settings where masculine norms and styles predominate.

In a model she calls "equality as acceptance," Christine Littleton argues for a gender-conscious approach to policy directed at rendering femininely gendered cultural attributes costless for women. This model begins with the assumption of structured social gender differences—for example, gender-dominated occupational categories, woman-dominated childrearing and other family member caretaking, and gender differences in the sports people wish to pursue. None of these are essences; it is not as though all men or all women follow the gendered patterns, but the patterns are identifiable and apply broadly to many people's lives. Littleton's model of equality as acceptance supports policies which not only will not disadvantage women who engage in traditionally feminine activity or behavior, but which value the feminine as much as the masculine:

> The focus of equality as acceptance, therefore, is not on the question of whether *women* are different, but rather on the question of how the social fact of gender asymmetry can be dealt with so as to create some symmetry in the lived-out experience of all members of the community. I do not think it matters so much whether differences are "natural" or not; they are built into our structures and selves in either event. As social facts, differences are created by the interaction of person with person or person with institution; they inhere in the relationship, not in the person. On this view, the function of equality is to make gender differences, perceived or actual, costless relative to each other, so that anyone may follow a male, female, or androgynous lifestyle according to their natural inclination or choice without being punished for following a female lifestyle or rewarded for following a male one. (Littleton, 1987, p. 1297)

The acceptance model of equality, then, publicly acknowledges culturally based gender differences, and takes steps to ensure that these differences do not disadvantage. Though Littleton does not emphasize it, this model implies, first, that gender differences must not be used implicitly or explicitly as a basis for excluding persons from institutions, positions, or opportunities. That is, general rights to equal opportunity, as well as other civil and political rights, must obtain. Over and above this, equality as acceptance explicitly revalues femininely coded activity and behavior as the equal of masculine-coded activity.

Comparable worth policies are a widely discussed strategy for revaluing the culturally feminine. Schemes of equal pay for work of comparable worth require that predominantly male and predominantly female jobs have similar wage structures if they involve similar degrees of skill, difficulty, stress, and so on. The problem in implementing these policies, of course, lies in designing methods of comparing different jobs. Most schemes of comparison still choose to minimize sex differences by using supposedly gender-neutral criteria, such as educational attainment, speed of work, whether the work involves manipulation of symbols, pleasantness of work conditions, decisionmaking ability, and so on. Some writers have suggested, however, that standard classifications of job traits may be systematically biased to keep specific kinds of tasks involved in many female-dominated occupations hidden. . . . Many female-dominated occupations involve gender-specific kinds of labor—such as nurturing, smoothing over social relations, or the exhibition of sexuality—which most task observation ignores. . . . A fair assessment of the skills and complexity of many female-dominated jobs may therefore involve paying explicit attention to gender differences rather than applying gender-blind categories of comparison (cf. Littleton, 1987, p. 1312).

Littleton offers sports as another area of revaluation. An "equality as acceptance" approach, she suggests, would support an equal division of resources between male and female programs rather than divide up the available sports budget per capita (Littleton, 1987, p. 1313). If the disparities in numbers of people involved were too great, I do not think this proposal would be fair, but I agree with the general principle Littleton is aiming at. Women who wish to participate in athletic activities should not be disadvantaged because there are not more women who currently wish to; they should have as many well-paid coaches, for example, as do men, their locker room facilities should be as good, and they should have access to all the equipment they need to excel. More importantly, femininely stereotyped sports, such as synchronized swimming or field hockey, should receive a level of support comparable to more masculine sport like football or baseball.

(2) In November 1986 the majority of voters in California supported a referendum declaring English the official language of that state. The ramifications of this policy are not clear, but it means at least that state institutions have no obligation to print ballots and other government literature or provide services in any language other than English. The California success has spurred a national movement to declare English the official language of the United States, as well as many additional local movements, especially in regions with fast-growing populations of people whose first language is not English. In winter 1989, for example, an English-only proposal went before the legislature of Suffolk County, Long Island, that even some English-first advocates thought was too strong. Not only would it have made English the official language of Suffolk County, but it would have forbidden public service providers from speaking to clients in any language other than English.

Many English-only advocates justify their position as another of many measures that should be taken to cut the costs of government. But the movement's primary appeal is to a normative ideal of the unity of the polity. As a nation, the United States was founded by English speakers; non-English speakers are not "real" Americans, no matter how many generations they can trace on American soil. A polity cannot sustain itself without significant commonality and mutual identification among its citizens, this argument goes, and a common language is one of the most important of such unifying forces. Linguistic and cultural pluralism leads to conflict, divisiveness, factionalism, and ultimately disintegration. Giving public preference to English supports this unity and encourages non-English speakers to assimilate more quickly.

There are at least three arguments against this appeal to unity of a single harmonious polity. First, it is simply unrealistic. From its beginnings the United States has always harbored sizeable linguistic and cultural minorities. Its history of imperialism and annexation and its immigration policy have resulted in more. In the past twenty-five years U.S. military and foreign policy has led to a huge influx of Latin Americans and Asians. Some estimate, moreover, that by the year 2000 Hispanic and Asian populations in the United States will have increased by 84 and 103 percent respectively (Sears and Huddy, 1987). Many individuals belonging to cultural minorities choose to assimilate, as do some whole groups. But many do not. Even without official support for their doing so and with considerable pressures against it, many groups have retained distinct linguistic and cultural identities, even some whose members have lived in the United States for several generations. Spanish speakers may be the most salient here because their relative numbers are large, and because their connections with Puerto Rico, Mexico, or other parts of Latin America remain strong. Given the determination of many linguistic and cultural minorities to maintain a specific identity even as they claim rights to the full benefits of American citizenship, a determination which seems to be increasing, the desire of the English-only movement to create unity through enforced language policy is simply silly.

Second, as I have already argued at several points, this norm of the homogeneous public is oppressive. Not only does it put unassimilated persons and groups at a severe disadvantage in the competition for scarce positions and resources, but it requires that persons transform their sense of identity in order to assimilate. Self-annihilation is an unreasonable and unjust requirement of citizenship. The fiction, poetry, and songs of American cultural minorities brim over with the pain and loss such demands inflict, documenting how thoroughly assimilationist values violate basic respect for persons.

Thus, third, the normative ideal of the homogeneous public does not succeed in its stated aim of creating a harmonious nation. In group-differentiated societies conflict, factionalism, divisiveness, civil warfare, do often occur between groups. The primary cause of such conflict, however, is not group difference per se, but rather the relations of domination and oppression between groups that produce resentment, hostility, and resistance among the oppressed. Placing a normative value on homogeneity only exacerbates division and conflict, because it gives members of the dominant groups reason to adopt a stance of self-righteous intractability.

... A just polity must embrace the ideal of a heterogeneous public. Group differences of gender, age, and sexuality should not be ignored, but publicly acknowledged and accepted. Even more so should group differences of nation or ethnicity be accepted. In the twentieth century the ideal state is composed of a plurality of nations or cultural groups, with a degree of self-determination and autonomy compatible with federated equal rights and obligations of citizenship. Many states of the world embrace this ideal, though they often realize it only very imperfectly. . . . English-only advocates often look with fear at the large and rapidly growing cultural minorities in the United States, especially the Spanish-speaking minority, and argue that only enforcing the primacy of English can prevent us from becoming a culturally plural society like Canada. Such arguments stubbornly refuse to see that we already are.

The difference between an assimilationist and a culturally pluralist ideal becomes particularly salient in educational policy. Bilingual education is highly controversial in the United States today, partly because of the different cultural meanings given to it. In 1974 the Supreme Court ruled that the state has an obligation to remedy the English-language deficiency of its students so they will have equal opportunity to learn all subjects; but the Court did not specify how this should be done. The Bilingual Education Act, passed in 1978 and amended several times, sets aside federal funds for use by school systems to develop bilingual education programs. Even so, in 1980, 77 percent of Hispanic children in the United States received no form of special programming corresponding to their linguistic needs (Bastian, 1986, p. 46). In 1986 in Texas, 80 percent of school districts were found out of compliance with a state-mandated bilingual education program (Canter, 1987).

There are several different models of language support programs. Some, like English as a Second Language, provide no instruction in the student's native language, and are often not taught by persons who can speak the student's language. Others, called immersion programs, involve English-language instruction primarily, but are taught by bilingual instructors whom the student can question in his or her native language. Transitional bilingual education programs involve genuinely bilingual instruction, with the proportions of English and native language changing as the student progresses. Transitional programs instruct students in such subjects as math, science and history in their native language at the same time that they develop English-language skills; they aim to increase the amount of time of instruction in English.

All these programs are assimilationist in intent. They seek to increase English proficiency to the point where native-language instruction is unnecessary; none has the goal of maintaining and developing proficiency in the native language. The vast majority of programs for students with limited English proficiency in the United States take one of these forms. The use of transitional bilingual programs instead of ESL or immersion programs is hotly debated. The majority of Americans support special language programs for students with limited English, in order to help them learn English; but the more programs instruct in a native language, especially when they instruct in subjects like math or science, the more they are considered by English speakers to be unfair coddling and a waste of taxpayer dollars (Sears and Huddy, 1987). Transitional bilingual educational programs, on the other hand, are usually preferred by linguistic minorities.

Another model of bilingual education is rarely practiced in the United States, and is hardly on the public agenda: bilingual-bicultural maintenance programs. These aim to reinforce knowledge of the students' native language and culture, at the same time that they train them to be proficient in the dominant language, English. Few advocates of cultural pluralism and group autonomy in the United States would deny that proficiency in English is a necessary condition for full participation in American society. The issue is only whether linguistic minorities are recognized as full participants in their specificity, with social support for the maintenance of their language and culture. Only bilingual-bicultural maintenance programs can both ensure the possibility of the full inclusion and participation of members of linguistic minorities in all society's institutions and at the same time preserve and affirm their group-specific identity.

(3) American Indians are the most invisible oppressed group in the United States. Numbering just over one million, they are too small a proportion of most regional populations to organize influential pressure groups or threaten major disruptions of the lives of white society. Federal and state policy often can safely ignore Indian interests and desires. Many Indians live on reservations, where non-Indians have little contact with them. Even in cities Indians often form their own support systems and networks, mingling little with non-Indians. Whether on or off the reservation, Indians suffer the most serious marginalization and deprivation of any social group; by every measure—income, unemployment rates, infant mortality, and so on—Indians are the poorest Americans.

At the same time, Indians are the most legally differentiated people in the United States, the only group granted formally special status and rights by the federal government. Indians represent the *arche*-difference that from the beginning subverts the claim to origin, to a New World, that founds the myth of America as the home of English-speaking farmers, traders, and inventors. Agents of the U.S. government have poisoned, burned, looted, tricked, relocated, and confined Indians many times over, in persistently genocidal policies, attempting to purge this difference within. Legal history and the string of federal treaties, however, also testify to a begrudging acknowledgment of the Indian peoples as independent political entities with which the government most negotiate. Until the twentieth century the special legal status of Indians was conceptualized almost entirely as a relation of wardship and dependence between an inferior savage people and a superior civilized sovereign, and the shadow of this conceptualization darkens even recent legal decisions. As with women, Blacks, and the feebleminded, Indian difference was codified in normalizing law as an inferior infantile nature that justified less than full citizenship.

At the turn of the century policymakers assumed that an end to this position of tutelage and wardship implied assimilation to the dominant culture. Thus the land reallocation policies of the late 1800s were intended to encourage Indians to value private property and the virtues of yeoman husbandry. In the 1920s, when Congress voted to grant Indians full U.S. citizenship, federal policy forced assimilation by forbidding Indian children to speak their native language in the boarding schools to which they were transported, sometimes thousands of miles from home. During the same period Indians were prohibited from practicing many of their traditional religious rites.

In the 1930s the Indian Reorganization Act eliminated and reversed many of these policies, creating the contemporary system of federally recognized tribal governments. But in the 1950s the pendulum swung back with the effort by Congress to terminate the federal relationship with tribes, withdrawing all recognition of Indians as distinct peoples, and once again attempting to force Indians to assimilate into white society. This brutal seesaw history of U.S.-Indian relations caused Indians to change and adapt their values, practices, and institutions and even their identities. Many distinct Indian identities have disappeared, as Indian groups merged or reorganized their relations with one another under the oppression of white policies. Throughout this history, however, assimilation was not a live option for the Indians. While many individuals may have left their groups and successfully integrated into the dominant white culture, Indians as groups persistently preserved their differences from white society against the fiercest opposition. Many Indians today find much fault with the present organization of the tribes, the definition of their role, and their legal relationship with the U.S. government, but few would propose the elimination of the tribal system that formally recognizes specific independently defined Indian groups and guarantees them specific rights in defining and running tribal affairs.

The case of American Indians especially exemplifies the arguments of this chapter because it is perhaps clearest here that justice toward groups requires special rights, and that an assimilationist ideal amounts to genocide. Such special rights, however, should not justify exclusion from full participation in the American dream of liberty, equal opportunity, and the like. The justice of recognizing both specific needs of a group and rights of full participation and inclusion in the polity has clear precedence in U.S. Indian law. Indians are the only group to have what almost amounts to a dual citizenship: as members of a tribe they have specific political, legal, and collective rights, and as U.S. citizens they have all the civil and political rights of other citizens. Recognized Indian tribes have specific rights to jurisdictional and territorial sovereignty, and many specific religious, cultural, and gaming rights.

Many Indians believe this system of particular rights remains too much at the discretion of the federal government, and some have taken their claims for greater self-determination to international judicial bodies. . . . Justice in the form of unambiguous recognition of American Indian groups as full and equal members of American society requires, in my view, that the U.S. government relinquish the absolute power to alter or eliminate Indian rights.

Even in the absence of full justice the case of Indians provides an important example of the combination of general rights and particular rights which, I have argued, is necessary for the equality of many oppressed or disadvantaged groups. The system of tribal rights, and their relation to general rights, is certainly complex, and there is often disagreement about the meaning and implications of these rights. Many Indians believe, moreover, that their rights, especially territorial rights to make decisions about land, water, and resources, are not sufficiently recognized and enforced because economic interests profit from ignoring them. I do not wish to argue that this system of particular rights, or the bureaucratic form it takes, should extend to other oppressed or disadvantaged social groups. The specificity of each group requires a specific set of rights for each, and for some a more comprehensive system than for others. The case of American Indians, however, illustrates the fact that there is a precedent for a system of particular rights that a group wants for reasons of justice, namely, because they enforce the group's autonomy and protect its interests as an oppressed minority.

The Heterogeneous Public and Group Representation

I have argued that participatory democracy is an element and condition of social justice. Contemporary participatory democratic theory, however, inherits from republicanism a commitment to a unified public that in practice tends to exclude or silence some groups. Where some groups are materially privileged and exercise cultural imperialism, formal democratic processes often elevate the particular experiences and perspectives of the privileged groups, silencing or denigrating those of oppressed groups.

In her study of the functioning of a New England town meeting government, for example, Jane Mansbridge demonstrates that women, Blacks, working-class people, and poor people tend to participate less and have their interests represented less than whites, middle-class professionals, and men. White middle-class men assume authority more than others, and they are more practiced at speaking persuasively; mothers and old people find it more difficult than others to get to meetings. . . . If the unified public does not transcend group differences and often allows the perspective and interests of privileged groups to dominate, then a democratic public can counteract this bias only by acknowledging and giving voice to the group differences within it.

I assert, then, the following principle: a democratic public should provide mechanisms for the effective recognition and representation of the distinct voices and perspectives of those of its constituent groups that are oppressed or disadvantaged. Such group representation implies institutional mechanisms and public resources supporting (1) self-organization of group members so that they achieve collective empowerment and a reflective understanding of their collective experience and interests in the context of the society; (2) group analysis and group generation of policy proposals in institutionalized contexts where decisionmakers are obliged to show that their deliberations have taken group perspectives into consideration; and (3) group veto power regarding specific policies that affect a group directly, such as reproductive rights policy for women, or land use policy for Indian reservations.

Specific representation for oppressed groups in the decisionmaking procedures of a democratic public promotes justice better than a homogeneous public in several ways, both procedural and substantial. First, it better assures procedural fairness in setting the public agenda and hearing opinions about its items. Social and economic privilege means, among other things, that the groups which have it behave as though they have a right to speak and be heard, that others treat them as though they have that right, and that they have the material, personal, and organizational resources that enable them to speak and be heard. As a result, policy issues are often defined by the assumptions and priorities of the privileged. Specific representation for oppressed groups interrupts this process, because it gives voice to the assumptions and priorities of other groups.

Second, because it assures a voice for the oppressed as well as the privileged, group representation better assures that all needs and interests in the public will be recognized in democratic deliberations. The privileged usually are not inclined to protect or advance the interests of the oppressed, partly because their social position prevents them from understanding those interests, and partly because to some degree their privilege depends on the continued oppression of others. While different groups may share many needs, moreover, their difference usually entails some special needs which the individual groups themselves can best express. If we consider just democratic decisionmaking as a politics of need interpretation, as I have already suggested, then democratic institutions should facilitate the public expression of the needs of those who tend to be socially marginalized or silenced by cultural imperialism. Group representation in the public facilitates such expression.

In the previous section I argued for the assertion of a positive sense of difference by oppressed groups, and for a principle of special rights for those groups. I discussed there the legitimate fears of many in emancipatory social movements that abandoning group-blind policies and adopting group-specific ones will restigmatize the groups and justify new exclusions. Group representation can help protect against such a consequence. If oppressed and disadvantaged groups can self-organize in the public and have a specific voice to present their interpretation of the meaning of and reasons for group-differentiated policies, then such policies are more likely to work for than against them.

Group representation, third, encourages the expression of individual and group needs and interests in terms that appeal to justice, that transform an "I want" into an "I am entitled to," in Hannah Pitkin's words. [Earlier] I argued that publicity itself encourages this transformation because a condition of the public is that people call one another to account. Group representation adds to such accountability because it serves as an antidote to self-deceiving self-interest masked as an impartial or general interest. Unless confronted with different perspectives on social relations and events, different values and language, most people tend to assert their perspective as universal. When special privilege allows some group perspectives to dominate a public while others are silent, such universalizing of the particular will be reaffirmed by many others. Thus the test of whether a claim upon the public is just or merely an expression of self-interest is best made when those making it must confront the opinion of others who have explicitly different, though not necessarily conflicting, experiences, priorities, and needs. As a person of social privilege, I am more likely to go outside myself and have regard for social justice when I must listen to the voice of those my privilege otherwise tends to silence.

Finally, group representation promotes just outcomes because it maximizes the social knowledge expressed in discussion, and thus furthers practical wisdom. Group differences are manifest not only in different needs, interests, and goals, but also in different social locations and experiences. People in different groups often know about somewhat different institutions, events, practices, and social relations, and often have differing perceptions of the same institutions, relations, or events. For this reason members of some groups are sometimes in a better position than members of others to understand and anticipate the probable consequences of implementing particular social policies. A public that makes use of all such social knowledge in its differentiated plurality is most likely to make just and wise decisions.

I should allay several possible misunderstandings of what this principle of group representation means and implies. First, the principle calls for specific representation of social groups, not interest groups or ideological groups. By an interest group I mean any aggregate or association of persons who seek a particular goal, or desire the same policy, or are similarly situated with respect to some social effect—for example, they are all recipients of acid rain caused by Ohio smokestacks. Social groups usually share some interests, but shared interests are not sufficient to constitute a social group. A social group is a collective of people who have affinity with one another because of a set of practices or way of life; they differentiate themselves from or are differentiated by at least one other group according to these cultural forms.

By an ideological group I mean a collective of persons with shared political beliefs. Nazis, socialists, feminists, Christian Democrats, and anti-abortionists are ideological groups. The situation of social groups may foster the formation of ideological groups, and under some circumstances an ideological group may become a social group. Shared political or moral beliefs, even when they are deeply and passionately held, however, do not themselves constitute a social group.

A democratic polity should permit the expression of all interests and opinions, but this does not imply specific representation for any of them. A democratic public may wish to provide representation for certain kinds of interests or political orientations; most parliamentary systems, for example, give proportional representation to political parties according to the number of votes they poll. The principle of group representation that I am arguing for here, however, refers only to social groups.

Second, it is important to remember that the principle calls for specific representation only of oppressed or disadvantaged groups. Privileged groups are already represented, in the sense that their voice, experience, values, and priorities are already heard and acted upon. . . .

This principle of group representation, finally, does not necessarily imply proportional representation. . . . I am concerned with the representation of group experience, perspectives, and interests. Proportional representation of group members may sometimes be too little or too much to accomplish that aim. A system of proportional group representation in state and federal government in the United States might result in no seats for American Indians, for example. Given the specific circumstances and deep oppression of Indians as a group, however, the principle would certainly require that they have a specific voice. Allocating strictly half of all places to women, on the other hand, might be more than is necessary to give women's perspectives an empowered voice, and might make it more difficult for other groups to be represented. . . .

Some might object that implementing a principle of group representation in governing bodies would exacerbate conflict and divisiveness in public life, rendering decisions even more difficult to reach. Especially if groups have veto power over policies that fundamentally and uniquely affect members of their group, it seems likely, it might be claimed, that decision-making would be stalled. This objection presupposes that group differences imply essential conflicts of interest. But this is not so; groups may have differing perspectives on issues, but these are often compatible and enrich everyone's understanding when they are expressed. To the extent that group differences produce or reflect conflict, moreover, group representation would not necessarily increase such conflict and might decrease it. If their differences bring groups into conflict, a just society should bring such differences into the open for discussion. Insofar as structured relations of privilege and oppression are the source of the conflict, moreover, group representation can change those relations by equalizing the ability of groups to speak and be heard. Thus group representation should mitigate, though not eliminate, certain kinds of conflict. If, finally, the alternative to stalled decisionmaking is a unified public that makes decisions ostensibly embodying the general interest which systematically ignore, suppress, or conflict with the interests of particular groups, then stalled decisionmaking may sometimes be just. . . .

One might ask how the idea of a heterogeneous public which encourages self-organization of groups and group representation in decisionmaking differs from the interest-group pluralism. . . . Interest-group pluralism, I suggest, operates precisely to forestall the emergence of public discussion and decisionmaking. Each interest group promotes its own specific interest as thoroughly and forcefully as it can, and need not consider the other interests competing in the political marketplace except strategically, as potential allies or adversaries in its own pursuit. The rules of interest-group pluralism do not require justifying one's interest as right, or compatible with social justice. A heterogeneous public, however, is a *public*, where participants discuss together the issues before them and come to a decision according to principles of justice. Group representation, I have argued, nurtures such publicity by calling for claimants to justify their demands before others who explicitly stand in different social locations. . . .

BIBLIOGRAPHY

Bastian, Ann, et al. (1986). *Choosing Equality: the Case for Democratic Schooling*. Philadelphia: Temple University Press.

Boxill, Bernard. 1984. *Blacks and Social Justice*. Totowa, NJ: Rowman and Allenheld.

Canter, Norma V. 1987. "Testimony from Mexican American Legal Defense and Education Fund." *Congressional Digest* (March).

Karst, Kenneth. 1986. "Paths to Belonging: The Constitution and Cultural Identity." *North Carolina Law Review* 64: 303–77.

Littleton, Christine. 1987. "Reconstructing Sexual Equality." *California Law Review* 75 (July): 1279–1377.

Sears, David O. and Leonia Huddy. 1987. "Bilingual Education: Symbolic Meaning and Support Among Non-Hispanics." Paper presented at the annual meeting of the American Political Science Association, Chicago, September.

Taub, Nadine and Wendy Williams. 1985. "Will Equality Require More than Assimilation, Accommodation or Separation from the Existing Social Structure?" *Rutgers Law Review* 31: 825–44.

Wasserstrom, Richard. 1980. "On Racism and Sexism." In *Philosophy and Social Issues*. Notre Dame: Notre Dame university Press.

Read

ARTHUR M. SCHLESINGER, JR.

The Disuniting of America: Reflections on a Multicultural Society

I

The ethnicity rage in general and Afrocentricity in particular not only divert attention from the real needs but exacerbate the problems. The recent apotheosis of ethnicity, black, brown, red, yellow, white, has revived the dismal prospect that in happy melting-pot days Americans thought the republic was moving safely beyond—that is, a society fragmented into separate ethnic communities. The cult of ethnicity exaggerates differences, intensifies resentments and antagonisms, drives ever deeper the awful wedges between races and nationalities. The endgame is self-pity and self-ghettoization.

Now there is a reasonable argument in the black case for a measure of regrouping and self-reliance as part of the preparation for entry into an integrated society on an equal basis. Integration on any other basis, it is contended, would mean total capitulation to white standards. Affirmation of racial and cultural pride is thus essential to true integration. One can see this as a psychological point, but as a cultural point?

For generations blacks have grown up in an American culture, on which they have had significant influence and to which they have made significant contributions. Self-Africanization after 300 years in America is play-acting. Afrocentricity as expounded by ethnic ideologues implies Europhobia, separatism, emotions of alienation, victimization, paranoia. Most curious and unexpected of all is a black demand for the return of black-white segregation.

"To separate [black children] from others of similar age and qualifications solely because of their race," Chief Justice Warren wrote in the school-integration case, "generates a feeling of inferiority as to their status in the community that may affect their hearts and minds in a way unlikely ever to be undone." In 40 years doctrine has come full circle. Now integra-

226

tion is held to bring feelings of inferiority, and segregation to bring the cure.

This revival of separatism will begin, if the black educator Felix Boateng has his way, in the earliest grades. "The use of standard English as the only language of instruction," Boateng argues, "aggravates the process of deculturalization." A "culturally relevant curriculum" for minority children would recognize "the home and community dialect they bring to school." (Not all black educators, it should be said, share this desire to handicap black children from infancy. "One fact is clear," notes Janice Hale-Benson of Cleveland State University. "Speaking standard English is a skill needed by Black children for upward mobility in American society and it should be taught in early childhood.")

If any educational institution should bring people together as individuals in friendly and civil association, it should be the university. But the fragmentation of campuses in recent years into a multitude of ethnic organizations is spectacular—and disconcerting.

One finds black dormitories, black student unions, black fraternities and sororities, black business and law societies, black homosexual and lesbian groups, black tables in dining halls. Stanford, Dinesh D'Souza reports, has "ethnic theme houses." The University of Pennsylvania gives blacks—6 percent of the enrollment—their own yearbook. Campuses today, according to one University of Pennsylvania professor, have "the cultural diversity of Beirut. There are separate armed camps. The black kids don't mix with the white kids. The Asians are off by themselves. Oppression is the great status symbol."

Oberlin was for a century and half the model of a racially integrated college. "Increasingly," Jacob Weisberg, an editor at *The New Republic,* reports, "Oberlin students think, act, and live apart." Asians live in Asia House, Jews in "J" House, Latinos in Spanish House, blacks in African-Heritage House, foreign students in Third World House. Even the Lesbian, Gay, and Bisexual Union has broken up into racial and gender factions. "The result is separate worlds."

Huddling is an understandable reaction for any minority group faced with new and scary challenges. But institutionalized separatism only crystallizes racial differences and magnifies racial tensions. "Certain activities are labeled white and black," says a black student at Central Michigan University. "If you don't just participate in black activities, you are shunned." A recent study by the black anthropologist Signithia Fordham of Rutgers concludes that a big reason for black underachievement is the fear that academic success will be taken as a sellout to the white world. "What appears to have emerged in some segments of the black community," Fordham says, "is a kind of cultural orientation which defines academic learning in school as 'acting white.'"

Militants further argue that because only blacks can comprehend the black experience, only blacks should teach black history and literature, as, in the view of some feminists, only women should teach women's history and literature. "True diversity," according to the faculty's Budget Committee at the University of California at Berkeley, requires that courses match the ethnic and gender identities of the professors.

The doctrine that *only* blacks can teach and write black history leads inexorably to the doctrine that blacks can teach and write *only* black history as well as to inescapable corollaries: Chinese must be restricted to Chinese history, women to women's history, and so on. Henry Louis Gates criticizes "ghettoized programs where students and members of the faculty sit around and argue about whether a white person can think a black thought." As for the notion that there is a "mystique" about black studies that requires a person to have black skin in order to pursue them—that, John Hope Franklin observes succinctly, is "voodoo."

The voodoo principle is extended from scholarship to the arts. Thus the fine black playwright August Wilson insists on a black director for the film of his play *Fences*. "We have a different way of responding to the world," Wilson explains. "We have different ideas about religion, different manners of social intercourse. We have different ideas about style, about language. We have different esthetics [*sic*]. . . . The job requires someone who shares the specifics of the culture of black Americans. . . . Let's make a rule. Blacks don't direct Italian films. Italians don't direct Jewish films. Jews don't direct black American films." What a terrible rule that would be!

In the same restrictive spirit, Actors' Equity tried to prevent the British actor Jonathan Pryce from playing in New York the role he created in London in *Miss Saigon,* announcing that it could not condone "the casting of a Caucasian actor in the role of a Eurasian." (Pryce responded that, if this doctrine prevails, "I'd be stuck playing Welshmen for the rest of my life.") Equity did not, however, apply the same principle to the black actors Morgan Freeman and Denzel Washington who were both acting in Shakespeare at that time in New York. *The Wall Street Journal* acidly suggested that, according to the principle invoked, not only whites but the disabled should protest the casting of Denzel Washington as Richard III because Washington lacked a hunchback.

The distinguished black social psychologist Kenneth B. Clark, whose findings influenced the Supreme Court's decision in the school-integration case, rejects the argument that blacks and whites must be separated "because they represent different cultures and that cultures, like oil and water, cannot mix." This, Clark says, is what white segregationists have argued for generations. He adds, "There is absolutely no evidence to support the contention that the inherent damage to human beings of primitive exclusion on the basis of race is any less damaging when demanded or enforced by the previous victims than when imposed by the dominant group."

II

The separatist impulse is by no means confined to the black community. Another salient expression is the bilingualism movement, ostensibly conducted in the interests of all non-English speakers but particularly a Hispanic-American project.

Bilingualism is hardly a new issue in American history. Seven years after the adoption of the Constitution, a proposal to print 3,000 sets of federal laws in German as well as English was narrowly defeated in the House of Representatives. (This incident gave rise to the myth, later cherished by Nazi propagandists like Colin Ross, that German had nearly displaced English as America's official language.) In the nineteenth century, newly arrived immigrants stayed for a season with their old language, used it in their homes, churches, newspapers, and not seldom in bilingual public schools, until acculturation reduced and the First World War discouraged the use of languages other than English.

In recent years the combination of the ethnicity cult with a flood of immigration from Spanish-speaking countries has given bilingualism new impetus. The presumed purpose is transitional: to move non-English-speaking children as quickly as possible from bilingual into all-English classes. The Bilingual Education Act of 1968 supplies guidelines and funding; the 1974 Supreme Court decision in *Lau v. Nichols* (a Chinese-speaking case) requires school districts to provide special programs for children who do not know English.

Alas, bilingualism has not worked out as planned: rather the contrary. Testimony is mixed, but indications are that bilingual education retards rather than expedites the movement of Hispanic children into the English-speaking world and that it promotes segregation more than it does integration. Bilingualism shuts doors. It nourishes self-ghettoization, and ghettoization nourishes racial antagonism. Bilingualism "encourages concentrations of Hispanics to stay together and not be integrated," says Alfredo Mathew Jr., a Hispanic civic leader, and it may well foster "a type of apartheid that will generate animosities with others, such as Blacks, in the competition for scarce resources, and further alienate the Hispanic from the larger society."

Using some language other than English dooms people to second-class citizenship in American society. "Those who have the most to lose in a bilingual America," says the Mexican-American writer Richard Rodriguez, "are the foreign-speaking poor." Rodriguez recalls his own boyhood: "It would have pleased me to hear my teachers address me in Spanish.... But I would have delayed ... having to learn the language of public society.... Only when I was able to think of myself as an American, no longer an alien in *gringo* society, could I seek the rights and opportunities necessary for full public individuality."

Monolingual education opens doors to the larger world. "I didn't speak English until I was about 8 years of age," Governor Mario Cuomo recently recalled, "and there was a kind of traumatic entry into public school. It made an immense impression on me." Traumatic or not, public school taught Cuomo the most effective English among politicos of his generation.

Yet a professor at the University of Massachusetts, told Rosalie Pedalino Porter, whose long experience in bilingual education led to her excellent book *Forked Tongue,* that teaching English to children reared in another language is a form of political oppression. Her rejoinder seems admirable: "When we succeed in helping our students use the majority language fluently . . . we are empowering our students rather than depriving them."

Panicky conservatives, fearful that the republic is over the hill, call for a constitutional amendment to make English the official language of the United States. Seventeen states already have such statutes. This is a poor idea. The English language does not need statutory reinforcement and the drive for an amendment will only increase racial discrimination and resentment.

Nonetheless, a common language is a necessary bond of national cohesion in so heterogeneous a nation as America. The bilingual campaign has created both an educational establishment with a vested interest in extending the bilingual empire and a political lobby with a vested interest in retaining a Hispanic constituency. Like Afrocentricity and the ethnicity cult, bilingualism is an elitist, not a popular, movement—"romantic ethnicity," as Myrdal called it; political ethnicity too. Still, institutionalized bilingualism remains another source of the fragmentation of America, another threat to the dream of "one people."

III

Most ominous about the separatist impulses is the meanness generated when one group is set against another. What Harold Isaacs, that acute student of racial sensitivities and resentments, called the "built-in we-they syndrome" has caused more dominating, fearing, hating, killing than any other single cause since time began.

Blacks, having suffered most grievously (at least in America) from persecution, have perhaps the greatest susceptibility to paranoia—remembering always that even paranoids may have real enemies. After all, considering what we now know about the plots against black Americans concocted by J. Edgar Hoover and executed by his FBI, who can blame blacks for being forever suspicious of white intentions?

Still, the *New York Times*–WCBS-TV poll of New Yorkers in 1990 is startling. Sixty percent of black respondents thought it true or possibly true that the government was making drugs available in black neighborhoods in order to harm black people. Twenty-nine percent thought it true or possibly true that the AIDS virus was invented by racist conspirators to kill blacks.

When Mayor Edward Koch invited the irrepressible Leonard Jeffries of CCNY to breakfast to discuss the "ice people-sun people" theory, Jeffries agreed to "but said he would not eat because white people were trying to poison him. When he arrived," Koch reports, "I offered him coffee and danish, but he refused it. I then offered to be his food taster, but he still declined."

On another occasion, Jeffries observed that "AIDS coming out of a laboratory and finding itself localized in certain populations certainly has to be looked at as part of a conspiratorial process." After a Jeffries class, 10 black students told the Times reporter that AIDS and drugs were indeed part of a white conspiracy. "During the Carter administration," one said, "there was a document put out that said by the year 2000, one hundred billion Africans had to be destroyed." "Because of who's being devastated the most, and growing up in the U.S. and knowing the history of slavery and racism in this country," an older black man said, "you can't be black and not feel that AIDS is some kind of experiment, some kind of plot to hit undesirable minority populations."

Nor is such speculation confined to the feverish sidewalks of New York. "Let me make a speech before a black audience," testifies William Raspberry, "and sometime during the Q & A someone is certain to ask if I believe there is a conspiracy against black Americans. It doesn't matter whether the subject is drugs or joblessness, school failure or teen pregnancy, politics or immigration. I can count on hearing some version of the conspiracy question."

The black case is only a more extreme version of the persecution complex—the feeling that someone is out to get them—to which nearly all minorities on occasion succumb. Mutual suspicion and hostility are bound to emerge in a society bent on defining itself in terms of jostling and competing groups.

IV

"The era that began with the dream of integration," Richard Rodriguez has observed, "ended up with scorn for assimilation." Instead of casting off the foreign skin as John Quincy Adams had stipulated, never to resume it, the fashion is to resume the foreign skin as conspicuously as can be. The cult of ethnicity has reversed the movement of American history, producing a nation of minorities—or at least of minority spokesmen—less interested in joining with the majority in common endeavor than in declaring their alienation from an oppressive, white, patriarchal, racist, sexist, classist society. The ethnic ideology inculcates the illusion that membership in one or another ethnic group is the basic American experience.

Most Americans, it is true, continue to see themselves primarily as individuals and only secondarily and trivially as adherents of a group. Nor is harm done when ethnic groups display pride in their historic past or in their contributions to the American present. But the division of society into fixed ethnicities nourishes a culture of victimization and a contagion of inflammable sensitivities. And when a vocal and visible minority pledges primary allegiance to their groups, whether ethnic, sexual, religious, or, in rare cases (communist, fascist), political, it presents a threat to the brittle bonds of national identity that hold this diverse and fractious society together. . . .

V

Is Europe really the root of all evil? The crimes of Europe against lesser breeds without the law (not to mention even worse crimes—Hitlerism and Stalinism—against other Europeans) are famous. But these crimes do not alter other facts of history: that Europe was the birthplace of the United States of America, that European ideas and culture formed the republic, that the United States is an extension of European civilization, and that nearly 80 percent of Americans are of European descent.

When Irving Howe, hardly a notorious conservative, dared write, "The Bible, Homer, Plato, Sophocles, Shakespeare are central to our culture," an outraged reader ("having graduated this past year from Amherst") wrote, "Where on Howe's list is the *Quran,* the *Gita,* Confucius, and other central cultural artifacts of the peoples of our nation?" No one can doubt the importance of these works nor the influence they have had on other societies. But on American society? It may be too bad that dead white European males have played so large a role in shaping our culture. But that's the way it is. One cannot erase history.

These humdrum historical facts, and not some dastardly imperialist conspiracy, explain the Eurocentric slant in American schools. Would anyone seriously argue that teachers should conceal the European origins of American civilization? or that schools should cater to the 20 percent and ignore the 80 percent? Of course the 20 percent and their contributions should be integrated into the curriculum too, which is the point of cultural pluralism.

But self-styled "multiculturalists" are very often ethnocentric separatists who see little in the Western heritage beyond Western crimes. The Western tradition, in this view, is inherently racist, sexist, "classist," hegemonic; irredeemably repressive, irredeemably oppressive. The spread of Western culture is due not to any innate quality but simply to the spread of Western power. Thus the popularity of European classical music around the world—and, one supposes, of American jazz and rock too—is evidence not of wide appeal but of "the pattern of imperialism, in which the conquered culture adopts that of the conqueror."

Such animus toward Europe lay behind the well-known crusade against the Western-civilization course at Stanford ("Hey-hey, ho-ho, Western culture's got to go!"). According to the National Endowment for the Humanities, students can graduate from 78 percent of American colleges and universities without taking a course in the history of Western civilization. A number of institutions—among them Dartmouth, Wisconsin, Mt. Holyoke—require courses in third-world or ethnic studies but not in Western civilization. The mood is one of divesting Americans of the sinful European inheritance and seeking redemptive infusions from non-Western cultures.

VI

Is the Western tradition a bar to progress and a curse on humanity? Would it really do America and the world good to get rid of the European legacy?

No doubt Europe has done terrible things, not least to itself. But what culture as not? History, said Edward Gibbon, is little more than the register of the crimes, follies, and misfortunes of mankind. The sins of the West are no worse than the sins of Asia or of the Middle East or of Africa.

There remains, however, a crucial difference between the Western tradition and the others. The crimes of the West have produced their own antidotes. They have provoked great movements to end slavery, to raise the status of women, to abolish torture, to combat racism, to defend freedom of inquiry and expression, to advance personal liberty and human rights.

Whatever the particular crimes of Europe, that continent is also the source—the *unique* source—of those liberating ideas of individual liberty, political democracy, the rule of law, human rights, and cultural freedom that constitute our most precious legacy and to which most of the world today aspires. These are *European* ideas, not Asian, nor African, nor Middle Eastern ideas, except by adoption.

The freedoms of inquiry and of artistic creation, for example, are Western values. Consider the differing reactions to the case of Salman Rushdie: what the West saw as an intolerable attack on individual freedom the Middle East saw as a proper punishment for an evildoer who had violated the mores of his group. Individualism itself is looked on with abhorrence and dread by collectivist cultures in which loyalty to the group overrides personal goals—cultures that, social scientists say, comprise about 70 percent of the world's population.

There is surely no reason for Western civilization to have guilt trips laid on it by champions of cultures based on despotism, superstition, tribalism, and fanaticism. In this regard the Afrocentrists are especially absurd. The West needs no lectures on the superior virtue of those "sun people" who sustained slavery until Western imperialism abolished it (and, it is reported, sustain it to this day in Mauritania and the Sudan), who still keep women in subjection and cut off their clitorises, who carry out racial persecutions not only against Indians and other Asians but against fellow Africans from the wrong tribes, who show themselves either incapable of operating a democracy or ideologically hostile to the democratic idea, and who in their tyrannies and massacres, their Idi Amins and Boukassas, have stamped with utmost brutality on human rights.

Certainly the European overlords did little enough to prepare Africa for self-government. But democracy would find it hard in any case to put down roots in a tribalist and patrimonial culture that, long before the West invaded Africa, had sacralized the personal authority of chieftains and ordained the submission of the rest. What the West would call corruption is regarded through much of Africa as no more than the prerogative of power. Competitive political parties, an independent judiciary, a free press, the rule of law are alien to African traditions.

It was the French, not the Algerians, who freed Algerian women from the veil (much to the irritation of Frantz Fanon, who regarded deveiling as symbolic rape); as in India it was the British, not the Indians, who ended (or did their best to end) the horrible custom of *suttee*—widows burning themselves alive on their husbands' funeral pyres. And it was the West, not the non-Western cultures, that launched the crusade to abolish slavery—and in doing so encountered mighty resistance, especially in the Islamic world (where Moslems, with fine impartiality, enslaved whites as well as blacks). Those many brave and humane Africans who are struggling these days for decent societies are animated by Western, not by African, ideals. White guilt can be pushed too far.

The Western commitment to human rights has unquestionably been intermittent and imperfect. Yet the ideal remains—and movement toward it has been real, if sporadic. Today it is the *Western* democratic tradition that attracts and empowers people of all continents, creeds, and colors. When the Chinese students cried and died for democracy in Tiananmen Square, they brought with them not representations of Confucius or Buddha but a model of the Statue of Liberty. . . .

BERNARD R. BOXILL

Separation or Assimilation?

Dubois's Dilemma

To assimilate, or not to assimilate. To black cultural nationalists, such the poet Imamu Amiri Baraka (Leroi Jones), the political theorists Stokely Carmichael and Charles V. Hamilton, and, most important, W. E. B. Dubois, that has been *the* question in the race issue. Not, of course, that they imagined that blacks have had much of a choice about assimilation. Their question was and is about goals. Should the goal be to assimilate, to become as much like the white majority as possible, to blend in? Or should it be not to assimilate, to keep and even accentuate the differences from the majority, to stand out? These thinkers consider that question as crucial and fundamental as Hamlet's. They maintain that to choose assimilation is to choose self-obliteration, to choose, in some important sense, not to be. In their estimation, if black people are not to cave in under the slings and arrows of the majority, they must affirm, maintain, and even accentuate their distinctiveness. But their position has not gone unchallenged. There are black thinkers who have seen nothing crucial in the question of whether or not to assimilate, and no obligation to avoid assimilation. These so-called assimilationists, whose number included Henry Highland Garnet and Frederick Douglass in the 19th century and most of the leadership of the NAACP today, do not say that blacks must necessarily assimilate, though they usually believe that assimilation is inevitable. But they do say that black people are not obliged *not* to assimilate.

But even assimilationists concede that self-segregation may sometimes be desirable, if only as a temporary strategy. Thus, even Frederick Douglass, the most consistent and thorough-going assimilationist, conceded reluctantly that "although it may seem to conflict with our views of human brotherhood, we shall undoubtedly for many years be compelled to have institutions of a complexional character, in order to obtain this very idea of human brotherhood.[1]

Now, there is in this comment of Douglass's the suggestion of a paradox or dilemma. On the one hand, we must overcome segregation because it

235

denies the idea of human brotherhood; on the other hand, to overcome segregation we must self-segregate and therefore also deny the idea of human brotherhood. Although Douglass evidently believed that this only "seemed" to be a problem, his great successor W. E. B. Dubois thought it a major dilemma. The "only effective defense" that a "segregated and despised group has against complete spiritual and physical disaster," he wrote, "is internal self-organization."[2] But internal self-organization, Dubois admitted, involves "more or less active segregation and acquiescence in segregation."[3] Consequently a paradox does seem to exist: To combat the evil of segregation blacks must acquiesce in the very evil they would combat. "The dilemma," Dubois declared, "is complete and there is no escape.[4]

Cultural Pluralism

Why did Dubois believe that by self-segregating blacks would be acquiescing in racism? On the face of it, that idea seems as confused as the idea— which is nevertheless often put forward—that in defending oneself against aggression one acquiesces in the very aggression one condemns. But offence is not defence. Things one may not do in offence one may do in defence— and not thereby acquiesce in offence. And one could reason similarly in the case of racial segregation. In response to white segregation laws, the black community could conceivably have imposed its own segregation laws. This would have been as justifiable as one nation compulsorily "segregating" its citizens from another aggressive foreign nation. In neither case would there be any invidious "acquiescence." If Dubois believed that black self-segregation was in some sense an acquiescence to the segregation imposed by racism, he must have believed that, independent of the pressures of racism, there was some reason for self-segregation. Why did he believe that? The answer lies in his lifelong sympathy for the doctrine of cultural pluralism.

Cultural pluralism boils down to four main points: (1) Each race has its own distinct and peculiar culture. (2) Different races can accept a common conception of justice and can live together at peace in one nation-state. (For this reason cultural pluralism is to be distinguished from separatism, which maintains that the races cannot live together at peace in one nation-state.) (3) Individuals must develop more and closer ties to the other members of their own race in order to preserve and enhance those cultural traits which mark it off from others. (4) To forestall charges of chauvinism and exclusivity, the cultural pluralist hastens to add that he does not say that any particular culture is superior or inferior to any other, only that they are different, and that the members of each race must make a concerted effort to develop their own culture, not solely for their own self-realization, but also because each race must present its culture as a gift to the other races at "the meeting place of conquest,"[5] where all will benefit from, and participate as, equals in a universal world culture.

Many black thinkers have endorsed the idea of cultural pluralism. Even Booker T. Washington, with his feet planted so firmly on the ground— some would say trapped in the sand—toyed with it. It is "not too much to hope," he wrote, "that the very qualities which make the Negro different from the peoples by whom he is surrounded will enable him, in the fulness [sic] of time, to make a peculiar contribution to the nation of which he forms a part."[6]

And in Senegal and Martinique the poets and statesmen Leopold Sedar Senghor and Aimé Cesaire gave the theory powerful expression in the philosophy of Negritude, which favorably contrasted the communality and closeness to nature of African culture with the soullessness and materialism of European culture. However, Dubois was cultural pluralisim's original architect, and had spelled out its essentials in the closing years of the 19th century. If "there is substantial agreement in laws, language and religion;" and "if there is a satisfactory adjustment of economic life, then," he wrote, "there is no reason why in the same country and on the same street, two or three great national ideals may not thrive and develop."[7] And black people should develop their peculiar culture not only for themselves. ". . . other race groups," Dubois wrote, "are striving, each in its own way to develop for civilization its particular message, its particular ideal, which shall help to guide the world nearer and nearer that perfection of human life for which we all long, that one far off Divine event." The Negro race, he believed, has "not given to civilization the full spiritual message [it is] capable of giving."[8]

Although Dubois never again gave such eloquent and extended expression to the idea of cultural pluralism as he did in "The Conservation of Races," from which I quoted, he always clung to it. Thus, in 1934, nearly forty years after he wrote it, he cited the essay, observing "I am rather pleased to find myself still so much in sympathy with myself;"[9] and in 1954, nearly sixty years after the "The Conservation of Races" appeared, its shadow is still evident in his warning that the "price" of the desegregation promised by *Brown* was that black people "must eventually surrender race 'solidarity' and the idea of an American Negro culture."[10]

This last comment reveals why Dubois believed that self-segregation acquiesced in racism, and why it was his sympathy for cultural pluralism that made him believe this. For, according to the ideals of cultural pluralism, there is something positively good about self-segregation, independent of its function as a defensive response to imposed segregation. It is for this reason that Dubois could speak of the "price'" of desegregation, although he was willing to pay that price. Moreover, it is quite clear that for the cultural pluralist the good offered by self-segregation is of such importance as to impose on blacks a duty to self-segregate. Since racists make precisely the same claim when instituting segregation, it is not surprising that to a cultural pluralist like Dubois, self-segregation seems to acquiesce in racism. The question we face then is whether cultural pluralism is a defensible doctrine.

Dubois offered three arguments for cultural pluralism: (1) It inspires black pride, (2) it maintains black cultural authenticity, and (3) it gives to the world the gift of black culture. I will address each argument separately.

Black Pride

There is no question that black pride is a necessary and desirable feeling. A person who lacks due pride in his race will probably lack self-esteem, self-respect, and autonomy, and racism has, of course, done all it can to undermine that pride in black people. But these are generalities. What exactly is black pride?

Black pride may mean several things. Cultural pluralism probably defines it as pride in being a member of a cultural group that has a particular "message" or "ideal" which, in Dubois's words, "shall help to guide the world nearer and nearer that perfection of human life for which we all long, that one far off Divine event." At the other extreme, black pride may simply mean pride in being black, that is, pride in have black skin and the other physical qualities typical of black people. . . .

There is nothing wrong with black pride as the cultural pluralist understands it. There is nothing wrong in a Senegalese being proud that he participates in the culture which produced the "particular message" of the poetry of Leopold Sedar Senghor, just as there is nothing wrong with an Englishman being proud that he participates in the culture which produced Dickens, that most English of English novelists.

Also, despite Douglass's view, there is nothing wrong with being proud that one has a black skin. Douglass thought that the very idea of "race pride" was "supercilious nonsense." "The only excuse for pride in individuals or races," he wrote, "is in the fact of their own achievements," and, of course, a person's race or color is not his achievement. "If the sun has curled our hair and tanned our skin," Douglass remarked sardonically, "let the sun be proud of its achievement." He also thought that race pride was "mischievous" and a positive evil because it led to complacency. It was race pride, he believed, which led "The poorest and meanest white man, drunk or sober, when he has nothing else to commend him [to say] 'I am a white man, I am.'" Black race pride would endorse and justify "American race pride; an assumption of superiority upon the ground of race or color," and the "mountain devil, the lion in the way of our progress."[11]

But Douglass was mistaken. Race pride is not necessarily an assumption of superiority on the grounds of race or color. If, as Douglass observed, "Our color is the gift of the Almighty," race pride may simply be a rejoicing in the gift of the Almighty. No assumption of superiority need be implied. And since we can, and indeed *should* rejoice in these gifts, there is no impropriety in being proud—in that sense—of our color. Finally, in that sense race pride need not lead to complacency. On the contrary, it may be necessary in order to develop the only kind of pride Douglass countenances—pride in achievement. For it is not implausible to assume that, unless one rejoices in and appreciates one's natural gifts, one will achieve nothing.

Therefore, I do not object to the idea of black pride either in the sense of pride in one's physical being, or in the sense of pride in one's cultural being. But there is a third sense in which black pride can be interpreted which is distinct from these two, and which better enhances black self-esteem.

In this third definition of black pride, a person is simply proud of the fact that there are black people who have made great achievements. This kind of black pride is distinct from cultural or physical pride. If a black person is proud of the achievements of outstanding black people, his culture need not be their culture, and their achievements need not be exemplifications of a peculiar black culture. I am proud that St. Augustine was a black man, but I am sure that my culture is not his, and I am not less proud—for I do not really care—that his *The Holy City* shows no traces of Negritude. Of course, it goes without saying that pride in the achievements of black people can mean pride in black culture. Dubois was proud of the art of the ancient West African nation of Benin and well he might be. But he could be proud of these products of black cultures because these cultures and these products were the achievements of black people.

It may be objected that I have begged the question. I say that a person can be proud of the achievements of outstanding black people, but I do not say what I mean by black people. Dubois defined a race as a "vast family of human beings, generally of common blood and language, always of common history, tradition and impulses, who are both voluntarily and involuntarily striving together for the accomplishment of certain more or less vividly conceived ideals of life."[12] If he is right, then, since black Americans do form a race, the black American who is proud of the achievements of outstanding black people must share a culture with the people who make him proud.

But in fact it is Dubois who has begged the question. It is he who has defined a race as a family of human beings sharing a common culture. Armed with this definition it is possible to draw the tautological inference that every member of a race shares a culture. However, it is not possible to draw the substantive inference that every black American shares a culture.

For since it is a false or at least controversial point, that black Americans are a family of human beings sharing a common culture, it is also false or controversial to maintain that they are a race as defined by Dubois.

In opposition to Dubois's cultural definition of race, I propose a physical definition of race. This definition is, for reasons which will presently emerge, the racist's definition. Individual differences in culture are supremely irrelevant to the way in which the racist classifies people into races. A man with blue eyes and blond hair who loves chitlins and jazz is still a white man, though perhaps a depraved one. A man with black skin and nappy hair who loves Shakespeare and ballet is still a black man, though certainly one who needs putting in his place. And when the black who "passes" is unmasked, it is not because he reveals a secret weakness for chitlins, but because it is revealed that he has black-skinned ancestors. The racist, we observe, takes a race to be a group of people distinguished either by their physical appearance or biology, or else descended from such a group of people, and since I have adopted their conception, I propose that, insofar as black people are a race, they are people who either themselves look black—that is, have a certain kind of appearance—or are, at least in part, descended from such a group of people.[13]

This definition of race better supports the idea of black pride and autonomy than the cultural definition and is more useful for an understanding of racism. Consider black pride. If to be black one must share in a particular culture, how can people who have black skins or black ancestors but who do not share in that culture have black pride? The cultural definition of race is evasive. When the racist tells black people that they can accomplish nothing because of their race, he is not telling them that they can accomplish nothing because of their culture. He is telling them that they can accomplish nothing because of their biological being. For racism is based predominantly on biology. Of course, it also maintains that black culture is degenerate, but it assumes that this is because blacks are biologically degenerate. Thus, to rebut racism's lie, to confront it directly, we must use words the way it uses words; we cannot use "race" to mean a cultural group. We must use "race," as racism uses it, to mean a group defined biologically. Only in this way can "race pride" mean "black pride" for all the victims of racism.

And Dubois's definition of race sometimes seriously misled him. It is, for example, what led him to define race prejudice as "nothing but the friction between different groups of people; it is the difference in aim, in feeling, in ideals of two different races."[14] If races are cultural groups this definition is plausible. There does tend to be friction between people with different aims and ideals. But that friction is not the friction between the races. The white racist does not hate blacks because they prefer jazz to country-and-western. He couldn't, because many prefer country-and-western to jazz. He hates them simply because they look black or are descended from people who look black. I do not deny that this hate may *arise* from a clash of cultures. But I am not describing here the origins of race prejudice. I am defining what it is. Neither do I deny that some, perhaps much, of the friction between blacks and whites is friction between people with different aims. Such friction is inevitable, given the difference in economic status of the two races. But the same kind of friction exists between the white lower class and the white middle and upper classes. It is not *racial* friction. And because Dubois's definition of prejudice is thus irrelevant it is also seriously misleading. It is often eminently reasonable to want to be widely separated from people with aims widely different from our own. When they pursue their aims, they are apt to prevent us from achieving our aims. Dubois's definition of race prejudice as a clash of cultures misleadingly allies it with this kind of reasonable attitude and thus obscures its utter irrationality.[15]

Cultural Authenticity

To be authentic, and true to oneself, one must first know oneself. Dubois evidently thought that this was a special problem for black Americans. In a widely admired passage he wrote: "No Negro who has given earnest thought to situation of his people in America has failed, at some time in life, to find himself at these crossroads; has failed to ask himself at some time: What, after all, am I? Am I an American or am I a Negro? . . ."[16] But Dubois felt that he had the "reading of the riddle." He maintained that farther than birth, citizenship, political ideals, language, and religion, black "Americanism does not go. At that point we are Negroes, members of a vast historic race that from the very dawn of creation has slept, but half-awakening, in the dark forests of its African fatherland. We are the first fruits of this new nation, the harbinger of that black tomorrow which is yet destined to soften the whiteness of the Teutonic today."[17]

But what of the assimilated black? Dubois's "reading of the riddle" does not really tell him much about what or who he is. Now, strictly speaking, in Dubois's definition of race a person with a black skin or ancestors, but who has assimilated, is white. But Dubois never let his ideas about race mislead him to that extent. He continued to accept the true, and commonsensical, view that such a person was black. However, he implied that a person with black skin or black ancestors *ought* to be culturally black if he wished to be authentic and true to himself. The destiny of black Americans, Dubois wrote, is "not absorption by the white Americans," nor "self-obliteration," nor a "servile imitation of Anglo-Saxon culture." It is a "stalwart originality which shall unswervingly follow Negro ideals."[18] If it is true, as these passages suggest, that cultural and individual authenticity, stalwartness, originality, and self-respect are undermined by acculturation, then, to the extent that blacks have a duty to be authentic, stalwart, original, and self-respecting, they have a duty to resist acculturation, that is, a duty to self-segregate.

It is widely believed that in some vague though deep sense, assimilated blacks are inauthentic, imitative, copy cats, unoriginal, ashamed of their color, morally flabby, so full of self-hate that they seek to be absorbed or obliterated, and, ultimately, servile. Thus, they are referred to derisively as "Afro-Saxons," or "oreos," black on the outside, white on the inside. If a person with a black skin writes a book or a poem, he must explicitly show his "blackness." Otherwise, he is trying to "pass," or, reverting inconsistently—since this view stresses color—to the cultural definition of race, he is not "really" black. Is there any basis to these extraordinary charges?

Attacks of this kind are sometimes based on the supposition that the assimilated black does not think of himself as black and therefore cannot be trusted as an ally. But this supposition begs the question. According to the cultural definition of race, the assimilated black will not, of course, see himself as black. But he is quite capable of seeing that he is black in the sense that racism puts him in the same boat as other people with black skins, and because he can see that, he can also see that he had better ally himself with them.

No doubt there are black people who are servile in part because they are assimilated. Indisputably, some aspects of white culture affirm that black people are inferior, and, to the extent that black people assimilate them, they will think of themselves as inferior. Some cultural pluralists go further and argue that the idea that white is superior and black is inferior is embedded in the very languages of Europe and North America, and, accordingly, that to speak those languages is to absorb a world-view which determines that one accept whites as superior to blacks.[19] But this theory is simplistic. Cultures are not seamless webs, their parts are not always consistent, and they are far more flexible than the theory supposes. For it is just as clear that some aspects of white culture affirm the equality of peoples, and black—and white—poets have not had to "destroy" English or European language before they could use them to say that black can be beautiful, and white can be ugly.[20]

And no doubt there are black people who pretend to a white culture which is not their own in order to "pass," or, if this is not possible, in order—they hope—to at least be accepted by that culture; and some black writers who imitate white writers because they believe that if they don't they won't be published, or the right people won't like their work, or simply because they despise themselves. The Martiniquan poet Éttienne Léro delivered a scathing indictment of this kind of writer: "The very reason for his entire social and poetic existence," he wrote, "is to be a faithful copy of the pale-skinned gentleman. . . . In his poetry too he tries not to 'act like a

Negro.' He takes a special pride in the fact that a white man can read his book without ever guessing the color of his skin."[21] Now, such people and such writers are certainly imitative, and possibly servile too, but it is false and vicious to infer that every assimilated black, or every black-skinned writer or poet who does not display "soul," is imitative and servile.

We do, I admit, have some grounds for suspecting a black poet or novelist—or moral philosopher—whose work appears to studiously avoid the question of the color bar. The color bar has caused too many tragedies, and raises too many personal and moral issues about the human condition—the subject of serious writing and philosophy—for one of its victims, who happens to be a serious writer or philosopher, to ignore it. But we must distinguish between writing about and protesting against the color bar, and displaying "soul," or, in Léro's words, "the black man's sensuous and colorful imagination." The serious black writer or philosopher sufficiently demonstrates his authenticity by coming to grips with, and condemning the color bar. He may, but need not do so with any particularly "black" style or diction.

But the world of white culture, it may be argued, is a world created by white-skinned people; black-skinned people feel like strangers in it, and white racism will make sure they continue to feel that way. In an essay significantly titled "Stranger in the Village," James Baldwin described this feeling of alienation when he visited an obscure hamlet in Europe. The inhabitants, Baldwin writes, "move with an authority I shall never have . . . the most illiterate among them is related, in a way that I am not, to Dante, Shakespeare, Michelangelo . . . Out of their hymns and dances come Beethoven and Bach. Go back a few centuries and they are in their full glory—but I am in Africa watching the conquerors arrive."[22]

I acknowledge the seductiveness of the feeling Baldwin describes. I deny, however, that it is rationally based, and deny therefore that we must cave in to it. The fallacy behind it is not that what is called "white culture" has been, to a considerable degree, created by black-skinned people, though, of course, this is true. The fallacy behind it is the assumption that people own cultures. Leaving aside the racist belief that a person's biology determines his culture or makes certain cultures more "natural" to him than others, only on that assumption does it even begin to make sense that blacks have any reason to feel "out of place" in white culture, or that whites have any right to make them feel that way. But the assumption is senseless. If the use or enjoyment of an object or idea by many different people causes a loss to someone, he may sensibly, and sometimes justifiably, claim ownership of it. But this does not apply to culture or the process of cultural assimilation. Except, perhaps as affronts to their racist beliefs—which count for nothing—assimilated blacks cause no loss to whites. Of course, many blacks do profess to feel truly ill at ease and out of place in white culture. But that may be simply because they are not assimilated. We succor the enemy if we let this unease be used to bolster the racist's argument that the assimilated black will inevitably still be alienated.

The Gift of Black Culture

According to Dubois, ". . . the Negro people, as a race have a contribution to make to civilization and humanity which no other race can make . . ." and ". . . it is duty of the Americans of Negro descent, as a body, to maintain their race identity until this mission of the Negro people is accomplished. . . ."[23] This suggests that black people have an obligation to self-segregate because they have a duty to help make the race's cultural contribution to civilization and humanity. But on what sense of obligation is that duty based?

The most likely candidate is the obligation of reciprocity. Such an obligation does exist. Since each person benefits from the contributions to society of others, he or she has a duty to contribute to it as well. It is wrong, and a dereliction of duty, to be a parasite. Everyone has a duty to "pull his own weight." But although this is true, it does not imply that black people have a duty to self-segregate.

It is not necessary to deny that "the Negro people," if they were to retain their "race identity," would make a peculiar and worthy contribution to the world. Certainly their historical experience has been peculiar and ought to give us privileged insights into the human condition. And certainly, as John Stuart Mill noted, groups of individuals pursuing a way of life together are experiments in living and therefore furnish mankind with valuable information. Thus, I disagree with Harvard sociologist Orlando Patterson, author of the widely-acclaimed *Slavery and Social Death,* who, in his critique of ethnic pluralism, professed to see no great value in a diversity of groups.[24] Neither is it necessary to deny that black people who choose to self-segregate for the purpose of helping to make the race's cultural contribution to humanity are fulfilling the duty of reciprocity, and fulfilling it in perhaps the most exalted way they can. Both these things will be true if the cultural contribution is likely to be, as I suspect it is, of great value.

What it is necessary and correct to deny is that black people—or white people—must fulfill the duty of reciprocity in the most exalted possible way, the way urged by Dubois. For although each person has a fundamental duty to reciprocate the contributions made by others to the world, each person also has an equally fundamental right to choose the way in which he or she will make that contribution. For example, a black person may choose to become a serious writer in order to distill and express the black experience, but he also may—and will commit no wrong if he does—

choose to become a plumber. If he has literary talent we may fairly attempt to persuade him that writing is, for him, a worthier goal. But it is sleight of hand to convert goals into duties because they are worthy.

These conclusions dissolve Dubois's dilemma about the choice of separation or integration for blacks. For that dilemma exists only if we accept cultural pluralism's claim that, independent of the pressures of racism, black people have an obligation to self-segregate. It is that claim which makes black self-segregation seem to acquiesce in racism, for, as we have noted, racism makes the same claim about the need for cultural integrity. But when black people self-segregate they need not be acquiescing to the dangerous nonsense of racism and cultural pluralism. They must admit, of course, that they have a common color or ancestry, and that they possess this commonality independent of separateness imposed by racism. And they may also admit that, independent of racist claims, they possess a common culture and that this makes it in some sense natural for them to self-segregate. But they may, and indeed should, deny that either of these identifications imposes on them an obligation to self-segregate. They should insist that the only circumstance that imposes such an obligation is the fact that they are all the victims of discrimination on the basis of their color or ancestry and that this commonality is not independent of racism, but, on the contrary, exists precisely because of racism. Consequently, since we have refuted the assumptions of pluralism, there is no dilemma. Black people may self-segregate in self-defense and may, simultaneously, and without the slightest inconsistency, protest the racism which makes this self-segregation necessary.

Nor does a dilemma reemerge if we grant that self-segregation may be necessary for the race to make a cultural contribution. Fighting and protesting against compulsory segregation does not mean fighting and protesting against every kind of segregation. It means precisely what it says: Fighting compulsory segregation. This is quite compatible with permitting, and even urging, black people to voluntarily self-segregate, and I see no reason why voluntary self-segregation cannot be a sufficient means of enabling the race to make its cultural contribution to the world.

Dubois's fear was that, if compulsory segregation were abolished, black people would *not* choose to self-segregate, but would assimilate as fast as they could. That was why he thought that the "price" of *Brown* would be the end of "American Negro culture." Perhaps his fears were well-founded. Perhaps blacks are assimilating as fast as they can, and perhaps the price of this is the disappearance of American Negro culture. I feel deeply the force of Dubois's concern. The price of desegregation may be high. And it may well be that, however much black people achieve in "white culture"—even if Keats, Dickens, and Newton had been black—black people would still not be esteemed as equals, unless they produced something peculiarly black, something completely and totally their own. People might still say—and are already saying—that, while blacks manage well among white people doing, and even improving, things white people started, they can't start anything or do anything at all by themselves. But even if we admit all this, and I don't think we have to, self-segregation and assimilation still pose no dilemma. For there is no dilemma about, no confusion between, securing justice and securing some other good, be it cultural integrity or maximizing welfare. Compulsory racial segregation is unjust. Even if its end means the end of "Negro culture" we seize no horn of a dilemma in striving to abolish it.

Authenticity as Autonomy

The conclusions of the preceding section point to a further, more fundamental, flaw in cultural pluralism. "What am I?" the black person asks. Cultural pluralism's answer is: "I am a being who springs from a people with a certain history and tradition; because of this I share with them certain impulses and strivings, both voluntary and involuntary, and to be true to myself and to help fulfill the Negro mission, I have a duty to retain that identity." This is a false, or at least, not fundamental, answer. The true answer is, "I am a being capable and worthy of making my own choices; because of this, I have certain basic duties and rights; among my duties is a duty to contribute to society, but among my rights is a right to choose how I shall contribute; I must allow neither history, tradition, nor seer to make my choices for me; I may choose, consistent with performing my duties and exercising my rights, any identity I please; only if my choices are thus autonomous can I really be true to myself." Frantz Fanon may have expressed himself too succinctly, but it is all there in his words: "There is no Negro mission; there is no white burden . . . I have one right alone: That of demanding human behavior from the other. One duty alone: That of not renouncing my freedom through my choices—I am not a prisoner of history. I should not seek there for the meaning of my destiny."[25]

In Dubois's mind, the cause of the dilemma was that, while he felt an allegiance to cultural pluralism, he also felt an allegiance to the truths summarized by Fanon. The first seduced him into believing that blacks had a duty to self-segregate; the second showed him clearly that each person has a right to choose for himself. Fortunately, Dubois's allegiance to human autonomy and individual rights was stronger than his allegiance to cultural pluralism. . . .

NOTES

1. Douglass, "An Address to the Colored People of the United States," *Negro Social and Political Thought 1850–1920, Representative Texts.* ed. Howard Brotz (New York: Basic Books, 1966), 211.

2. Dubois, "Separation and Self-Respect" in *The Seventh Son: The Thought and Writing of W.E.B. Dubois* ed. Julius Lester (New York: Vantage Books, 1971), 237.

3. Ibid., 247.

4. Ibid., 237.

5. Ainé Cesaire, *Return to My Native Land* (Paris: Présence Africaine, 1971), 138.

6. Washington, "On Making Our Race Life Count in the Life of the Nation," in Brotz, 380.

7. Dubois, "The Conservation of Races," in Brotz, 488.

8. Ibid., 487.

9. Dubois, "Counsels of Despair," in Lester, 254.

10. W.E.B. Dubois, "Two Hundred Years of Segregated Schools," in *W.E.B. Dubois Speaks: Speeches and Addresses 1920-1963,* ed. Phillip S. Foner (New York: Pathfinder Press, 1970), 283.

11. Douglass, "The Nation's Problem," in Brotz, 316, 317.

12. Dubois, "The Conservation of Races," in Brotz, 485.

13. Dubois often objected to definitions of this sort on the ground that they were imprecise. "Physical characteristics," he pointed out, "are not so inherited as to make it possible to divide the world into races" ("The White World," in Lester, 501). But though this is true, it is also irrelevant. First, all definitions of physical phenomena are imprecise; no matter how carefully we frame our definitions, new phenomena can always arise which elude them. Second, as Dubois himself was certainly aware, these theoretical problems in defining race did not matter one whit to practical racism. Third, they can be applied with even greater force against his cultural definition of race.

14. Dubois, "The Conservation of Races," in Brotz, 488.

15. That he would have agreed with me is indicative of Dubois's ambivalence. Thus, in the same essay in which he emphasized the theoretical problems in a definition of race, he also acknowledged the practical irrelevance of these problems. To the question of how he would differentiate the "black" race from others when he admitted it was "not black," he answered: "the black man is a person who must ride 'Jim Crow' in Georgia" ("White World," in Lester, 512). And this also acknowledges, of course, the complete irrelevance of culture to race. Similarly, when Dubois tacitly employed the physical definition of race, he was as clear as anyone of racism's irrationality. "I refuse," he wrote "to assent to the silly exaltation of a mere tint of skin or curl of hair" (Dubois, "A Philosophy for 1913," in Lester, 380).

16. Dubois, "Conservation of Races," in Brotz, 488.

17. Ibid., 489.

18. Ibid., 488.

19. This idea is suggested by some of the poets of negritude and by James Baldwin. See, for example, his "Stranger in the Village," in *What Country Have I? Political Writings by Black Americans,* ed. Herbert J. Storing (New York: St. Martin's Press, 1970), 219.

20. The necessity to "destroy" European language is suggested by J. P. Sartre in *Black Orpheus* (Paris: Présence Africaine, n.d.), 26.

21. Quoted in "Negritude Black Poetry From Africa and the Caribbean," ed. and trans. Norman R. Shapiro (New York: October House, 1970), 7.

22. Baldwin, "Stranger in the Village," 218.

23. Dubois, "The Conservation of Races," in Brotz, 491.

24. Orlando Patterson, "Ethnic Pluralism," *Change* (March 1975): 10.

25. Frantz Fanon, *Black Skin, White Masks,* (New York: Grove Press, 1967), 228, 229.

The Politics
of Recognition

I

A number of strands in contemporary politics turn on the need, some-times the demand, for *recognition*. The need, it can be argued, is one of the driving forces behind nationalist movements in politics. And the demand comes to the fore in a number of ways in today's politics, on behalf of minority or "subaltern" groups, in some forms of feminism and in what is today called the politics of "multiculturalism."

The demand for recognition in these latter cases is given urgency by the supposed links between recognition and identity, where this latter term des-ignates something like a person's understanding of who they are, of their fundamental defining characteristics as a human being. The thesis is that our identity is partly shaped by recognition or its absence, often by the *mis*recognition of others, and so a person or group of people can suffer real damage, real distortion, if the people or society around them mirror back to them a confining or demeaning or contemptible picture of themselves. Nonrecognition or misrecognition can inflict harm, can be a form of op-pression, imprisoning someone in a false, distorted, and reduced mode of being.

Thus some feminists have argued that women in patriarchal societies have been induced to adopt a depreciatory image of themselves. They have internalized a picture of their own inferiority, so that even when some of the objective obstacles to their advancement fall away, they may be incapa-ble of taking advantage of the new opportunities. And beyond this, they are condemned to suffer the pain of low self-esteem. An analogous point has been made in relation to blacks: that white society has for generations pro-jected a demeaning image of them, which some of them have been unable to resist adopting. Their own self-depreciation, on this view, becomes one of the most potent instruments of their own oppression. Their first task ought to be to purge themselves of this imposed and destructive identity. Recently, a similar point has been made in relation to indigenous and colo-nized people in general. It is held that since 1492 Europeans have projected an image of such people as somehow inferior, "uncivilized," and through the force of conquest have often been able to impose this image on the conquered. The figure of Caliban has been held to epitomize this crushing portrait of contempt of New World aboriginals.

Within these perspectives, misrecognition shows not just a lack of due respect. It can inflict a grievous wound, saddling its victims with a crippling self-hatred. Due recognition is not just a courtesy we owe people. It is a vital human need.

In order to examine some of the issues that have arisen here, I'd like to take a step back, achieve a little distance, and look first at how this discourse of recognition and identity came to seem familiar, or at least readily understandable, to us. For it was not always so, and our ancestors of more than a couple of centuries ago would have stared at us uncomprehendingly if we had used these terms in their current sense. How did we get started on this?

Hegel comes to mind right off, with his famous dialectic of the master and the slave. This is an important stage, but we need to go a little farther back to see how this passage came to have the sense it did. What changed to make this kind of talk have sense for us?

We can distinguish two changes that together have made the modern preoccupation with identity and recognition inevitable. The first is the collapse of social hierarchies, which used to be the basis for honor. I am using *honor* in the ancien régime sense in which it is intrinsically linked to inequalities. For some to have honor in this sense, it is essential that not everyone have it. This is the sense in which Montesquieu uses it in his description of Monarchy. Honor is intrinsically matter of "préférences."[1] It is also the sense in which we use the term when we speak of honoring someone by giving her some public award, for example, the Order of Canada. Clearly, this award would be without worth if tomorrow we decided to give it to every adult Canadian.

As against this notion of honor, we have the modern notion of dignity, now used in a universalist and egalitarian sense, where we talk of the inherent "dignity of human beings," or of citizen dignity. The underlying premise here is that everyone shares in it.[2] It is obvious that this concept of dignity is the only one compatible with a democratic society, and that it was inevitable that the old concept of honor was superseded. But this has also meant that the forms of equal recognition have been essential to democratic culture. For instance, that everyone be called "Mr.," "Mrs.," or "Miss," rather than some people being called "Lord" or "Lady" and others simply by their surnames—or, even more demeaning, by their first names— has been thought essential in some democratic societies, such as the United States. More recently, for similar reasons, "Mrs." and "Miss" have been collapsed into "Ms." Democracy has ushered in a politics of equal recognition, which has taken various forms over the years, and has now returned in the form of demands for the equal status of cultures and of genders.

But the importance of recognition has been modified and intensified by the new understanding of individual dignity that emerges at the end of the eighteenth century. We might speak of an *individualized* identity, one that is particular to me, and that I discover in myself. This notion arises along with an ideal, that of being true to myself and my own particular way of being. Following Lionel Trilling's usage in his brilliant study, I will speak of this as the ideal of "authenticity."[3] It will help to describe in what it consists and how it came about.

One way of describing its development is to see its starting point in the eighteenth-century notion that human beings are endowed with a moral sense, an intuitive feeling for what is right and wrong. The original point of this doctrine was to combat a rival view, that knowing right and wrong was a matter of calculating consequences, in particular, those concerned with divine reward and punishment. The idea was that understanding right and wrong was not a matter of dry calculation, but was anchored in our feelings.[4] Morality has, in a sense, a voice within.

The notion of authenticity develops out of a displacement of the moral accent in this idea. On the original view, the inner voice was important because it tells us what the right thing to do is. Being in touch with our moral feelings matters here, as a means to the end of acting rightly. What I'm calling the displacement of the moral accent comes about when being in touch with our feelings takes on independent and crucial moral significance. It comes to be something we have to attain if we are to be true and full human beings.

To see what is new here, we have to see the analogy to earlier moral views, where being in touch with some source—for example, God, or the Idea of the Good—was considered essential to full being. But now the source we have to connect with is deep within us. This fact is part of the massive subjective turn of modern culture, a new form of inwardness, in which we come to think of ourselves as beings with inner depths. At first, this idea that the source is within doesn't exclude our being related to God or the Ideas; it can be considered our proper way of relating to them. In a sense, it can be seen as just a continuation and intensification of the development inaugurated by Saint Augustine, who saw the road to God as passing through our own self-awareness. The first variants of this new view were theistic, or at least pantheistic.

The most important philosophical writer who helped to bring about this change was Jean-Jacques Rousseau. I think Rousseau is important not because he inaugurated the change; rather, I would argue that his great popularity comes in part from his articulating something that was in a sense already occurring in the culture. Rousseau frequently presents the issue of morality as that of following a voice of nature within us. This voice is often drowned out by the passions that are induced by our dependence on others, the main one being *amour propre,* or pride. Our moral salvation comes from recovering authentic contact with ourselves. Rousseau even gives a name to the intimate contact with oneself, more fundamental than any moral view, that is a source of such joy and contentment: "le sentiment de l'existence."[5]

The ideal of authenticity becomes crucial owing to a development that occurs after Rousseau, which I associate with the name of Herder—once again, as its major early articulator, rather than its originator. Herder put forward the idea that each of us has an original way of being human: each person has his or her own "measure."[6] This idea has burrowed very deep into modern consciousness. It is a new idea. Before the late eighteenth century, no one thought that the differences between human beings had this kind of moral significance. There is a certain way of being human that is *my* way. I am called upon to live my life in this way, and not in imitation of anyone else's life. But this notion gives a new importance to being true to myself. If I am not, I miss the point of my life; I miss what being human is for *me.*

This is the powerful moral ideal that has come down to us. It accords moral importance to a kind of contact with myself, with my own inner nature, which it sees as in danger of being lost, partly through the pressures toward outward conformity, but also because in taking an instrumental stance toward myself, I may have lost the capacity to listen to this inner voice. It greatly increases the importance of this self-contact by introducing the principle of originality: each of our voices has something unique to say. Not only should I not mold my life to the demands of external conformity; I can't even find the model by which to live outside myself. I can only find it within.[7]

Being true to myself means being true to my own originality, which is something only I can articulate and discover. In articulating it, I am also defining myself. I am realizing a potentiality that is properly my own. This is the background understanding to the modern ideal of authenticity, and to the goals of self-fulfillment and self-realization in which the ideal is usually couched. I should note here that Herder applied his conception of originality at two levels, not only to the individual person among other persons, but also to the culture-bearing people among other peoples. Just like individuals, a *Volk* should be true to itself, that is, its own culture. Germans shouldn't try to be derivative and (inevitably) second-rate Frenchmen, as Frederick the Great's patronage seemed to be encouraging them to do. The Slavic peoples had to find their own path. And European colonialism ought to be rolled back to give the of what we now call the Third World their chance to be themselves unimpeded. We can recognize here the seminal idea of modern nationalism in both benign and malignant forms.

This new ideal of authenticity was, like the idea of dignity, also in part an offshoot of the decline of hierarchical society. In those earlier societies, what we would now call identity was largely fixed by one's social position. That is, the background that explained what people recognized as important to themselves was to a great extent determined by their place in society, and whatever roles or activities attached to this position. The birth of a democratic society doesn't by itself do away with this phenomenon, because people can still define themselves by their social roles. What does decisively undermine this socially derived identification, however, is the ideal of authenticity itself. As this emerges, for instance, with Herder, it calls on me to discover my own original way of being. By definition, this way of being cannot be socially derived, but must be inwardly generated.

But in the nature of the case, there is no such thing as inward generation, monologically understood. In order to understand the close connection between identity and recognition, we have to take into account a crucial feature of the human condition that has been rendered a most invisible by the overwhelmingly monological bent of mainstream modern philosophy.

This crucial feature of human life is its fundamentally *dialogical* character. We become full human agents, capable of understanding ourselves, and hence of defining our identity, through our acquisition of rich human languages of expression. For my purposes here, I want to take *language* in a broad sense, covering not only the words we speak, but also other modes of expression whereby we define ourselves, including the "languages" of art, of gesture, of love, and the like. But we learn these modes of expression through exchanges with others. People do not acquire the languages needed for self-definition on their own. Rather, we are introduced to them through interaction with others who matter to us—what George Herbert Mead called "significant others."[8] The genesis of the human mind is in this sense not monological, not something each person accomplishes on his or her own, but dialogical.

Moreover, this is not just a fact about *genesis*, which can be ignored later on. We don't just learn the languages in dialogue and then go on to use them for our own purposes. We are of course expected to develop our own opinions, outlook, stances toward things, and to a considerable degree through solitary reflection. But this is not how things work with important issues, like the definition of our identity. We define our identity always in dialogue with, sometimes in struggle against, the things our significant others want to see in us. Even after we outgrow some of these others—our parents, for instance—and they disappear from our lives, the conversation with them continues within us as long as we live.[9]

Thus, the contribution of significant others, even when it is provided at the beginning of our lives, continues indefinitely. Some people may still want to hold on to some form of the monological ideal. It is true that we can never liberate ourselves completely from those whose love and care shaped us early in life, but we should strive to define ourselves on our own to the fullest extent possible, coming as best we can to understand and thus get some control over the influence of our parents, and avoiding falling into any more such dependent relationships. We need relationships to fulfill, but not to define, ourselves.

The monological ideal seriously underestimates the place of the dialogical in human life. It wants to confine it as much as possible to the genesis. It forgets how our understanding of the good things in life can be transformed by our enjoying them in common with the people we love; how some goods become accessible to us only through such common enjoyment. Because of this, it would take a great deal of effort, and probably many wrenching break-ups, to *prevent* our identity's being formed by the people we love. Consider what we mean by *identity*. It is who we are, "where we're coming from." As such it is the background against which our tastes and desires and opinions and aspirations make sense. If some of the things I value most are accessible to me only in relation to the person I love, then she becomes part of my identity.

To some people this might seem a limitation, from which one might aspire to free oneself. This is one way of understanding the impulse behind the life of the hermit or, to take a case more familiar to our culture, the solitary artist. But from another perspective, we might see even these lives as aspiring to a certain kind of dialogicality. In the case of the hermit, the interlocutor is God. In the case of the solitary artist, the work itself is addressed to a future audience, perhaps still to be created by the work. The very form of a work of art shows its character as *addressed*.[10] But however one feels about it, the making and sustaining of our identity, in the absence of a heroic effort to break out of ordinary existence, remains dialogical throughout our lives.

Thus my discovering my own identity doesn't mean that I work it out in isolation, but that I negotiate it through dialogue, partly overt, partly in internal, with others. That is why the development of an ideal of inwardly generated identity gives a new importance to recognition. My own identity crucially depends on my dialogical relations with others.

Of course, the point is not that this dependence on others arose with the age of authenticity. A form of dependence was always there. The socially derived identity was by its very nature dependent on society. But in the earlier age recognition never arose as a problem. General recognition was built into the socially derived identity by virtue of the very fact that it was based on social categories that everyone took for granted. Yet inwardly derived, personal, original identity doesn't enjoy this recognition *a priori*. It has to win it through exchange, and the attempt can fail. What has come about with the modern age is not the need for recognition but the conditions in which the attempt to be recognized can fail. That is why the need is now acknowledged for the first time. In premodern times, people didn't speak of "identity" and "recognition"—not because people didn't have (what we call) identities, or because these didn't depend on recognition, but rather because these were then too unproblematic to be thematized as such.

It's not surprising that we can find some of the seminal ideas about citizen dignity and universal recognition, even if not in these specific terms, in Rousseau, whom I have wanted to identify as one of the points of origin of the modern discourse of authenticity. Rousseau is a sharp critic of hierarchical honor, of "préférences." In a significant passage of the *Discourse on Inequality,* he pinpoints a fateful moment when society takes a turn toward corruption and injustice, when people begin to desire preferential esteem.[11] By contrast, in republican society, where all can share equally in the light of public attention, he sees the source of health.[12] But the topic of recognition is given its most influential early treatment in Hegel.[13]

The importance of recognition is now universally acknowledged in one form or another; on an intimate plane, we are all aware of how identity can be formed or malformed through the course of our contact with significant others. On the social plane, we have a continuing politics of equal recognition. Both planes have been shaped by the growing ideal of authenticity, and recognition plays an essential role in the culture that has arisen around this ideal.

On the intimate level we can see how much an original identity needs and is vulnerable to the recognition given or withheld by significant others. It is not surprising that in the culture of authenticity, relationships are seen as the key loci of self-affirmation. Love relationships are not just important because of the general emphasis in modem culture on the fulfillments of ordinary needs. They are also crucial because they are the crucibles of inwardly generated identity.

On the social plane, the understanding that identities are formed in open dialogue, unshaped by a predefined social script, has made the politics of equal recognition more central and stressful. It has, in fact, considerably raised the stakes. Equal recognition is not just the appropriate mode for a healthy democratic society. Its refusal can inflict damage on those who are denied it, according to a widespread modern view, as I indicated at the outset. The projection of an inferior or demeaning image on another can actually distort and oppress, to the extent that the image is internalized. Not only contemporary feminism but also race relations and discussions of multiculturalism are undergirded by the premise that the withholding of recognition can be a form of oppression. We may debate whether this factor has been exaggerated, but it is clear that the understanding of identity and authenticity has introduced a new dimension into the politics of equal recognition, which now operates with something like its own notion of authenticity, at least so far as the denunciation of other-induced distortions is concerned.

II

And so the discourse of recognition has become familiar to us, on two levels: First, in the intimate sphere, where we understand the formation of identity and the self as taking place in a continuing dialogue and struggle with significant others. And then in the public sphere, where a politics of equal recognition has come to play a bigger and bigger role. Certain feminist theories have tried to show the links between the two spheres.[14]

I want to concentrate here on the public sphere, and try to work out what a politics of equal recognition has meant and could mean.

In fact, it has come to mean two rather different things, connected, respectively, with the two major changes I have been describing. With the move from honor to dignity has come a politics of universalism, emphasizing the equal dignity of all citizens, and the content of this politics has been the equalization of rights and entitlements. What is to be avoided at all costs is the existence of "first-class" and "second-class" citizens. Naturally, the actual detailed measures justified by this principle have varied greatly, and have often been controversial. For some, equalization has affected only civil rights and voting rights; for others, it has extended into the socioeconomic sphere. People who are systematically handicapped by poverty from making the most of their citizenship rights are deemed on this view to have been relegated to second-class status, necessitating remedial action through equalization. But through all the differences of interpretation, the principle of equal citizenship has come to be universally accepted. Every position, no matter how reactionary, is now defended under the colors of this principle. Its greatest, most recent victory was won by the civil rights movement of the 1960s in the United States. It is worth noting that even the adversaries of extending voting rights to blacks in the southern states found some pretext consistent with universalism, such as "tests" to be administered to would-be voters at the time of registration.

By contrast, the second change, the development of the modern notion of identity, has given rise to a politics of difference. There is, of course, a universalist basis to this as well, making for the overlap and confusion between the two. *Everyone* should be recognized for his or her unique identity. But recognition here means something else. With the politics of equal dignity, what is established is meant to be universally the same, an identical basket of rights and immunities; with the politics of difference, what we are asked to recognize is the unique identity of this individual or group, their distinctness from everyone else. The idea is that it is precisely this distinctness that has been ignored, glossed over, assimilated to a dominant or majority identity. And this assimilation is the cardinal sin against the ideal of authenticity.[15]

Now underlying the demand is a principle of universal equality. The politics of difference is full of denunciations of discrimination and refusals of second-class citizenship. This gives the principle of universal equality a point of entry within the politics of dignity. But once inside, as it were, its demands are hard to assimilate to that politics. For it asks that we give acknowledgment and status to something that is not universally shared. Or, otherwise put, we give due acknowledgment only to what is universally present—everyone has an identity—through recognizing what is peculiar to each. The universal demand powers an acknowledgment of specificity.

The politics of difference grows organically out of the politics of universal dignity through one of those shifts with which we are long familiar, where a new understanding of the human social condition imparts a radically new meaning to an old principle. Just as a view of human beings as conditioned by their socioeconomic plight changed the understanding of second-class citizenship, so that this category came to include, for example, people in inherited poverty traps, so here the understanding of identity as formed in interchange, and as possibly so malformed, introduces a new form of second-class status into our purview. As in the present case, the socioeconomic redefinition justified social programs that were highly controversial. For those who had not gone along with this changed definition of equal status, the various redistributive programs and special opportunities offered to certain populations seemed a form of undue favoritism.

Similar conflicts arise today around the politics of difference. Where the politics of universal dignity fought for forms of nondiscrimination that were quite "blind" to the ways in which citizens differ, the politics of difference often redefines nondiscrimination as requiring that we make these distinctions the basis of differential treatment. So members of aboriginal bands will get certain rights and powers not enjoyed by other Canadians, if the demands for native self government are finally agreed on, and certain minorities will get the right to exclude others in order to preserve their cultural integrity, and so on.

To proponents of the original politics of dignity, this can seem like a reversal, a betrayal, a simple negation of their cherished principle. Attempts are therefore made to mediate, to show how some of these measures meant to accommodate minorities can after all be justified on the original basis of dignity. These arguments can be successful up to a point. For instance, some of the (apparently) most flagrant departures from "difference-blindness" are reverse discrimination measures, affording people from previously unfavored groups a competitive advantage for jobs or places in universities. This practice has been justified on the grounds that historical discrimination has created a pattern within which the unfavored struggle at a disadvantage. Reverse discrimination is defended as a temporary measure that will eventually level the playing field and allow the old "blind" rules to come back into force in a way that doesn't disadvantage anyone. This argument seems cogent enough—wherever its factual basis is sound. But it won't justify some of the measures now urged on the grounds of difference, the goal of which is not to bring us back to an eventual "difference-blind" social space but, on the contrary, to maintain and cherish distinctness, not just now but forever. After all, if we're concerned with identity, then what is more legitimate than one's aspiration that it never be lost? . . .

One of the key authors in th[e] transition [to the demand for recognition] is undoubtedly the late Frantz Fanon, whose influential *Les Damnés de la Terre (The Wretched of the Earth)*[16] argued that the major weapon of the colonizers was the imposition of their image of the colonized on the subjugated people. These latter, in order to be free, must first of all purge themselves of these depreciating self-images. Fanon recommended violence as the way to this freedom, matching the original violence of the alien imposition. Not all those who have drawn from Fanon have followed him in this, but the notion that there is a struggle for a changed self-image, which takes place both within the subjugated and against the dominator, has been very widely applied. The idea has become crucial to certain strands of feminism, and is also a very important element in the contemporary debate about multiculturalism.

The main locus of this debate is the world of education in a broad sense. One important focus is university humanities departments, where demands are made to alter, enlarge, or scrap the "canon" of accredited authors on the grounds that the one presently favored consists almost entirely of "dead white males." A greater place ought to be made for women, and for people of non-European races and cultures. A second focus is the secondary schools, where an attempt is being made, for instance, to develop Afrocentric curricula for pupils in mainly black schools.

The reason for these proposed changes is not, or not mainly, that all students may be missing something important through the exclusion of a certain gender or certain races or cultures, but rather that women and students from the excluded groups are given, either directly or by omission, a demeaning picture of themselves, as though all creativity and worth inhered in males of European provenance. Enlarging and changing the curriculum is therefore essential not so much in the name of a broader culture for everyone as in order to give due recognition to the hitherto excluded. The background premise of these demands is that recognition forges identity, particularly in its Fanonist application: dominant groups tend to entrench their hegemony by inculcating an image of inferiority in the subjugated. The struggle for freedom and equality must therefore pass through a revision of these images. Multicultural curricula are meant to help in this process of revision.

Although it is not often stated clearly, the logic behind some of these demands seems to depend upon a premise that we owe equal respect to all cultures. This emerges from the nature of the reproach made to the designers of traditional curricula. The claim is that the judgments of worth on which these latter were supposedly based were in fact corrupt, were marred by narrowness or insensitivity or, even worse, a desire to downgrade the excluded. The implication seems to be that absent these distorting factors, true judgments of value of different works would place all cultures more or less on the same footing. Of course, the attack could come from a more radical, neo-Nietzschean standpoint, which questions the very status of judgments of worth as such, but short of this extreme step (whose coherence I doubt), the presumption seems to be of equal worth.

I would like to maintain that there is something valid in this presumption, but that the presumption is by no means unproblematic, and involves something like an act of faith. As a presumption, the claim is that all human cultures that have animated whole societies over some considerable stretch of time have something important to say to all human beings. I have worded it in this way to exclude partial cultural milieux within a society, as well as short phases of a major culture. There is no reason to believe that, for instance, the different art forms of a given culture should all be of equal, or even of considerable, value; and every culture can go through phases of decadence.

But when I call this claim a "presumption," I mean that it is a starting hypothesis with which we ought to approach the study of any other culture. The validity of the claim has be demonstrated concretely in the actual study of the culture. Indeed, for a culture sufficiently different from our own, we may have only the foggiest idea *ex ante* of in what its valuable contribution might consist. Because, for a sufficiently different culture, the very understanding of what it is to be of worth will be strange and unfamiliar to us. To approach, say, a raga with the presumptions of value implicit in the well-tempered clavier would be forever to miss the point. What has to happen is what Gadamer has called a "fusion of horizons."[17] We learn to move in a broader horizon, within which we have formerly taken for granted as the background to valuation can be situated as one possibility alongside the different background of the formerly unfamiliar culture. The "fusion of horizons" operates through our developing new vocabularies of comparison, by means of which we can articulate these contrasts.[18] So that if and when we ultimately find substantive support for our initial presumption, it is on the basis of an understanding of what constitutes worth that we couldn't possibly have had at the beginning. We have reached the judgment partly through transforming our standards.

We might want to argue that we owe all cultures a presumption of this kind. I will explain later on what I think this claim might be based. From this point of view, withholding the presumption might be seen as the fruit merely of prejudice or of ill-will. It might even be tantamount to a denial of equal status. Something like this might lie behind the accusation leveled by supporters of multiculturalism against defenders of the traditional canon. Supposing that their reluctance to enlarge the canon comes from a mixture of prejudice and ill-will, the multiculturalists charge them with the arrogance of assuming their own superiority over formerly subject peoples.

This presumption would help explain why the demands of multiculturalism build on the already established principles of the politics of equal respect. If withholding the presumption is tantamount to a denial of equality, and if important consequences flow for people's identity from the absence of recognition, then a case can be made for insisting on the universalization of the presumption as a logical extension of the politics of dignity. Just as all must have equal civil rights, and equal voting rights, regardless of race or culture, so all should enjoy the presumption that their traditional culture has value. This extension, however logically it may seem to flow from the accepted norms of equal dignity, fits uneasily within them, as described [earlier], because it challenges the "difference-blindness" that was central to them. Yet it does indeed seem to flow from them, albeit uneasily.

I am not sure about the validity of demanding this presumption as a right. But we can leave this issue aside, because the demand made seems to be much stronger. The claim seems to be that a proper respect for equality requires more than a presumption that further study will make us see things this way, but actual judgments of equal worth applied to the customs and creations of these different cultures. Such judgments seem to be implicit in the demand that certain works be included in the canon, and in the implication that these works have not been included earlier only because of prejudice or ill-will or the desire to dominate. (Of course, the demand for inclusion is *logically* separable from a claim of equal worth. The demand could be: Include these because they're ours, even though they may well be inferior. But this is not how the people making the demand talk.)

But there is something very wrong with the demand in this form. It makes sense to demand as a matter of right that we approach the study of certain cultures with a presumption of their value, as described above. But it can't make sense to demand as a matter of right that we come up with a final concluding judgment that their value is great, or equal to others'. That is, if the judgment of value is to register something independent of our own wills and desires, it cannot be dictated by a principle of ethics. On examination, either we will find something of great value in culture C, or we will not. But it makes no more sense to demand that we do so than it does to demand that we find the earth round or flat, the temperature of the air hot or cold. . . .

Perhaps we don't need to ask whether it's something that others can demand from us as a right. We might simply ask whether this is the way we ought to approach others.

Well, is it? How can this presumption be grounded? One ground that has been proposed is a religious one. Herder, for instance, had a view of divine providence, according to which all this variety of culture was not a mere accident but was meant to bring about a greater harmony. I can't rule out such a view. But merely on the human level, one could argue that it is reasonable to suppose that cultures that have provided the horizon of meaning for large numbers of human beings, of diverse characters and temperaments, over a long period of time—that have, in other words, articulated their sense of the good, the holy, the admirable—are almost certain to have something that deserves our admiration and respect, even if it is accompanied by much that we have to abhor and reject. Perhaps one could put it another way: it would take a supreme arrogance to discount this possibility *a priori*.

There is perhaps after all a moral issue here. We only need a sense of our own limited part in the whole human story to accept the presumption. It is only arrogance, or some analogous moral failing, that can deprive us of this. But what the presumption requires of us is not peremptory and inauthentic judgments of equal value, but a willingness to be open to comparative cultural study of the kind that must displace our horizons in the resulting fusions. What it requires above all is an admission that we are very far away from that ultimate horizon from which the relative worth of different cultures might be evident. This would mean breaking with an illusion that still holds many "multiculturalists"—as well as their most bitter opponents—in its grip.

NOTES

1. "La nature de l'honneur est de demander de préférences et des distinctions. . . ." Montesquieu, *De l'esprit des lois,* Bk. 3, chap. 7.

2. The significance of this move from "honor" to "dignity" is interestingly discussed by Peter Berger in his "On the Obsolescence of the Concept of Honour," in *Revisions: Changing Perspectives in Moral Philosophy,* ed. Stanley Hauerwas and Alasdair MacIntyre (Notre Dame, Ind.: University Notre Dame Press, 1983), pp. 172–81.

3. Lionel Trilling, *Sincerity and Authenticity* (New York: Norton, 1969).

4. I have discussed the development of this doctrine at greater length, at first in

the work of Francis Hutcheson, drawing on the writings of the Earl of Shaftesbury, and its adversarial relation to Locke's theory in *Sources of the Self* (Cambridge, Mass.: Harvard University Press, 1989), chap. 15.

5. "Le sentiment de l'existence dépouillé de toute autre affection est par lui-même un sentiment précieux de contentment et de paix qui suffiroit seul pour rendre cette existence chére et douce à qui sauroit écarter de soi toutes les impressions sensuelles et terrestres qui viennent sans cesse nous en distraire et en troubler ici bas la douceur. Mais la pluspart des hommes agités de passions continuelles connoissent peu cet état et ne l'ayant gouté qu'imparfaitement durant peu d'instans n'en conservent qu'une idée obscure et confuse qui ne leur en fait pas sentir le charme." Jean-Jacques Rousseau, *Les Rêveries du promeneur solitaire,* "Cinquième Promenade," in *Oeuvres complètes* (Paris: Gallimard, 1959), 1:1047.

6. "Jeder Mensch hat ein eigenes Maass, gleichsam eine eigne Stimmung aller seiner sinnlichen Gefühle zu einander." Johann Gottlob Herder, *Ideen,* chap., 7, sec. 1, in *Herders Sämtliche Werke,* ed. Bernard Suphan (Berlin: Weidmann, 1877–1913), 13:291.

7. John Stuart Mill was influenced by this Romantic current of thought when he made something like the ideal of authenticity the basis for one of his most powerful arguments in *On Liberty.* See especially chapter 3, where he argues that we need something more than a capacity for "ape-like imitation": "A person whose desires and impulses are his own—are the expression of his own nature, as it has been developed and modified by his own culture—is said to have a character." "If a person possesses any tolerable amount of common sense and experience, his own mode of laying out his existence is the best, not because it is the best in itself, but because it is his own mode." John Stuart Mill, *Three Essays* (Oxford: Oxford University Press, 1975), pp. 73, 74, 83.

8. George Herbert Mead, *Mind, Self, and Society* (Chicago: University of Chicago Press, 1934).

9. This inner dialogicality has been explored by M. M. Bakhtin and those who have drawn on his work. See, of Bakhtin, especially *Problems of Dostoyevsky's Poetics,* trans. Caryl Emerson (Minneapolis: University of Minnesota Press, 1984). See also Michael Holquist and Katerina Clark, *Mikhail Bakhtin* (Cambridge, Mass.: Harvard University Press, 1984); and James Wertsch, *Voices of the Mind* (Cambridge, Mass.: Harvard University Press, 1991).

10. See Bakhtin, "The Problem of the Text in Linguistics, Philology and the Human Sciences," in *Speech Genres and Other Late Essays,* ed. Caryl Emerson and Michael Holquist (Austin: University of Texas Press, 1986), p. 126, for this notion of a "super-addressee," beyond our existing interlocutors.

11. Rousseau is describing the first assemblies: "Chacun commença à regarder les autres et à vouloir être regardé soi-même, et l'estime publique eut un prix. Celui qui chantait ou dansait le mieux; le plus beau, le plus fort, le plus adroit ou le plus éloquent devint le plus considéré, et ce fut là le premier pas vers l'inégalité, et vers le vice en même temps." *Discours sur l'origine et leas fondements de l'inégalité parmi les hommes* (Paris: Granier-Flamarion, 1971), p. 210.

12. See, for example, the passage in the *Considerations sur le gouvernement de Pologne* where he describes the ancient public festival, in which all the people took part, in *Du contrat social* (Paris: Garnier, 1962), p. 345; and also the parallel

passage in *Lettre à D'Alembert sur les spectacles,* in *Du contrat social,* pp. 224–25. The crucial principle was that there should be no division between performers and spectators, but that all should be seen by all. "Mais quels seront enfin les objets de ces spectacles? Qu'y montrera-t-on? Rien, si l'on veut. . . . Donnez les spectateurs en spectacles; rendez-les acteurs eux-mêmes; faites que chacun se voie et s'aime dans les autres, que tous en soient mieux unis."

13. See Hegel, *The Phenomenology of Spirit,* trans. A. V. Miller (Oxford: Oxford University Press, 1977), chap. 4.

14. There are a number of strands that have linked these two levels, but perhaps special prominence in recent years has been given to a psychoanalytically oriented feminism, which roots social inequalities in the early upbringing of men and women. See, for instance, Nancy Chodorow, *Feminism and Psychoanalytic Theory* (New Haven: Yale University Press, 1989); and Jessica Benjamin, *Bonds of Love: Psychoanalysis, Feminism and the Problem of Domination* (New York: Panthron, 1988).

15. A prime example of this charge from a feminist perspective is Carol Gilligan's critique of Lawrence Kohlberg's theory of moral development, for presenting a view of human development that privileges only one facet of moral reasoning, precisely the one that tends to predominate in boys rather than girls. See Gilligan, *In a Different Voice* (Cambridge, Mass.: Harvard University Press, 1982).

16. (Paris: Maspero, 1961).

17. *Wahrheit und Methode* (Tübingen: Mohr, 1975), pp. 289–90.

18. I have discussed what is involved here at greater length in "Comparison, History, Truth," in *Myth and Philosophy,* ed. Frank Reynolds and David Tracy (Albany: State University of New York Press, 1990); and in "Understanding and Ethnocentricity," in *Philosophy and the Human Sciences* (Cambridge: Cambridge University Press, 1985).

Pragmatism, Relativism, and the Justification of Democracy

I. Introduction

I want to discuss a philosopher whose work at its best illustrates the way in which American pragmatism (at *its best*) avoided both the illusions of metaphysics and the pitfalls of skepticism: John Dewey. . . . I shall call it *the epistemological justification of democracy* and although I shall state it in my own words, I shall deliberately select words which come from Dewey's own philosophical vocabulary.

The claim, then, is this: Democracy is not just a form of social life among other workable forms of social life; it is the precondition for the application of intelligence to the solution of social problems. The notions from Dewey's vocabulary that I have employed are, of course, *intelligence* (which Dewey contrasts with the traditional philosophical notion of *reason*) and *problem solving*. First, let me say a word about the sense in which such a claim, if supported, can be called *a justification* of a form of social life. . . .

II. The Noble Savage and the Golden Age

Although John Dewey's arguments are largely ignored in contemporary moral and political philosophy, his enterprise—the enterprise of justifying democracy—is alive and well. John Rawls's monumental *A Theory of Justice* for example, attempts both to produce a rationale for democratic institutions and a standpoint from which to criticize the failures of those institutions. This could also serve Dewey's project. But there are scholars in disciplines other than philosophy and to some extent even scholars of philosophy, who consider the very enterprise of justifying democracy a wrongheaded one. One objection comes from anthropologists and other social scientists,[1] although it is by no means limited to them. These relativist social scientists are sometimes also radicals when it comes to their own cultures, but they strongly oppose any attempt by members of liberal democratic cultures to prescribe change for traditional societies. In the most extreme case (the case I have in mind is an essay by a radical economist, Stephen Marglin[2]) they reject the idea that we can criticize traditional societies even for such sexist practices as female circumcision. . . . Not to be too nice about it, what I think we are seeing is the revival of the myth of the Noble Savage.

Basically, traditional societies are viewed by these thinkers as so superior to our own societies that we have no right to disturb them in any way. To see what is wrong with this view, let us for the moment focus on the case of male chauvinism in traditional societies.

One argument that is often used to justify a relativistic standpoint is virtually identical to an argument that is used by reactionaries in our own culture, and it is surprising that these social scientists fail to see this. At bottom, the idea is that people in traditional societies are "content"—they are not asking for changes and we have no right to say that they should be asking for changes, because in so doing we are simply imposing a morality that comes from a different social world. It is important in discussing this to separate two questions: the question of paternalistic intervention on one hand, and the question of moral judgment, moral argument, and persuasion on the other. It is not part of Dewey's view, for example, that benevolent despots should step in and correct social ills wherever they may exist. It is time to let Dewey speak for himself:

> The conception of community of good may be clarified by reference to attempts of those in fixed positions of superiority to confer good upon others. History shows that there have been benevolent despots who wished to bestow blessings on others. They have not succeeded except when their actions have taken the indirect form of changing the conditions under which those lived who were disadvantageously placed. The same principle holds of reformers and philanthropists when they try to do good to others in ways which leave passive those to be benefited. There is a moral tragedy inherent in efforts to further the common good which prevent the result from being either good or common—not good, because it is at the expense of the active growth of those to be helped, and not common because these have no share in bringing the result about. The social welfare can be advanced only by means which enlist the positive interest and active energy of those to be benefitted or improved. The traditional notion of the great man, of the hero, works harm. It encourages the idea that some "leader" is to show the way; others are to follow in imitation. It takes time to arouse minds from apathy and lethargy, to get them to thinking for themselves, to share in

making plans, to take part in their execution. But without active cooperation both in forming aims and in carrying them out there is no possibility of
a common good.[3]

The true paternalists are those who object to *informing* the victims of
male chauvinism, or of other forms of oppression, of the injustice of their
situation and of the existence of alternatives. Their argument is a thinly
disguised utilitarian one. Their conception of the good is basically "satisfaction" in one of the classic utilitarian senses; in effect they are saying that
the women (or whoever the oppressed may be) are satisfied, and that the
"agitator" who "stirs them up" is the one who is guilty of creating *dissatis-
faction.* But Dewey is no utilitarian. (He was a consequentialist, but he was
no utilitarian.) The fact that someone feels satisfied with a situation means
little if the person has no information or false information concerning either her own capacities or the existence of available alternatives to her
present way of life. The real test is not what women who have never heard
of feminism say about their situation; indeed, it is hard to see how the situation of a chauvinist woman in India is different from the situation of a
chauvinist woman in this country thirty years ago who had never been exposed to feminist ideas. Such women might well have answered a question-
naire by saying that they were satisfied with their lives; but after realizing
the falsity of the beliefs on which the acceptance of their lives had been
based, the same women not only felt dissatisfied with those lives, but they
sometimes felt ashamed of themselves for having allowed such a belief system to be imposed upon them. One of Dewey's fundamental assumptions is
that people value growth more than pleasure. To keep the oppressed from
learning so that they remain "satisfied" is, in a phrase originated by Peirce,
to "block the path of inquiry."

What the radical social scientists are in fact proposing is an "immunizing
strategy," a strategy by which the rationales of oppression in other cultures
can be protected from criticism. If this is based on the idea that the aspirations to equality and dignity are confined to citizens of Western industrial
democracies, then the events of Tien-an-men Square in the spring of 1989
speak a more powerful refutation of that view than any words I could write
here.

At the other extreme, at least politically, from the "Noble Savage" argument against attempting to justify democratic institutions is an argument
found in the recent writings of Alasdair MacIntyre. MacIntyre gives a
sweeping philosophical resumé of the history of Western thought which en-
dorses the idea that one system of ethical beliefs can "rationally defeat"
another system and insists that there can be progress in the development of
world views. MacIntyre's argument, however, is haunted by the suggestion
that such progress fundamentally stopped somewhere between the twelfth

and fourteenth centuries, and that we have been retrogressing ever since. MacIntyre's conception of rationality is based largely on the work of Thomas Kuhn[4] but with certain interesting omissions. Like Kuhn, MacIntyre believes that world views such as Confucianism, or Aristotelianism, or utilitarianism cum empiricism are often incommensurable. At the same time, MacIntyre believes that the adherents of a world view can incorporate elements from another world view, or even in exceptional cases, scrap their world view and go over to another by a kind of wholesale conversion. What makes such a wholesale conversion rational is that the new paradigm dissolves difficulties that the old paradigm is unable to escape either by straightforwardly answering the questions, or by showing why and how they are not genuine questions at all. Moreover, the new paradigm solves problems in a way that an honest adherent of the old paradigm must acknowledge as superior to anything his or her paradigm can supply. Of course, the new paradigm must not at the same time lose the ability to answer what its adherents must admit are genuine questions that the old paradigm could answer. . . .

The fact is that the methodological conceptions that MacIntyre defends are deeply flawed. I said that MacIntyre leaves certain things out of Kuhn's account of paradigm change in science. What he leaves out, in fact, is simply *experiment*. But the pragmatists recognized the value of experimentation. Dewey, of course, comes from the pragmatist tradition, and while the founder of pragmatism, Charles Sanders Peirce, eventually repudiated both the label "pragmatism" and much that William James and Dewey associated with that word, the two famous articles that Peirce published in *Popular Science Monthly* in 1877 and 1878, "The Fixation of Belief" and "How to Make Our Ideas Clear,"[5] remain the founding documents of the movement to the present day. In the first of those articles, Peirce discusses a methodology closely related to the one that MacIntyre proposes. He calls that the methodology of "What Is Agreeable to Reason."[6] Peirce tells us, I think rightly, that what we have learned—learned by trying that method, and trying again and again throughout the long history of our culture—is that it simply does not work. The method of "What Is Agreeable to Reason" by itself, without fallibilism, without experimentation, has never been able to lead to the successful discovery of laws of nature, nor has it been able to lead to resolutions of metaphysical disputes that would command the consensus of intelligent men and women. In place of the method of "What Is Agreeable to Reason" (and the other failed methods that Peirce calls the methods of "tenacity" and "authority"),[7] Peirce proposes the "scientific method.". . . What he means is testing one's ideas in practice, and maintaining an attitude of fallibilism toward them. To judge ideas simply on the basis of their ability to resolve difficulties without putting them under strain, without testing them, without trying to falsify them is to proceed prescientifically. Peirce would agree with MacIntyre that rational decision between paradigms requires reflection and discussion. More than any scientific philosopher of his time, Peirce stressed that scientific method is not just a matter of experimentation, but experimentation and testing remain crucial in the formation of rational beliefs about matters of fact.

I know that MacIntyre will say that this criticism passes him by. Far from claiming that rationality is just "out there," available to all properly trained human minds, as traditional rationalists did, MacIntyre insists that rationality (but not truth) is relative to one's paradigm.[8] No historical or universalistic account of rationality can be given at all, he insists. And, he argues, rejecting claims to unrevisable possession of truth makes one a fallibilist. The charm of MacIntyre's writing lies precisely in displaying how such a "postmodern" mind can come to such traditional conclusions! But I cannot accept this defense for two reasons. First, although rationality is relative and historical (perhaps *too* relative and historical!), in MacIntyre's view, there is a fixed principle governing rational discussion *between* paradigms, which allows one paradigm to sometimes "rationally defeat" another. It is in the application of *this* principle that MacIntyre is forced back upon what amounts to "What Is Agreeable to [MacIntyre's] Reason." The claim that he is only conceding what any "honest" adherent of the defeated paradigm would have to concede is a bit of persiflage that, in a different context, MacIntyre would be the first to see through. Second, fallibilism in the sense of giving up the a priori is not all there is to Peirce's sense of fallibilism. Peirce's fallibilism requires that one see experimentation, in the widest sense of that term, as the decisive element in rational paradigm change. MacIntyre might reply that reliance on experimentation is only rational "relative to" the contemporary scientific paradigm. But if that were his reply, then this is just where MacIntyre and pragmatism decisively part company.

If I am disturbed by the suggestion haunting MacIntyre's writing that we have been retrogressing ever since the late Middle Ages (a suggestion that has been put forward much more blatantly in Allan Bloom's best seller, *The Closing of the American Mind*) it is because the politics which such views can justify are nothing less than appalling. As many historians have reminded us, the Roman Catholic Church practiced torture through much of its long history. There was a total contempt for what are today regarded as human rights (of course, MacIntyre knows this), and there was terrible persecution of religious minorities. As a Jew, I am particularly worried by the possibility that the sufferings that the Church inflicted upon Jews could someday be "justified" as exercises of a paradigm which had "rationally defeat" the Jewish world view.

What the defenders of the Noble Savage and the defenders of the Golden Age have in common is that their doctrines tend to immunize institutionalized oppression from criticism. The immunizing strategies are different, but they have this in common: They give up the idea that it would be good for the victims of oppression to know of alternative ways of life, alternative conceptions of their situation, and to be free to see for themselves which conception is better. Both Noble Savagers and Golden Agers block the path of inquiry.

III. Dewey's Metaphysics (or Lack Thereof)

From what "premises" does Dewey derive the claim that I imputed to him, that is, that democracy is a precondition for the full application of intelligence to solving social problems? As we shall shortly see, the underlying premises are some very "ordinary" assumptions. . . .

Dewey believes (as we all do, when we are not playing the skeptic) that there are better and worse resolutions to human predicaments—to what he calls "problematical situations."[9] He believes that of all the methods for finding better resolutions, the "scientific method" has proved itself superior to Peirce's methods of "tenacity," "authority," and "What Is Agreeable to Reason." For Dewey, the scientific method is simply the method of experimental inquiry combined with free and full discussion—which means, in the case of social problems, the maximum use of the capacities of citizens for proposing courses of action, for testing them, and for evaluating the results. And, in my view, that is all that Dewey really needs to assume.

Of course, a conventional analytic metaphysician would not hold this view. In analytic philosophy today, one cannot simply assume that intelligent people are able to distinguish better resolutions to problematical situations from worse resolutions even after experimentation, reflection and discussion; one first must show that better and worse resolutions to problematical situations exist. . . .

[The] distinction between facts which are relative in this way and facts which are "absolute" is omnipresent; there can not be "absolute" facts of the kind Dewey thinks intelligent people are able to discover. Dewey, as I read him, would reply that the whole notion of an "absolute" fact is nonsensical. . . .

In my view, Dewey's great contribution was to insist that we neither have nor require a "theory of everything," and to stress that what we need instead is insight into how human beings resolve problematical situations. But again, it is time to let Dewey speak for himself:

[Philosophy's] primary concern is to clarify, liberate and extend the goods which inhere in the naturally generated functions or experience. It has no call to create a world of "reality" *de novo,* nor to delve into secrets of Being hidden from common sense and science. It has no stock of information or body of knowledge peculiarly its own; if it does not always become ridiculous when it sets up as a rival of science, it is only because a particular philosopher happens to be also, as a human being, a prophetic man of science. Its business is to accept and to utilize for a purpose the best available knowledge of its own time and place. And this purpose is criticism of beliefs, institutions, customs, policies with respect to their bearing upon good. This does not mean their bearing upon *the* good, as something itself attained and formulated in philosophy. For as philosophy has no private store of knowledge or of methods for attaining truth, so it has no private access to good. As it accepts knowledge of facts and principles from those competent and inquiry and discovery, so it accepts the goods that are diffused in human experience. It has no Mosaic or Pauline authority of revelation entrusted to it. But it has the authority of intelligence, of criticism of these common and natural goods.[10]

Here Dewey uses the notion of "intelligence." This notion, however, is not meant to be a metaphysical notion. Dewey contrasts this notion of intelligence with the traditional philosophical notion of reason. Intelligence, for Dewey, is not a transcendental faculty; it is simply the ability to plan conduct, to learn relevant facts, to make experiments, and to profit from the planning, the facts, and the experiments. The notion is admittedly vague, but we do have the ability to determine whether persons are more or less intelligent with respect to the conduct of their activities in particular areas. In a number of places Dewey connects intelligence with the ability for developing new capacities for acting effectively in an environment with what he calls "growth.". . .

Dewey believes, and he recognizes that this is an empirical hypothesis, that it is simply not true that democratic societies (and Dewey was a democratic socialist) cannot survive without producing massive unhappiness, or that ordinary people are not capable of making the decisions and taking the responsibilities that they must make and take if democracy is to function effectively. As a matter of empirical fact, the arguments offered by the despot and by all who defend special privilege are rationalizations, that is, they are offered in what is, at bottom, bad faith. I quote:

All special privilege narrows the outlook of those who possess it, as well as limits the development of those not having it. A very considerable portion of what is regarded as the inherent selfishness of mankind is the product of an inequitable distribution of power—inequitable because it shuts out some from the conditions which direct and evoke their capacities, while it produces a one-sided growth in those who have privilege. Much of the alleged unchangeableness of human nature signifies only that as long as social conditions are static and distribute opportunity unevenly, it is absurd to expect change in men's desires and aspirations. Special privilege always induces a stand pat and reactionary attitude on the part of those who have it; in the end it usually provokes a blind rage of destruction on the part of those who suffer from it. The intellectual blindness caused by privileged and monopolistic possession is made evident in "rationalization" of the misery and cultural degradation of others which attend its existence. These are asserted to be the fault of those who suffer; to be the consequence of their own improvidence, lack of industry, willful ignorance, etc. There is no favored class in history which has not suffered from distorted ideas and ideals, just as the deprived classes suffered from inertia and underdevelopment.[11]

The critical thrust of this discussion is unmistakable. Democracy may, as Winston Churchill said, be "better than all the other systems which have actually been tried," but it by no means provides full opportunity for the use of "social intelligence" in Dewey's sense. For the use of "social intelligence," as Dewey makes clear, is incompatible, on the one hand, with denying the underprivileged the opportunity to develop and use their capacities, and, on the other hand, with the rationalization of entrenched privilege. Dewey's justification is a critical justification of democracy, one that calls as much for the reform of democracy as for its defense. . . . For Dewey, the justification of democracy rests at every point on arguments which are not at all transcendental, but which represent the fruit of our collective experience. Deweyan philosophy exemplifies the very methodology for which argues. . . .

I would like to close by saying a little more about this critical dimension of Dewey's thought. When Dewey speaks of using the scientific method to solve social problems, he does not mean relying on experts, who, Dewey emphasizes, could not solve social problems. For one thing, experts belong to privileged classes and are affected by the rationalizations of which Dewey spoke. As an elite, they are accustomed to telling others how to solve their social problems. For Dewey, social problems are not resolved by telling other people what to do. Rather, they are resolved by releasing human energies so that people will be able to act for themselves. Dewey's social philosophy is not simply a restatement of classical liberalism; for, as Dewey says,

The real fallacy [of classical liberalism] lies in the notion that individuals have such a native or original endowment of rights, powers and wants that all that is required on the side of institutions and laws is to eliminate the obstructions they offer to the "free equipment of individuals." The removal of obstructions did not have a liberating effect upon such individuals as were antecedently possessed of the means, intellectual and economic, to take advantage of the changed social conditions. But it left all others at the mercy of new social conditions brought about by the freed powers of those advantageously situated. The notion that men are equally free to act if only the same legal arrangements apply equally to all—irrespective of differences in education, in command of capital, and that control of the social environment which is furnished by the institution of property—is a pure absurdity, as facts have demonstrated. Since actual, that is effective, rights and demands are products of interactions, and are not found in the original and isolated constitution of human nature, whether moral or psychological, mere elimination of obstructions is not enough. The latter merely liberates force and ability as that happens to be distributed by past accidents of history. This "free" action operates disastrously as far as the many are concerned. The only possible conclusion, both intellectually and practically, is that the attainment of freedom conceived as power to act in accord with choice depends upon positive and constructive changes in social arrangements.[12]

We too often forget that Dewey was a radical. But he was a radical democrat, not a radical scoffer at "bourgeois democracy." For Dewey, our democracy is not something to be spurned, nor is it something with which we should be satisfied. Our democracy is an emblem of what could be. What could be is a society that develops the capacities of all its men and women to think for themselves, to participate in the design and testing of social policies, and to judge the results. Perhaps for Dewey education plays the role that revolution plays in the philosophy of Karl Marx. Not that education is enough. Education is a means by which people can acquire capacities, but they have to be empowered to use those capacities. In the above passage, Dewey lists a number of things that stand in the way of that empowerment. Nevertheless, education is a precondition for democracy if democracy is a precondition for the use of intelligence to solve social problems. The kind of education that Dewey advocated did not consist in a Rousseauistic belief in the native goodness of every child, or in an opposition to discipline in public schools, or in a belief that content need not be taught. As Dewey's writings on education show, he was far more hardheaded and realistic than the "progressive educators" in all of these respects. Dewey did insist, however, that education must not be designed to teach people their place, or to defer to experts, or to accept uncritically a set of opinions. Education must be designed to produce men and women who are capable of learning on their own and of thinking critically. The extent to which we take the commitment to democracy seriously is measured by the extent to which we take the commitment to education seriously. In these days, saying these words fills me with shame for the state of democracy at the end of the twentieth century.

NOTES

1. See, for example, Frédérique A. Marglin and Stephen A. Marglin, eds., *Dominating Knowledge* (Oxford: Clarendon Press, 1990).

2. Stephen Marglin, "Towards the Decolonization of the Mind," in *Dominating Knowledge*, 1–29.

3. John Dewey and J. H. Tufts, *Ethics,* rev. ed. (Now York: Holt, 1936).

4. Thomas Kuhn, *The Structure of Scientific Revolutions*, 2nd ed. (Chicago: University of Chicago Press, 1970).

5. Charles Sanders Peirce, *The Fixation of Belief;* Peirce, *How to Make our Ideas Clear,* reprinted in *Writings of Charles S. Peirce,* ed. Christian J. Kloescl (Bloomington: Indiana University Press, 1986), 3.242–276.

6. Peirce, *Fixation,* 256.

7. Ibid., 250, 251.

8. MacIntyre, *After Virtue,* 2nd ed, (Notre Dame, Ind.: University of Notre Dame Press, 1984), 9–10.

9. John Dewey, *Logic* (Now York: Holt, 1938), 280.

10. John Dewey, *Experience and Nature,* 2nd ed. (La Salle, Ill.: Open Court, 1958), 407–408.

11. Dewey and Tufts, *Ethics,* 385–386.

12. John Dewey, "Philosophies of Freedom," in *Freedom in the Modern World,* ed. Horace Meyer Kallen (New York: Coward-McCann, 1928), 249–250.

About the Book and Editors

Throughout its history, the United States has struggled with the inevitable tensions of a highly diverse society. With the opening of higher education to women, ethnic minorities, and members of other previously marginalized groups, these tensions are now visited most especially upon our nation's colleges and universities.

This collection addresses the most controversial issues now troubling our campuses: the content of the curriculum, sexual harassment and date rape, hate speech versus free speech, and affirmative action. In addition, several contributions probe the fundamental issues underlying the more specific problems of the "politics of difference."

The contributions to this volume represent a wide range of disciplines—including philosophy, history, literary theory, law, economics, and politics—as well as views from across the political spectrum. Readers will find both familiar essays and new ones, arranged so that the authors speak directly to one another, thus providing a genuine conversation.

There is no better source for investigating the urgent issues of race, sex, and culture that not only raise academic questions but also reflect practical problems of day-to-day life in contemporary U.S. higher education.

John Arthur is professor of philosophy at the State University of New York at Binghamton. He is author of *The Unfinished Constitution: Philosophy and Constitutional Practice* and *Words That Bind: Judicial Review and the Grounds of Modern Constitutional Theory* (Westview, 1995) as well as editor of many successful anthologies on topics including democracy, ethics, and the law. In 1992 he was awarded the SUNY Chancellor's and Binghamton University awards for excellence in teaching. **Amy Shapiro,** a graduate of Harvard Law School, has taught legal history and currently practices law in Binghamton, New York.

About the Contributors

Andrew Altman teaches philosophy at George Washington University. In addition to many articles in philosophy of law and political philosophy, he is the author of *Critical Legal Studies*.

Allan Bloom is on the faculty of the Committee of Social Thought at the University of Chicago. He is author of *The Closing of the American Mind* and *Shakespeare's Politics;* he has also translated Plato's *Republic* and Rousseau's *Emile*.

Bernard R. Boxill is professor of philosophy at the University of North Carolina–Chapel Hill. Besides many articles, he is the author of *Blacks and Social Justice*.

Stanley Fish is Arts and Sciences Professor of English, professor of law, and chair of the Department of English at Duke University. He is the author of *Is There a Text In This Class?, Doing What Comes Naturally, Surprised By Sin* and *The Living Temple*.

Lino A. Graglia is professor of law at the University of Texas–Austin. He is the author of numerous articles on constitutional law.

Gerald Gunther, professor of constitutional law at Stanford University Law School, is the author of *Constitutional Law: Cases and Materials* and *John Marshall's Defense of Judicial Review* as well as numerous articles in constitutional law.

Amy Gutmann is professor of politics at Princeton University and director of the University Center for Human Values. Among her publications are *Democratic Education* and *Democracy and the Welfare State*.

Duncan Kennedy is professor of law at Harvard University. In addition to many articles on law, he is author of *Sexy Dressing: Essays on the Power and Politics of Cultural Identity*.

Audre Lorde was a poet and author. She wrote *Sister Outsider, The Cancer Journals,* and *Zami*.

Catharine A. MacKinnon is professor of law at the University of Michigan Law School. In addition to many articles, she has written *Feminism Unmodified, Toward a Feminist Theory of the State,* and *Only Words*.

Camille Paglia is professor of humanities at the University of the Arts in Philadelphia. She is the author of *Sexual Personae: Art and Decadence from Nefertiti to Emily Dickinson* and *Sex, Art, and American Culture.*

Lois Pineau is professor of philosophy at Kansas State University. She has written articles in feminist theory and philosophy of mind.

Hilary Putnam is professor of philosophy at Harvard University. His works include *The Many Faces of Realism; Reason, Truth and History;* and *Representation and Reality* as well as many articles in philosophy of science and philosophy of mind.

Barry W. Sarchett is assistant professor of English at Colorado College. He has written on literary theory and criticism, American literature, and film and popular culture.

Arthur M. Schlesinger, Jr., teaches at the graduate school of the University Center of City University of New York. He has won two Pulitzer Prizes and is the author of many books, including *A Thousand Days: John F. Kennedy in the White House* and *The Disuniting of America: Reflections on a Multicultural Society.*

John R. Searle is professor of philosophy at the University of California–Berkeley. Among his many articles and books are *The Rediscovery of the Mind; Minds, Brains, and Science; Intentionality;* and *Speech Act Theory and Pragmatism.*

Shelby Steele is professor of English at San Jose State University. His work has appeared widely, including in *The New York Times Magazine,* and he won the National Magazine Award in 1989. He is author of *The Content of Our Character* along with numerous essays and articles.

Charles Taylor is professor of philosophy and political science at McGill University. He is the author of numerous articles and books, including *Sources of the Self.*

Iris Marion Young is professor of public and international affairs at the University of Pittsburgh. In addition to many articles, she is the author of *Throwing Like a Girl and Other Essays in Feminist Philosophy and Social Theory* and *Justice and the Politics of Difference.*

Credits

Allan Bloom, "The Closing of the American Mind," from Allan Bloom, *The Closing of the American Mind* (New York: Simon & Schuster, 1987), pp. 25–40, 62–64. Copyright © 1987 by Allan Bloom. Reprinted by permission of Simon & Schuster, Inc.

Barry W. Sarchett, "What's All the Fuss About This Postmodernist Stuff?" *Colorado College Bulletin,* February 1992. Reprinted by permission.

John R. Searle, "Postmodernism and the Western Rationalist Tradition" from John R. Searle, "Rationality and Realism, What Is at Stake?" *Daedalus* 122, 4 (Fall 1993): 55–83. Reprinted by permission.

Stanley Fish, "Is There a Text in This Class?" from Stanley Fish, *Is There a Text in This Class?* (Cambridge: Harvard University Press, 1980), pp. 305–321. Copyright © 1980 by the President and Fellows of Harvard College. Reprinted by permission of the publishers.

Amy Gutmann, "Introduction" in Charles Taylor, *Multiculturalism and the Politics of Recognition* (Princeton: Princeton University Press, 1992), pp. 12–22, Copyright © 1992 by PUP, and Amy Gutmann, "The Challenge of Multiculturalism to Political Ethics," *Philosophy and Public Affairs* 22, 3 (Summer 1993): 172–180, Copyright © 1993 by PUP. Reprinted by permission of Princeton University Press.

Catharine A. MacKinnon, "Sexuality," from Catharine A. MacKinnon, *Toward a Feminist Theory of the State* (Cambridge: Harvard University Press, 1989), pp. 127–137, 145–150, 153–154. Copyright © 1989 by Catharine A. MacKinnon. Reprinted by permission of the publishers. Some footnotes have been omitted.

Lois Pineau, "Date Rape: A Feminist Analysis," *Law and Philosophy* 8:217–243. Copyright © 1989 by Kluwer Academic Publishers. Reprinted by permission of Kluwer Academic Publishers.

Camille Paglia, "An Interview About Sex and Date Rape," conducted by Celia Farber in *Spin,* September and October 1991, and Sonya Friedman, *Sonya Live,* CNN Television, December 13, 1991. Copyright © 1991 by Camouflage Associates and CNN Television. Reprinted by permission.

Gerald Gunther, "Good Speech, Bad Speech—No," *Stanford Lawyer* 24 (1990): 7, 9, 41. Reprinted by permission.

Andrew Altman, "Liberalism and Campus Hate Speech," *Ethics* 103 (January 1993): 302–317. Copyright © 1993 by The University of Chicago. All rights reserved. Reprinted by permission.

Lino A. Graglia, "Affirmative Discrimination," *National Review,* July 5, 1993, pp. 26–31. Reprinted by permission.

Duncan Kennedy, "A Cultural Pluralist Case for Affirmative Action," *Duke Law Journal* (1990); also reprinted in *Sexy Dressing: Essays on the Power and Politics of Cultural Identity* (Cambridge: Harvard University Press, 1994). Reprinted by permission.

Shelby Steele, "The Recoloring of Campus Life: Student Racism, Academic Pluralism, and the End of a Dream," from Shelby Steele, *The Content of Our Character: A New Vision of Race in America* (New York: HarperCollins Publishers, 1990), pp. 129–148, 169–172. Copyright © 1990 by Shelby Steele. Reprinted by permission.

Audre Lorde, "Age, Race, Class, and Sex: Women Redefining Difference," from Audre Lorde, *Sister Outsider* (Trumansburg, New York: The Crossing Press, 1984). Copyright © 1984 by Audre Lorde. Reprinted by permission.

Iris Marion Young, "Social Movements and the Politics of Difference," from Iris Marion Young, *Justice and the Politics of Difference* (Princeton: Princeton University Press, 1990), pp. 157–159, 162–175, 178–181. Copyright © 1990 by PUP. Reprinted by permission of Princeton University Press. References have been omitted.

Arthur M. Schlesinger, Jr., "The Disuniting of America: Reflections on a Multicultural Society," from Arthur M. Schlesinger, Jr., *The Disuniting of America; Reflections on a Multicultural Society* (New York: W. W. Norton Co., 1992). Reprinted by permission.

Bernard R. Boxill, "Separation or Assimilation?" from Bernard R. Boxill, *Blacks and Social Justice* (Lanham, MD: Rowman and Littlefield, 1992). Copyright © 1992 by Rowman and Littlefield Publishers. Reprinted by permission.

Charles Taylor, "The Politics of Recognition," from Charles Taylor, *Multiculturalism and the Politics of Recognition* (Princeton: Princeton University Press, 1992), pp. 25–40. Copyright © 1992 by PUP. Reprinted by permission of Princeton University Press.

Hilary Putnam, "Pragmatism, Relativism, and the Justification of Democracy," from Hilary Putnam, "A Reconsideration of Deweyan Democracy," *S. Cal. L. Rev.* 63 (1990). Reprinted by permission of *Southern California Law Review.* Some footnotes have been omitted.